The Freedom to Remember

The Freedom to Remember

Narrative, Slavery, and Gender in Contemporary Black Women's Fiction

ANGELYN MITCHELL

RUTGERS UNIVERSITY PRESS
New Brunswick, New Jersey, and London

Library of Congress Cataloging-in-Publication Data

Mitchell, Angelyn, 1960–
   The freedom to remember : narrative, slavery, and gender in contemporary Black
women's fiction / Angelyn Mitchell.
      p. cm.
   Includes bibliographical references and index.
   ISBN 0-8135-3068-7 (cloth : alk. paper) — ISBN 0-8135-3069-5 (pbk. : alk. paper)
   1. American fiction—African American authors—History and criticism.
2. Slavery in literature. 3. Women and literature—United States—History—20th
century. 4. American fiction—Women authors—History and criticism. 5. American
fiction—20th century—History and criticism. 6. African American women in
literature. 7. African Americans in literature. 8. Sex role in literature. 9. Memory in
literature. 10. Narration (Rhetoric) I. Title.

PS374.S58 M58 2002
813'.54099287'08996073—dc21

                                                                                    2001048609

British Cataloging-in-Publication information is available from the British Library.

Manufactured in the United States of America

To Duane,
my soul mate

Contents

Preface

I have never lived, nor has any of us, in a world in which race did not matter.

          —TONI MORRISON

As a Black person and a woman I don't read history for facts. I read it for clues.

          —ALICE WALKER

Think of Slavery
as
Educational!

       —AMIRI BARAKA

I WAS BORN FREE, but race has colored my life from the beginning. I am a daughter of the South. In 1960, I was born in Dr. Vladimir Bensen's private medical clinic in Raleigh, North Carolina, because the hospitals were separate but not equal. Most of the local White hospitals did not admit Black patients, and the one hospital that did provided segregated, second-class care at best. The area's only Black hospital had a reputation for dubious conditions born of economic woes. Thus Dr. Bensen, a Russian general practitioner, delivered me with the assistance of his nurse in his clinic on Peace Street, as was his practice for his Black obstetrics patients. Something of a maverick, Dr. Bensen also defied the local custom of segregated waiting rooms.

The 1954 Supreme Court ruling of *Brown v. the Board of Education of Topeka* to desegregate public schools with "all deliberate speed" was slowly implemented in my home state. In Clayton, a town sixteen miles east of Raleigh, where I grew up, I attended a segregated kindergarten in 1966 (with outdoor

plumbing) and a segregated first grade in 1967 (where the books were out-
dated and resources were limited). My school district, the Johnston County
Public School System, was finally integrated in 1969. The year before, in 1968,
my parents sent my brother and me to the "White school" as this was the
"freedom of choice" transitional year—we were free to attend the "White
school," and they were free to allow us. I was one of five Black students in
the school. I was the only Black student in all of my classes. That fall when
my second grade social studies class held mock presidential elections, I made
and wore a "Hubert Humphrey for President" button because my Democratic
parents supported him. I suspect my classmates were also following the lead
of their parents: the majority of my White classmates wore "Richard Nixon
for President" buttons, while a few supported George Wallace's candidacy.
During that transitional school year, my parents were on guard for any possibility. Smithfield, our county seat just a few miles away, boasted a gigantic
red and white billboard that read, "Welcome to KKK Country." (This sign
was finally removed some years after I graduated from high school in 1978.) I
have vivid memories from the 1970s of huge crosses burning, surrounded by
shadowy figures, at Klan rallies on a farm not far from our home.

     In my small southern town, segregation reigned, well after the sit-ins, the
marches, the Civil Rights Act of 1964, the Voting Rights Act of 1965, and
school integration. In the 1970s, Blacks and Whites did not live in the same
neighborhoods (railroad tracks still speak to me of division); we did not pray
together; we did not eat together; we did not socialize together; we did not
even sit together in most public offices. While the signs of demarcation—"Colored" and "White"—that even I can remember were eventually removed, the
sentiment was not so easily eradicated. Thanks to the law of the land, we did
attend school together. What was taught, however, still reflected the hegemony of the day—White male patriarchy. There, to borrow from W.E.B. Du
Bois, I sat with Shakespeare, and he winced not. But I had few opportunities
to see myself or read the stories of people who looked like me and my folk in
what I formally learned. The local library and its bookmobile assisted my solitary endeavor to fill in the blanks as I read all of its limited holdings by or
about Black folk. In school, I remember feeling inexplicably uncomfortable
when the subject of slavery was discussed, however briefly; race was never discussed. I did not know then that I was dealing with the same existential question that Du Bois had already posed: How does it feel to be a problem? In the
context of our sketchy lessons on slavery, I wondered, how did enslaved Blacks
feel about themselves and their circumstances? Everything around me in my
little corner of the world proclaimed race mattered. How and why it mattered

were not as clear to my developing self. But I decided that how and why it mattered must have been forged in the historical and shameful moment of chattel slavery. There, I thought, might be some of the answers to the many questions I had but did not even know how to articulate. I have since observed that our country suffered and suffers from this same inability to articulate its pain and shame as they relate to slavery.

A voracious reader, I wanted to know more than the dates of the Civil War and the text of the Emancipation Proclamation; I wanted to better understand my world. I read not only biography and history but also fiction, where imagined people and their circumstance fueled my own imagination. I read such works as Harriet Beecher Stowe's *Uncle Tom's Cabin* (1852) and Margaret Mitchell's *Gone with the Wind* (1937). Of course, I read Faulkner in my quest to understand better the South. Still, I wondered what Eliza, Mammy, and Dilcey's stories would have been had they been told from their own perspectives. Where were their stories? At that time, I knew only about Frederick Douglass's 1845 narrative and nothing about Harriet A. Jacobs, Harriet E. Wilson, David Walker, William and Ellen Craft, or Henry "Box" Brown because White patriarchy was at the center of all that I learned. Where were the voices of my ancestors? What was this relationship between race and knowledge? How and why did race determine what I learned? Would race, this all-powerful entity, silently determine my fate and would it render me invisible? Looking back, it is interesting to consider how issues of race trumped issues of gender in the 1960s and 1970s because racism, not sexism, seemed more immediate and more insurmountable.

Given my personal history, it is not surprising then that slavery has been one of my primary research areas and that I have written this book on representations of slavery in contemporary Black women's writing. The fundamental issue that has shaped our country's history and identity has been race, and in complex ways, slavery has become synonymous with race as slavery may be read as a crucial metonym of our social history. As a professor of literature, my work has centered on examining how the cultural construct of race operates in American society. What does it mean to be raced and American in a country where racial identity supercedes national identity? How do African American and Anglo American literatures represent and reveal this meaning? While working on my master's degree in English at North Carolina Central University, I studied with the late John Sekora, a specialist in slave narratives, or as I prefer now, *emancipatory* narratives. Later, I was fascinated by what has been called the neoslave narrative, so much so that I wrote my doctoral dissertation on the ways in which the twentieth-century Black women

writers of neoslave narratives revised or signified on the nineteenth-century
female slave narrative. As an African Americanist scholar, I continue to
grapple with many of the same existential and epistemic questions of my youth.
As a womanist scholar, I am interested in Black women's fiction and history
as well as in textual representations of Black women. Having spent the last
ten years reading, thinking, teaching, and writing about textual envisionings
of slavery by Black women, I have identified a new genre—a genre I term the
liberatory narrative—one that derives from the nineteenth-century female
emancipatory narrative. As we know, the nineteenth-century female emancipatory narrative was written to advance the cause of abolition and freedom
by revealing the unspeakable realities of chattel slavery, especially for Black
women, helping to force our country to confront this issue. The twentieth-
century liberatory narrative differs, I believe, from the emancipatory narrative in that it reveals the unspeakable—indeed, the unacknowledged—*residuals*
of slavery in the context of Black womanhood as it illuminates the enduring
effects of our racist and sexist American history in today's society.

Quiet as it's kept, many debts are accumulated when one writes a book. The
debts can range from simple words of encouragement to reading and commenting on numerous drafts. I thank my colleagues at Georgetown University for
their generous support in a variety of ways, particularly Valerie Babb, Leona
Fisher, Lucy Maddox, James Slevin, and Kathryn Temple. I am particularly
grateful to Leona Fisher and Lucy Maddox who carefully read the manuscript
and offered insightful comments and suggestions that enriched this book tre-
mendously. My students at Georgetown, particularly those who have taken
my Slavery and the American Literary Imagination course, have also contributed greatly to this book's final form. Their infectious enthusiasm, indefati-
gable energy, and incredible intellect have sustained and nurtured my own
enthusiasm, energy, and intellect. Special thanks to Danny Levy (COL '01)
for his title suggestions and to Soyica Diggs (COL '01), Rayshad Holmes (GSB
'99), and Haven Ward (COL '01) for their research assistance. I am grateful
to the English department for the course releases that helped me complete
this book and to the Graduate School of Arts and Sciences for funding and a
junior faculty sabbatical, funded in part by the Andrew Mellon Foundation.
This book began as my doctoral dissertation and, for its support while I was a
Danforth-Compton Fellow at Howard University, the Danforth Foundation
will always have my gratitude.

One of the best decisions I ever made was attending graduate school at
Howard University. The gifts of the "Capstone," tangible and intangible, are

immeasurable. My then professors and now colleagues are models of excellence and collegiality. Whatever I ask of them, they eagerly and willingly give. I especially thank R. Victoria Arana, who patiently and graciously read and reread this manuscript and offered invaluable suggestions and advice. This book, and I, would be much less without her influence. Her continued support of me in this project as well as in other endeavors means more than she probably knows; I am inspired by her example of unselfish collegiality and generous friendship.

I am grateful to each of the authors whose work is examined here for their extraordinary literary gifts. Their words not only enrich me; they liberate me. I must remember here, as well, the all-too-short life of Sherley Anne Williams (1944–1999). We met once; her genuine warmth and gracious spirit were unforgettable.

Three very special friends passed on since I began this book. One of life's most precious gifts is to see one's best self through the eyes of another. My mentor, the late Ernest D. Mason of North Carolina Central University, afforded me this rare opportunity through his selfless mentoring and his enduring friendship. I owe so much of who I am to him. While I was at NCCU, he encouraged me to follow my passion. This book would not have existed without him. Much of what is written here reflects our many conversations over the years; we had so many but still too few. Since his death, I've tried to keep our conversations alive in my work, although I'm painfully aware of how much better my work, and I, would be if he were still here.

A relative who is also a friend is a special treat. My uncle, the late Rev. Garland F. Wiggins, was one of my closest confidants. As a girl in rural North Carolina, I was enamored with my handsome and debonair uncle who lived in New York. As an adult, I continued to admire him as I sought his wise counsel in both personal and professional matters. I miss, as he once described himself, my greatest admirer.

Finally, those who know me well know that my sheltie, Mac, was my heart. From 1987 to 1997, he gave me such joy. Pixie hasn't taken his place in my heart; she has her own.

I have been blessed with an incredible family by blood and by choice. In particular, I thank first my wonderful mother, Evelyn W. Mitchell, who taught me the beauty and the value of words; my late father, James J. Mitchell, who taught me the power of words; my late grandmother, Fannie P. Wiggins, who taught me how to read; and my late grandfather, Rev. Alonza M. Wiggins, who taught me through his words the power of the Divine. I thank my brother, Steven V. Mitchell, for being my lifelong friend and for being the co-trustee of our childhood *lieux de mémoire*; I am proud to be his "Baby Sister." My two very best sister-friends, Deborah H. Barnes and Lola A. Davis, make my life so much more phenomenal than it would be without them. Their gifts to me are many and varied, and they are overwhelmingly appreciated. Since meeting in graduate school, Deborah and I have collaborated on many projects. She is my ideal reader. She has lived this project with me: reading drafts, offering suggestions, and banishing doubts. I thank her for being my comrade in arms and my collaborator for life. Lola and I have been friends since childhood; she is the sister I always wanted. I appreciate her thoughtfulness, her reliability, and her laughter. I thank her for her unconditional love and lifelong friendship. I am especially grateful to my family by choice—my in-laws—for their love, their encouragement, and particularly their understanding when I was preoccupied with work. I especially thank my parents-in-law, Carolyn A. and George C. Cooper. Finally, I thank all of those who, through my own fault, may not know how very much I appreciate their presence in my life. I do.

I am delighted to be a part of the Rutgers University Press family; I am grateful to everyone at the Press who worked on this book, particularly Marg Sumner, my copyeditor. I am especially grateful to my editor, Leslie Mitchner, associate director and editor-in-chief, for her interest in my work, for her honesty and professionalism, and for being the very best in the business. My thanks as well to Farah Jasmine Griffin for her insightful and thoughtful comments on the manuscript that greatly improved this book's final form. I am grateful to Joseph Holston for allowing *Miz Emily* to grace this book's cover.

This book is dedicated to my husband, Duane A. Cooper, who passionately believes in me and who generously gives me his unwavering support. I thank him for being, to use Toni Morrison's marvelous phrase, both "ship and safe harbor" for me. There is no better definition—and no finer example—of a soul mate.

Angelyn Mitchell
Washington, D.C.
July 2001

The Freedom to Remember

Introduction

Visions and Revisions of Slavery

> History . . . is not merely something to be read. And it
> does not refer merely, or even principally, to the past.
> On the contrary, the great force of history comes from
> the fact that we carry it within us, are unconsciously
> controlled by it in many ways, and history is literally
> present in all that we do.
>
> —JAMES BALDWIN

> I know I can't change the future but I can change the
> past. It is the past, not the future, which is infinite.
>
> —TONI MORRISON

> The dominance of the past, which returns like a
> nightmare to hang over the unredeemed present, can
> only be smashed by the analytic power of a form of
> remembering which can look calmly at what has
> happened as history without seeing it as morally
> neutral.
>
> —JÜRGEN HABERMAS

A Conversation on Race?

In June of 1997, Representative Tony P. Hall (D–Ohio) proposed the following simple resolution that attempted to acknowledge and to correct one
of the greatest injustices in American history:

> Resolved by the House of Representatives that the Congress
> apologizes to African-Americans whose ancestors suffered as slaves
> under the Constitution and laws of the United States until 1865.
> (H.R. 96)

W.E.B. Du Bois was indeed prophetic in 1903: the problem of the twentieth
century was the problem of the color line (17). That the institution of chattel

slavery continued to affect American society even in the closing years of the twentieth century, as dramatized by the subsequently tabled resolution and the tremendous response it engendered, suggests how systemically pervasive the infinite pain and shame of slavery remain in the American consciousness. That House Resolution 96 died in session represents yet another example of how unwilling Americans are to discuss that pain and shame, much less to face it.

The responses to the unsuccessful resolution are illuminating as they reveal the complex and contentious nature of contemporary race relations. According to Representative Hall, most of the voluminous correspondence he received condemned his idea. Two of the most common arguments against the resolution were that slavery was a thing of the past and that no one living had participated or suffered in slavery. One might wonder, Why did Hall's proposed resolution prompt such strong and dismissive reactions from the American public? Even then-President William Jefferson Clinton (1993–2001), who wanted to have "a national conversation on race" and who commissioned a blue-ribbon panel of experts, led by noted historian John Hope Franklin, declined to support the resolution; former Speaker of the House Newt Gingrich (R–Georgia), the primary architect of the "Contract with America," dismissed the resolution as simply "emotional symbolism"; and civil rights activist Rev. Jesse L. Jackson characterized the gesture as "meaningless" because there was no accompanying discussion of economic reparations. As the controversy raged, various polls queried the public with this question: Should America apologize for slavery? Because human rights violations, sanctioned by the United States government, were committed against Americans of African descent during the period of chattel slavery, an apology from the government, even a long overdue one, could, as apologies do, begin the process of atonement needed to heal such a monumental breach of the American promise. Perhaps a more provocative question should have been posed in order to engender more meaningful discussion about this lingering and complex issue: Why should America apologize for slavery?

While House Resolution 96 may be read as an illuminating example of the way slavery continues to affect American society, it is not the only example. In addition to congressional discussions about apologies for slavery, cinematic representations abound, giving dimension to the institution of slavery for contemporary viewers. Movies such as *Amistad* (1997) and *Beloved* (1998), directed by Steven Spielberg and Jonathan Demme, respectively, revisited slavery and foundered at the box office. Haile Gerima's independent film *Sankofa* (1993) takes its audience on a voyage through the Middle Passage and back to Africa, and educational documentaries, such as PBS's six-hour series *Africans in America: America's Journey Through Slavery* (1998), provide viewers with the historical context of this epoch. In addition to the protracted national debate, fueled by DNA testing concerning the relationship between Sally Hemings and President Thomas Jefferson, a movie, *Jefferson in Paris* (1995), as well as a television mini-series oddly entitled *Sally Hemings: An American Scandal* (2000), attempted to depict their controversial relationship. In light of these recent examples, it is clear that the historical moment of slavery continues to haunt the American consciousness. The issue of slavery, it would seem, in twentieth-century North America was like a Möbius strip on which remembering and forgetting twist endlessly in the collective national consciousness. With slavery "bursting at the seam of our historical memory," as Michael Eric Dyson has observed (Alter 60), how will we prevent the rupture?

The calculus of slavery has also fueled the imaginations of a number of African American writers, especially women writers, who have dramatized the institution of slavery and/or the legacies of slavery—specifically, the pain and shame of that past—in their works.[1] The institution of slavery has informed the novels of the five contemporary Black women novelists at the center of this study—*Kindred* (1979) by Octavia E. Butler, *Dessa Rose* (1986) by Sherley Anne Williams, *Beloved* (1987) by Toni Morrison, *Family* (1992) by J. California Cooper, and *The Price of a Child* (1995) by Lorene Cary. Revisiting slavery, these writers all engage their historical and literary past by developing a new literary form. Bernard W. Bell has termed these types of narratives *neoslave narratives*, broadly defined as "residually oral, modern narratives of escape from bondage to freedom" (289).[2] This term has been useful in initiating critical discourse about these narratives. But the slave narrative of the eighteenth and nineteenth centuries has not simply been made anew by the writers examined here. Certainly, the same details are told about slavery in the twentieth-century narrative; its urgencies, however, have perdured and now take the form of contemporary communications about ways contemporary readers can free themselves from the pain and shame that are a residual of the legacy of slavery in the United States.

While Bell's term suggests that contemporary writers are inventing fictional slave narratives that revisit the historical period of slavery in much the same spirit as historical novels describe past lives, there is a more appropriate term for the cultural productions that interests me. The focus of these narratives by contemporary African American women writers is not, it seems to me, on the experience of enslavement but, more importantly, on the construct we call freedom. In other words, they do more than narrate movement from bondage to freedom. These narratives analyze freedom. Accordingly, these narratives are *liberatory narratives*. I define the liberatory narrative as a contemporary novel that engages the historical period of chattel slavery in order to provide new models of liberation by problematizing the concept of freedom. I prefer the term liberatory narrative as the contemporary narratives are more than "new": they are more complex in form and content than the eighteenth- and nineteenth-century slave narratives. Set primarily in nineteenth-century North America, the liberatory narrative is self-conscious thematically of its antecedent text, the slave narrative; is centered on its enslaved protagonist's attainment of freedom; is concerned with the protagonist's life as a free citizen; and is focused on the protagonist's conception and articulation of herself as a free, autonomous, and self-authorized self. In other words, the liberatory narrative is primarily concerned with the nature of freedom—of affranchisement— for those who were formerly enslaved. The contemporary narratives are certainly informed by their intertextuality, their resonance, with prior texts of slavery.

Liberatory narratives are concerned with more than a state of being; their primary function indeed is in describing how to achieve freedom. In doing so, the liberatory narrative seeks to eclipse the deterministic condition of racial enslavement. This move is important because one cannot proffer or embrace paradigms of freedom if one is still chained to the old paradigm with its language of bondage. For all of these reasons, I want to shift the gaze from slavery to freedom, from slave narrative to emancipatory narrative and from neoslave narrative to liberatory narrative. Of the need for this type of epistemological shift, Toni Cade Bambara explains, "we've been trained to call [narratives by enslaved African Americans] slave narratives for reasons too obscene to mention, as if the 'slave' were an identity and not a status interrupted by the very act of fleeing, speaking, writing, and countering the happy-darky propaganda" (250). I maintain that an epistemological liberation from the dominant narratives of our social, cultural, and political histories—the master narratives—must begin with a critique of the linguistic signs that construct and structure our reality. Because this study reconceptualizes issues of identity politics that have been historically presented as immutable, it is necessary for me, in order to shift the gaze, to employ terms that resist those heretofore fixed definitions concerning African Americans and African American literary traditions. For these reasons, in what follows, I eschew the term slaves and instead use as identifiers enslaved Black men and women or enslaved African American men and women. Likewise, I do not refer to the slave narrative but rather I refer to the emancipatory narrative, as Eleanor W. Traylor and others have, to identify the narrative written by the self-emancipated African American of the eighteenth and nineteenth centuries.[3]

As African American narrative begins with the depiction of bondage and the desire for freedom in the eighteenth and nineteenth centuries, it is telling that in the last years of the twentieth century a number of African American writers continue to probe the issues of bondage and freedom as these issues have colored the lives of African Americans from the inception of chattel slavery. Contemporary African American writers who engage the theme of slavery do so in order to bear witness to the "unspeakable," to correct enduring misrepresentations and misinterpretations of Black Americans forged in slavery, and to present history from a racialized perspective. Although contemporary Black men writers such as Ernest Gaines, Ishmael Reed, and Charles Johnson have also engaged the historical moment of chattel slavery in their novels and even though Alex Haley's *Roots* (1976), both the novel and the television series, made significant contributions to the discourse of slavery, contemporary Black women writers, beginning with Margaret Walker and her historical novel *Jubilee* (1966), have been at the forefront in revisiting slavery. A comparative examination of both the men's and women's texts is beyond the scope of this study as I do not find the narratives by Black men to be liberatory in the way that I have defined the genre. For that reason, I have chosen to examine here narratives by Black women from a feminist perspective as they are most evocative in their creation of the liberatory narrative. If one were to create a Venn diagram of the liberatory narrative's primary categories of narrative, slavery, and gender, one would find at its intersection—at its center—the self. If there exists a quintessential Black feminist theme, it is the self. Because of this, contemporary Black women writers, it seems to me, are acutely aware of the need to right the master narratives so that African Americans in general and African American women specifically are represented more authentically as agents, as subjects. The *written* narrative that a society writes about itself is considered the *master narrative*, and this narrative is always presented and interpreted from the perspective of the hegemonic power base. I am particularly interested in liberatory narratives written by Black women writers because they construct bold illustrations of a historical continuum of the self in terms of Black female identity.

The personal and political imperative of Black women writers like Butler, Williams, Morrison, Cooper, and Cary is to address the Black woman's legacy of enslavement and dispossession in the United States, and to utilize this knowledge in the reclamation and celebration of their racial and gendered selves and heritage. The challenge for these revisionary writers lies in conquering the silences and erasures concerning enslaved Black women that would otherwise inhibit the transformative potential of their endeavor. I offer that the liberatory narratives not only instruct contemporary readers about slavery, but more importantly instruct readers—in ways that are deliberately generative and healing—about the days when American identity was defined in circumscribed ways. Their objective is to engender a liberatory effect on the reader. Much work is needed, however, on the reader's part. As bell hooks has observed, "the liberatory voice . . . demands that paradigms shift—that we learn to talk—to listen—to hear in a new way" (*Talking Back* 15). Overall, the liberatory narrative engages the personal and the emotional as it depicts the history of slavery. Despite all that we know or think we know about slavery, the liberatory narratives remind us of how little we know, particularly if all we know are the facts.

Since the proliferation of contemporary texts that revisit slavery begins with Margaret Walker's *Jubilee* (1966), it might be argued that the Civil Rights Movement and its aftermath inspired a number of Black women writers to reveal aspects of the enslavement experience by revisiting the historical moment of American slavery from the "safe" vantage point of the late twentieth century that their literary ancestors could not reveal. Of the liberatory narratives as well as the recent cultural productions that have been enacted in such disparate public arenas as law and film one might ask: Why does slavery continue to haunt the American cultural and literary imagination? This study considers the ways in which the characters of contemporary imaginations inflect our understanding of slavery as an American historical phenomenon that involved and continues to affect all of its citizenry. In many ways, the liberatory narratives examined give witness to what has been historically unspeakable and, in some ways, unimaginable—not simply to aggravate old wounds but to offer narrative possibilities for healing the wounds caused by racism, institutionalized and otherwise.

History as Text and Context

A surprising number of contemporary Black women writers have written historical novels, novels that engage the past at specific historic moments. The majority of these contemporary novels revisit African American history and culture from the years of the Harlem Renaissance to the present. Four of Toni Morrison's novels—*The Bluest Eye* (1970), *Sula* (1973), *Song of Solomon* (1977), and *Jazz* (1992)—as well as Gloria Naylor's *The Women of Brewster Place* (1982), and Alice Walker's *The Third Life of Grange Copeland* (1970) and *The Color Purple* (1982) explore the African American woman's social and personal experiences during the 1920s, 1930s, or 1940s. The same novelists, as well as others, have also revisited their own recent history. Walker's *Meridian* (1976) and Toni Cade Bambara's *The Salt Eaters* (1979) both examine the aftermath of the turbulent 1960s, while Paule Marshall's *Praisesong for the Widow* (1982), Morrison's *Tar Baby* (1981), and Naylor's *Linden Hills* (1985) interrogate the effects of upward social and economic mobility among African Americans during the upheavals of the 1960s and 1970s. From these examples, one may surmise that history, not only as text but also as context, is a significant trope for Black women novelists in portraying African American experiences. In other words, history is accurately portrayed; the crucial differences are in matters of perspective and motivation.

Twentieth-century history, however, is not the only historic period of interest to contemporary Black women writers. Slavery, as a site of memory, has also captured the literary imaginations of Black women writers.[4] Preoccupied with reinterpreting the past by rewriting the master narrative of slavery, contemporary African American women writers who offer twentieth-century representations of slavery do not simply imitate their literary ancestors. Rather, they construct alternative versions of the enslaved female's life through transformative revisions of antecedent texts. These are more than parodic, but the concept of literary parody is useful in working toward a clarification of their intent. Literary parody, as Linda Hutcheon cautions in *A Poetics of Postmodernism*, should not be defined, as some might, in the narrow, eighteenth-century sense of a ridiculing imitation, but as "repetition with critical distance that allows ironic signaling of difference at the very heart of similarity" (26). Parody, Hutcheon contends, is double-voiced as it both enshrines and questions the past (126). Indeed, contemporary Black women writers have both enshrined and questioned their past by revising or signifyin(g) on precursive texts and history.[5] The liberatory narrative has designs on its contemporary readers that differ markedly from either the original narratives or parodic narratives like Ishmael Reed's *Flight to Canada* (1976).

In the nineteenth century, the institution of chattel slavery gave rise to a uniquely indigenous American literary form: the nineteenth-century emancipatory narrative. As John Sekora writes, the emancipatory narrative was important, then and now, because "[o]utside the narrative, slavery was a wordless, nameless, timeless time. It was time without history and without imminence. Slaveholders sought to reduce existence to the psychological present and to mandate their records as the only reliable texts" ("Comprehending Slavery" 163). Thus, the existence of the emancipatory narrative refuted the very

foundation of slavery. The emancipatory narrative has specific generic characteristics, as several critics have observed. For example, it typically begins
with the words "I was born" and reveals, among other events, vignettes of the
protagonist's life in bondage as well as the protagonist's flight from slavery to
freedom. The nineteenth-century emancipatory narrative also has political
import. These narratives were most often written to aid the cause of abolition and, consequently, were rich in the rhetoric of propaganda. The narrator
often wrote in order to reveal the material and immoral circumstances of slavery. Many events were recounted selectively and benignly so as not to offend readers, and much information (such as names of accomplices or specific
travel arrangements) was purposely omitted for obvious reasons. Consequently,
aspects of the interior lives of the enslaved Americans and other participants
in slavery remained cloaked and veiled. Frances Smith Foster defines the typical emancipatory narrative in these terms:

> The antebellum slave narrative featured a protagonist best described
> as a *heroic male* fugitive. The usual pattern of the narrative was to
> demonstrate examples of cruelty and degradation inherent in the
> institution of slavery, then to chronicle an individual's discovery that
> the concept and the condition of slavery were neither inevitable or
> irrevocable. Following that revelation, the typical slave narrator
> secretly plotted *his* escape and, at the opportune time, struck out alone
> but resolved to follow the North Star to freedom. Slave narratives
> generally ended when, upon arrival in the free territory, the former
> slave assumed a new name, obtained a job, married, and began a new
> happy-ever-after life. ("Resisting *Incidents*" 65; emphasis added)

One can see from Foster's overview, as well as from similarly delineated analyses
by Charles Davis, Williams Andrews, James Olney, and Deborah McDowell,
that the personal or inner self was not a part of the narrative's formula because that self had no currency in rhetorical value.[6] Additionally, until the
emergence of Black feminist thought and the explosion of Black women writers
in the 1970s, a wide range of scholarly studies, if they did not ignore Black
women, offered reductive and stereotypic analyses of Black women's lives. After
what I call the Black Woman's Creative Renaissance of the 1970s, ignoring
Black women's history was harder to do. Because Harriet Jacobs's *Incidents in
the Life of a Slave Girl, Written by Herself* (1861) was authenticated in 1986
by Jean Fagan Yellin, because a number of Black women historians, including
Deborah Gray White and Darlene Clark Hine, unearthed and made prominent the history of Black women in the 1980s, and because pioneering African Americanists like Mary Helen Washington and Henry Louis Gates, Jr.

presented the writings of nineteenth-century Black women writers in accessible volumes in the 1970s and 1980s, the Black woman's life in slavery has become better known.

Black Women Bearing Witness

Of the more than one hundred and thirty autobiographical narratives written or dictated by persons of African descent and published prior to 1865, only sixteen were written or dictated by women.[7] Perhaps the best known of the nineteenth-century female emancipatory narratives is Harriet Jacobs's *Incidents in the Life of a Slave Girl, Written by Herself* because of its place in the African American and American canons, its accessibility to readers, and its artfulness. Scholars now consider *Incidents* an Ur-text of the genre and, as such, it is taught with regularity. While the male emancipatory narrative and the female emancipatory narrative share similar features in form and content, as several critics have noted, the primary difference between the two arises from gender-related themes, such as the variance in treatments of sexual abuse and parenthood.[8] In Jacobs's *Incidents*, Linda Brent, Jacobs's pseudonymic alter ego, guardedly tells her story so as not to offend her audience even though the subject matter is offensive, and the audience should be offended by such brutality.

To have been completely authentic in constructing the enslaved Black woman's life would have jeopardized the potential power of the text as a fulcrum for social change; moreover, nineteenth-century constructs of womanhood (as well as nineteenth-century literary conventions) could not openly accommodate, for racist, sexist, and political reasons, the Black woman's story. Because the enslaved woman was not allowed to participate equally in mainstream nineteenth-century Anglo-American society and yet was unfairly evaluated by its ideological tenets of "true womanhood," any unveiled revelations of her sexual exploitation and victimization would have offended her audience's Victorian sensibilities.[9] The inner life of the enslaved woman, the sum of her thoughts and her emotions, was therefore, at best, circumscriptively depicted.

In exposing and reversing these enforced silences, twentieth-century Black women writers in the main allow their protagonists to assert their claims to selfhood as they interrogate the limits of their personal freedom in a racist and patriarchal society. Indeed, one of the primary defining traits of contemporary Black women's writing is the presentation of the self as central rather than marginal. Margaret Walker's acclaimed historical novel, *Jubilee* (1966), is one of the first novels to recuperate the Black woman's history by situating

the enslaved Black woman as central.[10] Walker's novel reads much like a documentary as she presents the material conditions of her enslaved heroine's life.
Interrogations of her protagonist's life or of the circumstances of her life are
not primary to Walker's endeavor. As such, *Jubilee* is not included in this study
because it does not fit the profile of the liberatory narrative. Deborah E.
McDowell maintains that *Jubilee* is indeed the mainspring, if not the catalyst,
for the numerous novels written in the last thirty years that depict the historical moment of chattel slavery in the United States ("Negotiating" 144).
While it may or may not be the mainspring, it certainly created a space for
representations of slavery and of enslaved Black women. Indeed, Walker can
be credited with providing the first accurate depiction of the material conditions of slavery, particularly in relation to the enslaved Black woman, for a
contemporary readership. And this in itself is a tremendous contribution. Of
the need for historical recuperation, Barbara Christian reminds us that

> [r]e-memory is a critical determinant in how we value the past, what
> we remember, what we select to emphasize, what we forget . . . . But
> that concept could not be at the center of a narrative's revisioning of
> history until the obvious fact that African-Americans did have a
> history and culture was firmly established in American society, for
> writers would be constrained not only by their readers' point of view
> but also by the dearth of available information about the past that
> might give their work authenticity. ("Somebody" 333)

Because *Jubilee* is a historical novel, it is primarily concerned with revealing
the social and material conditions of enslavement in the Black woman's life
and does not delve into her inner world and self. It is understandable that as
a first of its kind—the first novel to present the Black woman's life in slavery—it would necessarily provide a realistic rendering of that life and that
time. Its function is to recover the enslaved Black woman's life story; it does
not interrogate that life. Due to its historical and cultural moment of composition, *Jubilee* does offer its readers, as Hazel V. Carby suggests, a necessary
pedagogic recovery of history, even if it is "a severely limited historical, psychological, and aesthetic vision" ("Ideologies of Black Folk" 136). It is for precisely these reasons that I do not read it as a liberatory narrative.

   Although Walker's *Jubilee* may have provided the momentum for recent
revisions of slavery, more recent novels have moved away from the realistic
style that Walker employed. Novelists who write liberatory narratives often
eschew "life-like" characters, the organization of incidents into a plot with a
clearly defined beginning and ending, the chronological arrangement of events,

and the use of reliable and omniscient narrators as being no longer sufficient to portray their perceptions of enslaved Black women and their worlds. In short, the portrayal of the objective conditions of slavery, as in Walker's *Jubilee*, no longer assumes priority for Black female revisionists of slavery; these writers are far more interested in disclosing the subjectivity and interiority of enslaved Black women and their worlds. Such an emphasis tends to move contemporary African American fiction beyond the discursive practices of literary realism and the constraints inherent in historical fiction. Realism suggests that the past can be accurately represented and re-presented; postmodernism maintains that the past can never be accurately represented or re-presented. Therefore, one might say that realism remembers the past so as to forget it, while postmodernism remembers the past, rendering it impossible to forget. The liberatory narrative is self-reflexive yet historically centered in demanding a reevaluation of representation as well as of the processes by which representations are constructed. Liberatory narratives are not simply new narratives; rather, they are narratives that can move their readers into new and perhaps freer spaces.

Theorizing Rememory

As the liberatory narrative embodies postmodernist concerns, a brief discussion of postmodernism and of its relationship to the liberatory narrative may be useful. In A *Poetics of Postmodernism*, Linda Hutcheon employs the term "historiographic metafiction" to describe novels that incorporate literature, history, and theory in such a way that "theoretical self-awareness of history and fiction as human constructs . . . is made the grounds for . . . rethinking and reworking" experience (5). At the center of the narratives in question here is, of course, a concern for history and its representation; indeed, the liberatory narrative may be considered a postmodern historiographic metafiction. According to Matei Calinescu, the central questions related to postmodernism are (1) how can literature be other than self-referential, (2) how can literature be a representation of reality when reality itself is a construct, and (3) how does the construction of reality differ from the construction of possibility? (299). These questions are also central questions for these contemporary Black women writers as they create fictitious worlds based upon actual places, events, or persons. I am particularly struck by this irony: that the primary characteristics of postmodernism—fragmentation, non-linearity, discontinuity, and cognitive disruptiveness—are also the primary characteristics of the enslaved person's sense of self, memory, history, and culture in the liberatory narrative.

The liberatory narrative, I believe, seeks to transmute these postmodern char-acteristics that represent the psychic legacy of slavery.

If parody both enshrines and questions the past, the liberatory narrative reconfigures presentations and representations of African-American women. In her study of postmodernism, Brenda K. Marshall suggests that historio-graphic metafiction "comes with a warning and a challenge: the reader is warned that this story, like all others, will be skewed, and is then challenged to remain aware of the skewing" (156). In other words, the liberatory narra-tive, a form of historiographic metafiction, reenforces the idea that the pre-sentation and representation of reality are subjective constructs and as such may reveal discourses traditionally silenced by more powerful discourses.

The move from literary realism has not been the only development in contemporary revisions of slavery. Intertextuality—texts speaking to other texts—is one of the ways the liberatory narrative constructs what Morrison calls "rememory," the process of remembering not only what one has forgot-ten but also what one wants to forget and cannot.[11] Memory may be described as the selection of images; rememory is the replaying of selected images. Memory functions in these narratives as an imaginative recovery of the his-torical past. By imaginatively rewriting the prevailing themes—e.g., female sexuality, motherhood, individualism, and community—of antecedent female emancipatory narratives, most notably of Jacobs's *Incidents in the Life of a Slave Girl*, contemporary Black women novelists construct the interior life of the enslaved woman as they engage in feminine discourse, a discourse character-istically dialogic and relational. Characterizing the Black woman's literary tra-dition, Mary Helen Washington explains, "Women talk to other women in this tradition" literally and figuratively ("Darkened Eye" xxi). Of the inter-textual relations of Black women writers, Deborah E. McDowell concludes that each writer's text is "in dialogue with all previous texts, transforming and re-taining narrative patterns and strategies in endless possibility" ("The Chang-ing Same" 107). In other words, these novels speak to each other and to their antecedent texts in such ways as to involve the reader in the essentials which they evoke. Postmodernist intertextuality, dialogic and relational, seems to be "a formal manifestation of both a desire to close the gap between past and present . . . and a desire to rewrite the past in a new context" (Hutcheon 118). The liberatory narrative interrupts and challenges what we think we know about slavery. If one accepts the master narrative's version of slavery, then one is limited to a singular perspective as one constructs her or his individual re-sponse to that past.

Intertextual referentiality provides a historically grounded context in which to discuss contemporary literary texts as they seek to deepen and to broaden the representations of their cultural and historical past. Indeed, as contemporary readers of the liberatory narratives can only experience slavery through discursive word work, the narrative possibilities are infinite, as Hortense J. Spillers explains, because slavery involves "a repertoire of relationships of texts and among texts that is purely open to modes of improvisation and rearrangement" ("Changing the Letter" 42). Some discussion of the theory of intertextuality then is essential, since intertextuality, "the oldest troping . . . , the most ancient textual (con)figuration" (O'Donnell and Davis xiii), foregrounds my premise. The conception of intertextuality has much in common with Bakhtin's process of re-accentuation, in which "every age re-accentuates in its own way the works of its most immediate past" (*The Dialogic Imagination* 421). Specifically, Bakhtin theorizes that the reemphasizing of images is the foundation of literary histories:

> all subsequent re-accentuations of images in a given novel . . . [take] on an enormous heuristic significance, deepening and broadening our artistic and ideological understanding of them. . . . [G]reat novelistic images continue to grow and develop even after the moment of their creation; they are capable of being creatively transformed in different eras, far distant from the day and hour of their original birth. (422)

Williams's and Morrison's employment, for example, of the enslaved mother figure broadens our understanding of the mother image presented in Jacobs's *Incidents*.

Unlike the notion of literary influence, intertextuality is not based on Freudian psychology nor is it predicated on the centrality of the author; rather, as Julia Kristeva defines it, intertextuality denotes that "any text is constructed as a mosaic of quotations; any text is the absorption and transformation of another" text or generic form (66). Contemporary Black women novelists do not mimic their literary precursors; these writers have no allegiance, as Hortense J. Spillers explains, "to a hierarchy of dynastic meanings that unfolds in linear succession and according to [the] customary sense of 'influence'" ("Cross-Currents" 258). Rather, contemporary Black women novelists "reaccentuate" their precursor texts. "Any text," offers Roland Barthes, "is a new tissue of past citations" (39). Barthes continues:

> Bits of codes, formulae, rhythmic models, fragments of social languages, etc., pass into the text and are redistributed within it, for there is always language before and around the text. . . . The concept of intertext is what brings to the theory of the text the volume of sociality: the whole of language, anterior or contemporary, comes to the text, not following the path of a discoverable filiation or willed

imitation, but that of a dissemination—an image which makes sure the text has the status not of a reproduction but of a productivity. (39)

The liberatory narratives absorb and reply to their precursor texts. In so doing, the novelists reread the period of slavery as well as the prior discourses of slavery for a contemporary readership in need of strategies of affranchisement, resistance, survival, and recovery. Clearly, these liberatory narratives speak to Jacobs's *Incidents* by employing Henry Louis Gates's trope of "unmotivated signifyin(g)," the trope of revising.

In *The Signifying Monkey*, Gates builds upon the post-structuralist concept of intertextuality, what he calls *signifyin(g)*, to illustrate and to analyze the intertextual relations of the "canonical" texts of African American literature. Like Gates, I maintain that intertextuality is a foundational strategy for reading and for interpreting the African American literary tradition.[12] Among other things, signifyin(g) designates verbal skill in reversing, revising, or parodying another's speech or discourse and thus provides a literary tradition through "rhetorical self-definition" (*Figures in Black* 242). This indigenous African American form of intertextuality, according to Gates, is rooted in a literary tradition of "grounded repetition and difference" (*Signifying Monkey* 256). Gates further divides signifyin(g) into two categories: motivated and unmotivated. Unmotivated signifyin(g) employs pastiche and engages "in refiguration as an act of homage," while motivated signifyin(g) employs parody proper and seeks to erase previous texts through revision (*Signifying Monkey* xxvi). Differentiating between these two forms of parody—pastiche and parody proper—Gates states that pastiche announces through revision "its surface content [as] the displaced content of the intertextual relations" in the literary tradition (*Signifying Monkey* 124), while parody heightens the "characteristics of the thing imitated" (*Signifying Monkey* 107). In the liberatory narrative, intertextuality is a strategy used to highlight the primary concerns of bondage and freedom. Intertextuality facilitates an examination and discussion of slavery and its legacy, interrogates the dynamics and dialectics of bondage and freedom, and posits a usable past.

This distinction between pastiche and parody proper is significant. Like Harold Bloom, who viewed White male literary relations as contestable, some have viewed the formal literary relations between Black male writers as adversarial, or as Gates would have it, as motivated signifyin(g). Gates explains the distinction between the Black male (parody) and the Black female literary tradition (pastiche): "Whereas most older black male writers deny any influence at all—or eagerly claim a white paternity—black female authors often claim descent from other black women literary ancestors" (*Reading Black*

4). Thus, Gates characterizes Ishmael Reed's *Mumbo Jumbo* as an example of motivated signifyin(g), that is, of Reed's attempt to erase previous texts through revision. On the other hand, Gates concludes that the intertextualities in the women's texts he examines, Hurston's *Their Eyes Were Watching God* and Walker's *The Color Purple*, represent a tradition within a tradition; he views Walker's signifyin(g) on Hurston as a sign of renewal and continuance. Signifyin(g) and intertextuality, in this instance, are the processes that mark the complimentary as well as complementary nature of Black women writers's literary relations.

The authors' exploration of the enslaved Black woman in the liberatory narrative is also an extension of Black feminist thought. The liberatory narrative reveals questions, assertions, and conclusions crucially different from its antecedent narrative. My aim in this study is to give a dynamic account of major themes and strategies in the context of African American women's writing using the critical lens of feminist literary theory. To demonstrate how the liberatory narratives signify on Jacobs's narrative, I explore a number of Black feminist concerns—female sexuality, motherhood, individualism, and community—as inextricably linked themes. These themes reify pivotal junctures of self-realization for Black women in the process of negotiating their personal and political realities. Accordingly, their narratives foreground the problematic nature of constructing a unified self in a racist and sexist society. "Unified" should not be confused with "monolithic" as both Black feminist writers and critics have conscientiously sought to present and to chart the multiplicity of Black women's experiences and perspectives.[13]

The Feminist Emancipatory Narrative

Accordingly, as an Ur-text which has undergone numerous re-envisionings, Harriet Jacobs's narrative, *Incidents in the Life of a Slave Girl, Written by Herself*, is not merely a literary convention or even the formula for a literary convention. The narrative is, rather, the constructed discourse of the major concerns and issues that have organized and structured much of the African American woman's life. As Hazel Carby has observed, "The consequences of being a slave woman did not end with the abolition of slavery as an institution but haunted the texts of Black women throughout the nineteenth century and into the twentieth" (*Reconstructing Womanhood* 61). Indeed, that there are a number of narratives written in the closing years of the twentieth century, specifically set in the historical moment of chattel slavery, demonstrates its overwhelming influence. The same feminist concerns and issues, themes and gestures are rewritten with such frequency, I believe, because they encapsulate the polemics for Black women that have been constant from the time of chattel slavery to the present day.

Since Jacobs's narrative provides a dramatic account of the survival skills of the enslaved female protagonist, one might expect that the experiences charted would involve a movement from suffering to a conquering of that suffering. But the triumph over suffering does not provide the foundation for Jacobs's narrative. *Incidents* presents a Black woman who lived according to her own terms, in spite of her circumstances.[14] The sub-text that does shape the narrative is another fundamental concept in African-American culture and thought, a more abstract version of the suffering-survival dichotomy. In this version, "progress," however slight, occurs for the female protagonist not simply through an overcoming of suffering, but through the active engagement of the voluntaristic/deterministic dichotomy. In other words, that Jacobs succeeds in exercising her volition in the determinism of slavery (and racism) is cause for celebrating the human spirit. While Jacobs employs the literary conventions of the nineteenth-century sentimental novel, a genre that might be considered deterministic fiction because gender defines the outcome for the protagonist, Jacobs deliberately refigures these conventions to serve her political and polemical needs. She constructs an identity that appears to be without agency; in reality, the construction is an act of agency which reveals other agential acts.[15] In this dialectical model, "deterministic" refers to change which occurs independent of human will and which is the result of vast, transpersonal forces such as "reason" and "God." "Voluntaristic," on the other hand, means change which occurs as the result of the action of self-consciousness, "spirit," or outstanding effort. As Mary Helen Washington notes, Jacobs "eschews the sentimental novel's passive stand for one of power and authority" and does not succumb to a deterministic outlook ("Meditations" 6). In contrast, in the revisionist and signifyin(g) practices of the contemporary novelists, the path toward action and change in the volitional enslaved female protagonists is complicated by the workings of vast and impersonal forces directed against them. The protagonists of the liberatory narrative demonstrate how agency and the will to be free facilitate the liberation of the soul and the psyche. These protagonists exhibit infinite commitment and make inordinate sacrifices. How they prevail may offer paradigms of liberation for their readers. All of the protagonists recognize and accept responsibility for their destinies in spite of those forces that conspire against them. In this context, one can see self-liberation occur in the lives of the protagonists in nuanced and definitive ways, with or without divine intervention, as they *will* themselves to freedom.

Slavery as a Site of Memory

In a discussion of her literary craft, Toni Morrison identified the emancipatory narrative, the origin of African American narrative, as her site of memory. She observes that while "no slave society in the history of the world wrote more—or more thoughtfully—about its own enslavement," the interior lives of the self-emancipated narrators remained veiled and unexamined ("Site" 109). Therefore, her enterprise as an African American writer involves the desire "to extend, fill in and complement slave autobiographical narratives" ("Site" 120) through the use of memory and imagination in order to recover a usable past. In this sense, slavery becomes what Pierre Nora calls a *lieu de mémoire*. According to Nora, a site of memory encompasses objects, symbols, and texts that embody and condense memory and provoke explorations of how the past relates to the present and the future.[16] The liberatory narrative operates as a site of memory by allowing its readers to go beyond the events of slavery into the feelings and thoughts of the people who imaginatively had the experience. In the liberatory narrative, intertextuality is a means of encoding memory and creates for us a space for meeting and for understanding a different time and setting which, in turn, allows us to better understand our own. Because the liberatory narrative reveals much about its contemporary political and social environments, one's reading of the liberatory narrative is enriched by considering its historical or extra-textual manifestations. The liberatory narrative creates a new national discourse on American history and culture by destabilizing and revising the master narrative of history, creating what Athena Vrettos has called "curative domains" where healing may take place through discursive acts (456).

In what follows, I examine through close reading each narrative in order of publication as I believe that each relates to the previous in an intertextual continuum of memory, determination, and resilience. For example, Butler's *Kindred* initiates the postmodern discourse of slavery among contemporary Black women writers by juxtaposing the past with the present, highlighting the similarities and dissimilarities between the two. Female sexuality, motherhood, individualism, and community are themes interwoven in constructing the enslaved Black woman's identity and reality. Unable to claim herself, the enslaved Black woman was not allowed agency in expressing her sexuality or in the product of its expression, created by choice or by force. Motherhood, then, becomes pivotal in conjoining her personal and political realities. While all Black women are not mothers, either by choice or by circumstance, all Black women are participants in the procreative process in that all women are, to borrow from Adrienne Rich, of woman born. Individualism and communalism are not diametrically opposed concepts in the enslaved Black woman's life since, to borrow from a well-known African proverb, she is because her community is, and her community is because she is.

I maintain in chapter one that Jacobs in *Incidents in the Life of a Slave Girl, Written by Herself* begins a dialogue about the nature of Black womanhood in America to which the contemporary novelists respond; for this reason, an examination of her narrative is foundational to this study. Employing the conventions of the sentimental novel, Jacobs provides examples of the patriarchal abuses and misuses of female sexuality, the problematic nature of motherhood in the enslaved woman's life, the manifestations of volition for the enslaved woman, and the various functions and potentialities for community. Jacobs's narrative is her testimony, in which she bears witness to the tragedies and triumphs of her own life as well as the lives of her comrades in bondage. In spite of her seemingly insurmountable problems, Jacobs forcefully exerts her will and positively shapes her destiny. Thus, Jacobs's legacies are perseverance, self-reliance, self-definition, and self-authorized agency.

My second chapter focuses on Octavia E. Butler's *Kindred* (1979) in which I examine the juxtaposition of the historical moment of chattel slavery with contemporary history, specifically the bicentennial year of 1976. Primarily a science fiction writer, Butler employs the device of time travel to offer a bridge across a metaphoric Middle Passage between the two worlds. She establishes the dialogic relationship of these texts by portraying the symbiotic relationship, often forgotten, of Black Americans and White Americans during and after slavery. Indeed, Butler juxtaposes the past and the present to illuminate the similarities shared by the nineteenth-century enslaved Black woman and her twentieth-century free counterpart. By highlighting the similarities as well as the differences, Butler offers a type of liberation from the confines of history for her readers. We, like Butler's protagonist, learn that for all we may know about slavery, we really do not know as much as we think we do because what we have traditionally learned has been from one perspective only—the hegemonic. Butler illuminates the fluid relationship between past and present by blurring the distinction between the two, a technique through which she reveals the ironies pertaining to American doctrine and ideology.

Chapter three, on Sherley Anne Williams's *Dessa Rose* (1986), offers an evaluation of the nature and ramifications of freedom within a site of bondage, signaling that freedom is more than a physical attainment. Historical representation is at the heart of Williams's narrative. Williams confronts the singular "master narrative" of history by writing her versions of history, from multiple subject positions, as history comprises many narratives. Not only does she present the enslaved Black woman's narrative, she also presents the White man's narrative and the White woman's narrative as these intersect with the enslaved Black woman's narrative. In this way, Williams shows how one may disarm the authority of the dominant discourse. Additionally, Williams posits a type of beloved community in her integrated community. At the center of this community is an interracial sisterhood that provides a liberatory model for Black and White women as they seek to build feminist coalitions around feminist issues. Williams creates her narrative from two existing, disparate, and ignored texts of slavery involving two women, one White and one Black, who are both agents of their own liberation from societal constraints. To create this community and this sisterhood, Williams must deconstruct ideologies of racial identities bound by stereotype and gender. In turn, her readers are invited to participate in their own liberation from racist and sexist ideologies concerning nineteenth-century womanhood and slavery.

In chapter four, I argue that Toni Morrison's *Beloved* (1987) provides the opportunity to achieve a metaphysical liberation from the tyranny of the historic period the novel features. Morrison's response to Harriet Jacobs's call transcends all of Jacobs's concerns, voiced and silenced. We may know, for instance, of Jacobs's selfless love for her children, symbolized by her self-imposed exile in her grandmother's garret for their sake. Her sacrifice is of mythic proportions. But we have not had the opportunity to know women like Morrison's Sethe, whose characterization is based historically upon an enslaved woman named Margaret Garner. Like Jacobs, Sethe is motivated by her maternal love to free herself and her family. In the wake of the Fugitive Slave Law of 1850, Sethe exerts her volition by choosing an alternative form of freedom—death— for herself and her children, but her plan is only partially fulfilled. Sethe then has to live with the tragic consequences and the memories of her desperate act of self-possession. Intersecting the present with memories of the past, Morrison shows how the past impinges on one's present. Morrison, like Williams, returns to the historic moment of slavery to challenge traditional ways of theorizing both bondage and freedom. In so doing, Morrison proposes a paradigm of metaphysical liberation. She shows that freeing the soul requires the individual to take a journey, both physical and metaphysical. I read the character Beloved as a spirit, not a ghost, who challenges others to face the pain and shame of the past. Morrison further reveals the complexities of a newly free woman's attempt to construct a whole sense of self and community in a racialized society.

Chapter five centers on J. California Cooper's *Family* (1992), where indeterminacies abound. Like Morrison, Cooper relies upon issues of incorporeality to construct a liberatory narrative of epic proportions. Her narrator, Clora, dies early in the narrative but continues as a disembodied narrator who witnesses racism's wide sweep from the ships of captivity of the 1400s to the lynchings of the twentieth century and beyond. Only in her disembodied state can the narrator reclaim what is important to her—all of her family, splintered and scattered by the institution of slavery. Ironically, Clora is able in death to do what she could not in life: keep her children, particularly her daughter, under her watchful eye. Even the usual is made unusual in *Family*. In Cooper's hands, the creation myth is a narrative of miscegenation; therefore, there is really only one race—the human race. In this way, Cooper offers a liberation from the boundaries of race, time, and space, boundaries that are perpetuated, according to Cooper, by our own investments in those boundaries. Accordingly, the narrator experiences a psychological liberation, a catharsis if you will, from the pain and trauma of her past through the telling of her life story. In doing so, the narrator seeks to understand better human motivation and behavior as both have negatively influenced her life and the lives of her ancestors and her progeny. This, in turn, allows her readers to consider vicariously these dynamics as well. Additionally, the perspective of the enslaved daughter is more specifically foregrounded by Cooper's choice of the enslaved daughter, Always, as the protagonist. Her name, seemingly a promise, is really a question as Cooper asks her readers to consider if indeed the circumstances and effects of enslavement are permanent and immutable.

Finally, chapter six examines Lorene Cary's *The Price of a Child* (1995). Cary, like Morrison, takes an existing text of slavery from William Still's *The Underground Railroad* (1872) as her source material to create a meditation on freedom, motherhood, community, and self-possession. Known in her enslaved life as Ginnie, the self-emancipated and self-named Mercer is the mother of three children, two by her owner. In order to emancipate herself and two of her children, Mercer pays the ultimate price for her freedom—she sacrifices her third child, held ransom in bondage by her owner. Centered on economic issues, Cary's narrative depicts the economies of bondage and freedom in Mercer's new life in the city of brotherly love, Philadelphia. How does one establish a free self in urban nineteenth-century America? One is never certain of the cost of bondage or the cost of freedom in *The Price of a Child*. In this vein, Cary interrupts pedestrian thinking concerning this dialectic. Cary's narrative raises these questions: What is the cost of freedom? What does one continue to pay for one's humanity in a commodity-driven, free enterprise, capitalist society?

In the epilogue, I take up the following: What do the liberatory narratives add to the present discourse concerning identity, freedom, and race relations? What can be gained from examining slavery through the lens of freedom? What aesthetic, political, and social issues are related to the representation of slavery in contemporary African American literature? Additionally, how does one bear witness—as writer or reader—to a trauma one has not experienced but which still exists?

Examining the revisionary practices of these writers through the lens of intertextuality reveals a dynamic model of cultural, ideological, and aesthetic change in the literary tradition of African-American women novelists. These narratives are liberatory not only in content and form, but in their projected and ideal reception as well. They serve, as McDowell writes, to "posit a female-gendered subjectivity, more complex in dimension [than the female emancipatory narrative], that dramatizes not what was done to slave women, but what they did with what was done to them" ("Negotiating" 146). Overall, the great force of these liberatory narratives is not that they show the reader what slavery was like, but importantly that they show what slavery—the absence of personal freedom—felt like, which in turn allows the reader *to feel* what slavery was like. Thus the liberatory narrative can effect a release of this historic pain and shame. Ideally, after reading these narratives, the reader knows more acutely the concept of freedom. "Contemporary novels of slavery," Deborah McDowell observes,

> [witness] slavery after freedom in order to engrave that past on the memory of the present but, more importantly, on future generations that might otherwise succumb to the cultural amnesia that has begun to re-enslave us all in social and literary texts that impoverish our imaginations. ("Negotiating" 160–161)

Going beyond what McDowell identifies as their pedagogic value, I offer that the liberatory narratives by Butler, Williams, Morrison, Cooper, and Cary have a *civic* value: they can help to emancipate their readers from the cultural and historical amnesia that has surrounded the issue of slavery in the United States. By creating this discursive space of interrogation, these writers recast and augment our understanding of our sometimes painful, but always collective, past. In many ways, these narratives foster the conversation on race the country so sorely needs. The liberatory narrative does not simply present or chronicle the past; it disrupts history as we know it in order to illuminate what has not been told, what has been ignored, what has been silenced, and what has been forgotten.

Chapter 1

Harriet A. Jacobs's *Incidents in the Life of a Slave Girl, Written by Herself*

Slavery is terrible for men; but it is far more terrible for women. Superadded to the burden common to all, they have wrongs, and sufferings, and mortifications peculiarly their own.

   —*Incidents in the Life of a Slave Girl*

Pity me, and pardon me, O virtuous reader! You never knew what it is to be a slave; to be entirely unprotected by law or custom; to have the laws reduce you to the condition of a chattel, entirely subject to the will of another.

       —*Incidents*

My master had power and law on his side; I had a determined will. There is might in each.

       —*Incidents*

The Ur-Narrative of Black Womanhood

No STUDY OF CONTEMPORARY discourses of slavery can ignore Harriet A. Jacobs's *Incidents in the Life of a Slave Girl, Written by Herself* (1861) as an antecedent text. *Incidents in the Life of a Slave Girl* sets forth the terms of discussion for so many narratives that follow in the literary tradition of Black women by providing ample opportunity to examine the feminist themes of female sexuality, motherhood, individualism, and community.[1] These dominant themes, as portrayed by Jacobs in her feminist emancipatory narrative, not only relate to an enslaved woman's life, but also characterize the constructed discourse that gives rise to the contemporary Black woman's text. Employing the conventions of the sentimental novel, as rhetorical models for liberation were not possible for her, Jacobs creates her own paradigm in her portrayal of her fictional self, Linda Brent, an activist who forcefully exerts her free will—her volition—in her reductive environment. In the persona of Linda Brent (Harriet Jacobs's self-protective pseudonym), Jacobs redefines her commodified self as an African American woman in the nineteenth century. Linda Brent's personhood is predicated upon her ability to renegotiate the socially constructed boundaries of institutions and experiences forced upon her by White enslaving patriarchy. Accordingly, Jacobs inscribes Linda Brent as a volitional agent, capable of overruling the hegemony of the racist patriarchal and institutional forces that seek to defile all aspects of the enslaved Black woman's life. Although a number of critics have examined Jacobs's *Incidents in the Life of a Slave Girl* (hereafter referred to as *Incidents*) in terms of its generic qualities, contemporary feminist critics and novelists have clarified the place of this narrative as an Ur-text that establishes the constructed discourse of the Black woman's narrative. Before examining the particulars of Jacobs's narrative, a brief overview of the enslaved Black woman's life as it has been treated in historical studies may help to show how revolutionary Jacobs's narrative is.

Traditionally, historians have focused their critical attention primarily on the institution, not the culture, of slavery and secondarily on the enslaved Black *male*, so much so that feminist critical studies of the institution and of the enslaved Black woman are mostly quite recent.[2] The most comprehensive of such recent historical studies is Deborah Gray White's *Ar'n't I a Woman: Female Slaves in the Plantation South* (1985). White does what previous historians failed to do: she analyzes the enslaved Black woman as the embodiment and continuation of the African culture she preserved and utilized in constructing her African American culture. White corrects numerous stereotypical myths, including those myths which inform the themes examined herein concerning the nature of the African American woman's life in bondage.

The violation and exploitation of the enslaved Black woman's sexuality are among the most pervasive themes in African American history. While one's sex is an anatomical fact, one's sexuality is culturally constructed. It could be argued that this construction is the very way a society fictionalizes its relationship to the act of sex, creating gender-specific roles. Because White patriarchy constructed gender specifically in ways that served to control female sexuality and to ensure the interests of White male supremacy, the exploitation and misappropriation of the Black woman's sexuality are not surprising.

In her analysis, White notes that the Europeans were not interested in recognizing or understanding the cultural practices and behaviors of African women and constructed the myth of the Black female's sexual promiscuity or immorality for their own subjective reasons. For example, White explains,

> [t]he idea that black women were exceptionally sensual first gained credence when Englishmen went to Africa to buy slaves. Unaccustomed to the requirements of a tropical climate, Europeans mistook seminudity for lewdness. Similarly, they misinterpreted African cultural traditions, so that polygamy was attributed to the Africans' uncontrolled lust, tribal dances were reduced to the level of orgy, and African religions lost the sacredness that had sustained generations of ancestral worshipers. (29)

The African woman's sexuality was mistakenly interpreted by traders and enslavers who then placed a deliberately negative moral value on its expression and a purposefully positive monetary value on its production.

White's discussion of motherhood in African society sheds light on the assumptions and practices that the African woman brought with her to the institution of slavery. In Africa, White writes, the Black woman's primary role was motherhood (66). In West Africa, women perpetuated and sustained their society's cultural survival; they were the bearers of their heritage and tradition. As their society's primary nurturers, they established and maintained conventional behaviors among their families and their communities. African women were unquestionably the foundation of their society, and unlike their African American enslaved descendants, they were protected by laws, family, and customs.

White's illuminating analysis of the enslaved woman's African culture as it relates to sexuality and motherhood delineates how tragically alien the enslaved African American woman's life in the New World was from that of her African foremothers. In the New World, enslaved African American women struggled to recreate their ancestral and traditional kinship patterns in their immediate domains, the family and the community, which provided the strength and perseverance to survive servitude. In this manner, the enslaved African American woman endeavored to reclaim and to maintain the essence of her African legacy of womanhood.

In her discussions of female sexuality and of motherhood, White examines two prevalent and reductive images of Black women—those of the Jezebel and the mammy—both rooted in the historical circumstances of slavery. The Jezebel image, White observes, "in every way . . . was the counter image of the mid-nineteenth-century ideal of the Victorian lady. She did not lead men and children to God; piety was foreign to her" (29). The enslavers quickly learned that the fecund enslaved Black woman was the most profitable and economical means by which an enslaver could increase his stock, particularly after trans-Atlantic trading was abolished in 1808. As Angela Davis explains, "The right claimed by slaveowners and their agents over the bodies of female slaves was a direct expression of their presumed property rights over Black people as a whole. The license to rape emanated from and facilitated the ruthless economic domination that was the gruesome hallmark of slavery" (*Women, Race and Class* 175). Thus, the agents of slavocracy constructed the myth of the lewdly sensuous enslaved Black woman—the Jezebel—who animalistically and uninhibitedly acted upon her sexual urges when in reality her body became the site of White male licentiousness and economic desire.

Conversely, the mammy image was a mythical construct of asexuality. As an enslaved Black woman who worked in the enslaver's house, the religiously faithful mammy generally managed the household and cared for the physical and emotional needs of her owner and his family. In many cases, suckling and rearing the enslaver's children were the mammy's primary responsibilities. In her later years, the mammy, having been a good and faithful servant, generally held a position of respect within her surrogate family and a position of power within her own community. "As the personification of the ideal slave, and the ideal woman," White concludes, "Mammy was an ideal symbol of the patriarchal tradition" (58). I believe that the mammy image's cultural currency resided in its power to socialize and to condition its viewers to identify Black women in specifically circumscribed ways. This observation, of course, could be true of all of the stereotypes surrounding Black women. In particular, the mammy's singular aptitude for domestic servitude was distilled as the stereotype of an obedient, long-suffering, and dehumanized worker to be used in the service of those more powerful.

It is clear from the recent scholarship produced by Black feminist critics that female sexuality and motherhood, as well as individualism and communalism, are realities still subject to appropriation and revision by White patriarchal hegemony. For the enslaved African American woman, matters of sexuality generally equaled matters of fecundity as White enslavers commodified and exploited the Black woman's reproductive abilities. Thus, a discussion of the enslaved Black woman's sexuality is incomplete without a discussion of her disjunctive experience of motherhood. In slavery, the Black woman's positions as sexualized object and racialized worker met in her ability to replenish the enslaved labor force. Denied the right to own herself or her offspring, the enslaved mother had little or no control in choosing her sexual partner, in utilizing methods of contraception, and in the fates of her children. After giving birth, she lived in constant jeopardy of separation from her children. Incredibly, the role of mother, a communal role so valued in Africa as the conservator and transmitter of the general culture, was diminished by the institution of slavery, an institution sanctioned by United States law, to that of breeder—replenisher of her enslaver's stock—and of worker. In cases of infertility or age, her inability to reproduce further depreciated her value and her status in this commodity-driven economy.

The realization of the enslaved woman's individuality, of her personal worth and personal distinctiveness—a central feature of Jacobs's narrative and of the liberatory narrative—is striking, given that the patriarchal institution of slavery sought to eradicate all traces of the enslaved woman's self—her very humanity—in order to perpetuate and to preserve its domination and hegemony. Patricia M. Robinson observes, "Black slaves were . . . very costly 'beasts of burden' whose cultural sexual patterns had to be interrupted and broken, forcing them to conform to patterns that would profit the white farmer and plantation owner" (261). If the enslaved woman did not realize or acknowledge her own selfhood, she could not value her personhood; therefore, she was less likely to rebel against her enslavers. In other words, individualism precedes agency: *I am* precedes *I can*. Ironically, motherhood could cause the enslaved woman to feign complacency since escape or insurrection was more complicated for the enslaved mother. There were cases, nonetheless, where motherhood provided the impetus or inspiration for rebellion or escape. This compromised situation conditioned the convoluted roles and emotions relating to sexuality and motherhood for the enslaved Black woman.[3]

Generically, the emancipatory narrative may be considered a sub-genre of autobiography, as John Sekora has convincingly argued.[4] Recent post-structuralist critics, however, acknowledge the nebulous nature of autobiography's ability to (re)present truth and reality, inasmuch as "autobiography lives in the two worlds of history and literature, objective fact and subjective awareness" (Butterfield 1). Recognizing these opposing worlds, scholars of autobiography often question whether or not fact can remain separate from fiction or fantasy in relating one's life experience. As William L. Andrews argues in *To Tell a Free Story*, the antebellum emancipatory narrative, "written by himself or herself," may be examined within the genre of autobiography, for the enslaved narrator's "autobiography became a very public way of declaring oneself free, of redefining and then assigning [freedom] to oneself" (xi). As a public declaration, the emancipatory narrative is also an example of testimonial autobiography. Jacobs even refers to her narrative as "her testimony" (1). Because of the enslaved narrator's peculiar situation in regard to reader reception, the "demands of truthfulness and self-preservation were often at odds in the experience of blacks in America," and particularly, in the experiences of Black women (Andrews 3).

As others have observed in terms of genre, placing *Incidents* in the context of sentimental literature provides a greater understanding of Jacobs's narrative.[5] In her study of nineteenth-century Black women writers, Hazel V. Carby argues that we must consider the ideological construct of White womanhood in nineteenth-century America in order to assess accurately the cultural, material, and ideological condition of Black women in slavery. It is important, Carby insists, to situate the "narratives by black women within the dominant discourse of white female sexuality in order [for us] to be able to comprehend and analyze the ways in which black women, as writers, addressed, used, transformed, and on occasion, subverted the dominant ideological codes" (*Reconstructing* 20–21). The flourishing of nineteenth-century Anglo-American sentimental literature, the literature of "true [white] womanhood," occurred concomitantly with the antebellum proliferation of emancipatory narratives. The popularity of sentimental novels is just one of the reasons Jacobs chose to employ this literary mode in constructing her narrative. The emphasis on feeling and emotion, characteristics of sentimental literature, also worked well in delineating the experiences of slavery, an emotionally charged subject. Although traditionally defined in ways that reinscribe patriarchal definitions about and attitudes toward women, sentimental writing is now defined, thanks to recent feminist scholarship, as

> an imaginative mode generated by a dominant pattern of cultural perception, gender-related but not necessarily gender-specific, manifesting itself in narratives privileging affectional ties, characterized by plot conventions, character types, and language usage designed to address the primary vision of human connection in a dehumanized world. (Dobson 171)

Jacobs's narrative does indeed attempt to show humanity in a dehumanizing world, and her choice of genre assisted her endeavor. As Valerie Smith so aptly puts it, Jacobs "seized authority over her literary restraints in much the same way that she seized power in life" ("Loopholes" 213). Antithetical to the purpose and content of the emancipatory narrative, Anglo-American sentimental literature reflected the societal expectations of White womanhood. Sentimental literature "emphasized the cultivation of sensibility, the glorification of virtue, the preservation of family life, the revival of religion, and the achievement of a utopian society" (*Witnessing Slavery* 64). And as Carby reminds us, "the attributes of True Womanhood, by which a woman judged herself and was judged by her husband, her neighbors and society, could be divided into four cardinal virtues—piety, purity, submissiveness, and domesticity" (*Reconstructing* 23). Measured against constructs shaped by puritanical ideals and Christian morality, enslaved Black women were deemed the immoral instigators of their own fall from grace. The stereotype of the Jezebel helped to provide rationalization for the sexual exploitation of enslaved Black women by White men, while simultaneously providing justification for the White men's behavior in the eyes of their White wives, mothers, and sisters. In this context, Hortense J. Spillers observes, "The African American women's community and Anglo-American women's community under shared cultural conditions, were the twin actants on a common psychic landscape [and] were subject to the same fabric of dread and humiliation [as] [n]either could claim her body and its various productions as her own" ("Mama's Baby" 77). However shared their conditions, eighteenth- and nineteenth-century Black women and White women had one significant dissimilarity: they were not defined and interpreted by patriarchy in the same way.

Certainly, one of Jacobs's primary reasons for adapting the elements of the nineteenth-century woman's story is to utilize the literary conventions and sources of her nineteenth-century American readership to effect a political end, namely universal endorsement of the abolitionist cause. Of Jacobs's rhetorical choice, Claudia Tate theorizes:

> [t]he pedagogy of sentimentality had considerable influence on white
> and black American literary culture. Black writers apparently
> appropriated many sentimental conventions to give expression to
> their social concerns and to demonstrate their intellectual compe-
> tence in terms that the dominant culture respected. (*Domestic
> Allegories* 64–65)

To lessen the offensiveness of revealing unsavory incidents, Jacobs employs many of the conventions of the dominant discourse to make her narrative more palatable to her White audience. In other words, while Jacobs does not assume a White woman's persona, she uses the literary conventions "that would help her to establish rapport with her Northern white women readers" ("Meditations" 5) as she hoped they would be responsive to her call.

As Jacobs illustrates in her narrative, the enslaved Black woman was denied the opportunity to cultivate wholesomely her domestic life and was not allowed to retain her piety or "purity" in the midst of White male licentiousness. Additionally, the enslaved African American woman was not judged by her ability to synthesize or to mediate her two cultures. These circumstances are particularly evident in Jacobs's narrative. "Writing in the nineteenth-century and in the form of the domestic sentimental novel," as Mary Helen Washington concludes, Jacobs "had to observe conventions of decorum which demanded virginity, modesty, and delicacy of women" ("Meditations" 5). Ironically, that Jacobs's narrative so neatly fits the rubric of sentimental novels caused historian John Blassingame to doubt its validity as an authentic emancipatory narrative.[6] His reading is due in part to the pejorative ways that sentimental literature has been read and analyzed until recent feminist literary scholarship redeemed it. Jacobs's narrative, its validity firmly established by Jean Fagin Yellin's meticulous research, is a discourse of liberation that demands a revised definition of true womanhood to include, as Beth Doriani suggests, "the world of the black woman—as a person inextricably bound up with others yet responsible for her own survival" (207). *Incidents* then provides ample opportunity for readers to examine the ways Jacobs employs the themes of sentimental fiction—female sexuality, motherhood, individualism, community—to construct her discourse of liberation by utilizing these themes as well as the conventions of the emancipatory narrative and the sentimental novel.

The key feature of *Incidents* is its retrospective appropriation of the volitional self. At the beginning of Jacobs's narrative, there is no sense of a clearly defined individual self to be noted in the character of Linda Brent, Jacobs's fictional self. Employing the introductory sentence characteristic of the genre of the emancipatory narrative, Brent begins her narration self-consciously, as if her childhood experiences were typical for an enslaved child. "I was born a slave[,]" she relates, "but I never knew it till six years of happy childhood had passed away. . . . I was so fondly shielded that I never dreamed that I was a piece of merchandise, trusted to [my parents] for safe keeping, and liable to be demanded of them at any moment" (5). Only through retrospection does she view her selfhood as distinct from that of the many Black children in slavery, and, indeed, it is. Unlike most in bondage, Brent's first six years of life are spent with her nuclear family—her father, her mother, and her brother; she also enjoys a loving relationship with her maternal grandmother and her maternal uncle. These six years of familial and communal nurturing seem to be the source of Brent's perception of herself as a unique individual.

Indeed, a key feature of the text is that moment when the narrator recognizes her own will to live born of her perception of self-worth. Jacobs's narrative also clearly represents the need to repossess the self in a moment of clear objectification of her person and body. Brent's sense of selfhood first emerges in the text as she recounts the sexual advances of her master, Dr. Flint, in her fifteenth year. Thus, when Brent embarks on a journey for self-possession in order to eliminate the potential exploitation of her sexuality, her desire for freedom is both physical and spiritual. She seeks freedom from her socially imposed physical bondage as well as from her socially imposed psychic bondage. She confronts the institution of motherhood, the awareness of herself as a unique individual, and the continuing realization that she needs a community in order to possess and to complete herself as a unified being.

In *Incidents*, as Brent intimates, one of the greatest dangers for an enslaved Black woman in antebellum America was the abuse and misuse of the enslaved woman's sexuality because she was so often the object of White male sexual and economic desires. Locked into the conventions of the sentimental novel, Jacobs "presents Dr. Flint as a jealous lover and herself as a vulnerable, young woman undergoing a 'perilous passage' rather than a slave whose sexual exploitation was legally sanctioned. Her use of romantic language seems more suited to a story of seduction than to the slave woman's life" ("Meditations" 5). The trait of vulnerability and the act of violation are essential elements of female emancipatory narratives. It is another specific trait of the female emancipatory narrative to signal the function of sexuality as an impetus of enlightenment for the enslaved woman. Brent's developing sexuality causes her to differentiate perceptibly between the enslaved man's and the enslaved woman's experience of slavery: after her daughter is born, Brent concludes, "Slavery is terrible for men; but it is far more terrible for women. Superadded to the burden common to all, *they* have wrongs, and sufferings, and mortifications peculiarly their own" (77; emphasis in original). The enslaved Black woman lived in double jeopardy: she was both a potential victim of rape and a potential object of sexual commodification. Frances Smith Foster explains,

> As victim she became the assailant, since her submission to repeated
> violations was not in line with the values of sentimental heroines who
> died rather than be abused. Her survival of these ordeals and contin-
> ued participation in other aspects of slave life seemed to connote, if
> not outright licentiousness, at least a less sensitive and abused spirit
> than that of white heroines. (*Witnessing Slavery* 131–132)

Certainly, the nature of her womanhood could not conform to the standards set by the dominant and domineering Anglo-American culture. If the enslaved woman wished to reclaim herself from the delimiting and usurping circumstances of racist and sexist bondage, to do so she had also to redefine the construct of Black womanhood.

Incidents marks and characterizes the turning point as a moment born of introspection. "For most young slave women," Jacqueline Jones observes, "sexual maturity marked a crucial turning point" (32). Linda Brent provides strong evidence of this turning point in her fifteenth year—"a sad epoch in the life of a slave girl":

> My master began to whisper foul words in my ear. Young as I was, I could not remain ignorant of their import. I tried to treat them with indifference or contempt. The master's age, my extreme youth, and the fear that his conduct would be reported to my grandmother, made him bear this treatment for many months. . . . He tried his utmost to corrupt the pure principles my grandmother had instilled. He peopled my young mind with unclean images, such as only a vile monster could think of. I turned away from him with disgust and hatred. But he was my master. (27)

Without sustainable familial protection and without legal protection, young Linda Brent appears to have no initial recourse: she must seem outwardly accepting of her physical vulnerability and her fated victimization while inwardly rebelling against them. While in bondage, Linda Brent learns the difference between fraudulent and genuine morality, a key component to the recognition of her volitional self.

The heroine also discovers the difference between education and experience. Indeed, the reader is invited to consider what had been the effects on Brent's perception of her sexuality in light of her religious, social, and moral training and its antithesis in her dealings with Dr. Flint. The text establishes a record of her developing awareness of that difference. Inherited at the age of twelve by Dr. Flint's young daughter, Linda Brent is confronted by the reality of the enslaved woman's sexual life during her first few weeks at the Flints's home. Miscegenation in most instances signaled sexual relations born of misuse and abuse of power. For example, Brent witnesses both the vicious beating of an enslaved Black husband, who had previously argued in the presence of the overseer with his enslaved wife concerning the paternity of her unusually fair-skinned baby, *and* the subsequent sale of the enslaved couple. Brent recounts, "When the mother was delivered into the trader's hands, she said, 'You *promised* to treat me well.' To which [Dr. Flint] replied, 'You have let your tongue run too far; damn you!' She had forgotten that it was a crime for a slave to tell who was the father of her child" (13; emphasis in original).

Brent learns several lessons from this episode: (1) that marriages between enslaved African Americans are disrespected and disregarded by the enslavers,
(2) that the enslaved woman has no legal authority over her body and her
progeny, and (3) that sexually abusive enslavers could and would ruthlessly
sell their subjugated concubines as well as their own offspring with them.

As Linda learns of the pain and betrayal associated with enslaved/enslaver
relations, the lesson provides her with the cultural insight to examine this relationship critically. The dichotomous nature of female sexuality—the pleasure and the danger—emerges subtly from this episode as well. As Carole S.
Vance explains, female sexuality "is simultaneously a domain of restriction,
repression, and danger as well as a domain of exploration, pleasure, and agency"
(1). In slavery, the dangerous sphere dominated the enslaved woman's expression of sexuality, as dramatized overtly in the above story, while the pleasur-
able sphere necessarily remained cloaked, veiled, and only intimated, as in
the mother's complaint (quoted above), by the broken promise of some kind
of pleasure and by the stated disappointment of the woman, dejected upon
being betrayed. In other words, "sexual harassment, sexual intercourse, and
childbirth are not tangential to a narrative of enslavement, escape, and emancipation; they are that narrative" (Sanchez-Eppler 84).

In *Incidents*, Jacobs characterizes the vulnerability and victimization of
enslaved women in terms of isolated agony, sexual harassment, and psychological battering and posits the antidote—strategies of resistance—as avoidance, repression, and communal support. Dr. Flint, "a hoary-headed miscreant,"
(34) begins making sexual advances toward Brent when she is fifteen. In chapter five, revealingly entitled "The Trials of Girlhood," Brent describes the isolated agony she endures, unable to confide in others or in her free grandmother
about Dr. Flint's sexual and psychological abuse. She could not speak because
she had witnessed what would happen if she broke her silence. Equally important, she could not reveal what was occurring because to do so would compromise her community's perception of her purity. Her suppressed desire to
tell of her trials testifies to her awareness of her valued personhood. The enslaved community feared extreme punishment, and none spoke of Dr. Flint's
indiscretions. Additionally, Aunt Martha, Brent's grandmother, was morally
"strict on such subjects" (29). Linda's primary strategy of resistance, then, becomes avoidance—"by being in the midst of people" (53). She finds safety in
her community. Even the distance of years, however, does not erase the psychological effects of the degradation and humiliation caused by Dr. Flint's lechery. Jacobs confides, "I cannot tell how much I suffered in the presence of these
wrongs, nor how I am still pained by the retrospect" (28). Brent suggests that

her trauma led to the repression of her developing sexuality. The structure of the narrative depends, nonetheless, on the heroine's gradual discovery of the value of resistance, both individual and communal.

So interesting is this text's treatment of repressed sexuality that it bears discussion here. A telling episode of repression occurs in chapter seven, "The Lover." Significantly, Brent confines her acknowledgment of her erotic desires to the period of her youth. In those years, the young Brent appears to have assimilated the dominant culture's values of Christian morality by idealizing the notion of sexual relations within the notion of romantic love. Linda Brent falls in love with a free Black man, a young carpenter. "Youth will be youth," Brent recollects, "I loved, and I indulged the hope that the dark clouds around me would turn out a *bright* lining. . . . I loved him with all the *ardor* of a young girl's first love" (37; emphasis added). Linda romantically dreams, a characteristic convention of the sentimental novel, of a love that will rescue her from the turmoil of her life: "This love-dream had been my support through many trials; and I could not bear to run the risk of having it suddenly dissipated" (38). Inspired by love, Linda confides her dilemma to her grandmother and to an influential, neighboring White woman. Linda's dream of rescue ultimately dissipates, however, as Dr. Flint refuses to sell Brent to her lover or to anyone. Confronted by a jealous Dr. Flint, Linda again reveals her awareness of her individuality. In response to Dr. Flint's noxious demands, she asks, "Don't you suppose, sir, that a slave can have some preference about marrying? Do you suppose that all men are alike to her?" (39). Even though he strikes her and threatens to kill her, she continues to refuse his presumed right to do whatever he likes to her (39). Still, Dr. Flint continues his sexual harassment by proposing that she move with him to another state without Mrs. Flint and forbids any further exchange between young Linda and the object of her affection.

In spite of her romantic desires, Linda acquiesces, not wanting harm to come to her lover then or later, by sending him away. After Brent advises him to go to a free state, her lover leaves. For Brent, "the lamp of hope had gone out. The dream of [her] girlhood was over. [She] felt lonely and desolate" (42). After her loss, Linda finds comfort in having her grandmother and her brother to love, although she now realizes how tenuous all bonds of love are for the enslaved woman, and never again in the narrative does Brent mention marriage or even the notion of romantic love.[7] "Marriage and bondage, then, are not merely antithetical in *Incidents*," as Claudia Tate observes; "they are mutually exclusive" (*Domestic Allegories* 32). I would triangulate Tate's opposing thematics of *marriage* and *bondage* by adding a third—*romance*. Linda is not entitled to marriage or romance in her state of bondage. Because the economic value placed on her body by the institution of slavery mediates all aspects of her life, Linda concludes that she must revise her participation in such a morally bankrupt institution, not because she wishes to succumb to its immorality but rather to usurp its immoral authority in her life. Although she seems to be powerless, Brent realizes that she does have power over the choices open to her.

The text, at this point, offers strategies of resistance as Brent asserts her volition—her will—in her deterministic environment. Dr. Flint devises scheme after scheme; but, as a prominent physician, he wishes to conceal his base desires. Proposing to give to Brent her own secluded house in exchange for her sexual favors, Dr. Flint initiates "a *perilous passage* in the slave girl's life" (53; emphasis added). Brent explains, "I was determined that the master, whom I so hated and loathed, who had blighted the prospects of my youth, and made my life a desert, should not, after my long struggle with him, succeed at last in trampling his victim under his feet. I would do any thing, every thing, for the sake of defeating him" (53). The only way of subverting Dr. Flint, Brent concludes, is to choose an untouchable lover. Thus Brent's strategy of resistance is to reappropriate her sexuality by exercising her free will within the limits constructed around her. With deliberation, Brent selects a young, successful, unmarried White man as her lover because "[i]t seems less degrading to give one's self, than to submit to compulsion. There is something *akin to freedom* in having a lover who has no control over you, except that which he gains by kindness and attachment" (55; emphasis added).

In light of Brent's abovementioned confession, Saidiya V. Hartman insightfully probes Jacobs's use of seduction in the narrative. Hartman writes, "*Incidents* makes use of seduction and recasts it by emphasizing the degradation of enslavement, the perverse domesticity of the paternal institution, and the violence enacted on the captive body within an arena purportedly defined by ties of sentiment, mutual affection, and interest" (103). Key here is the phrase *purportedly*: seduction may indeed exist outside of Hartman's defined arena, as it does in *Incidents* and many other texts by women writers, usually for political reasons. Hartman further questions Brent's justification for choosing Mr. Sands as "something akin to freedom" (Jacobs 55). For Hartman, "akin to freedom" expresses "the limited possibilities, constraint, despair, and duress that condition the giving of the self, not unlimited options, freedom, or unencumbered choice" (104). My reading of Jacobs's narrative as well as other narratives in the Black woman's literary tradition suggests that choices are never unencumbered. For many reasons, Hartman doubts Brent's ability to choose authentically her lover in a property exchange governed by dominance. She explains, "[I]f desperation, recklessness, and hopelessness determine 'choosing one's lover,' absolute distinctions between compulsion and assent cannot be sustained" (111). While Hartman's argument is compelling, I find Brent's phrase, "akin to freedom," to be deliberately and appropriately meaningful. This phrase signals Brent's understanding of the parameters of her existence, parameters of "compulsion and assent" that she cannot simply vanquish by her sheer will. Brent may be desperate and even reckless in her choice, but she is not hopeless. Indeed, choosing Mr. Sands as her lover is a sign of hope.[8] She is hopeful that her act will give rise not only to her future children's freedom but to her own freedom. Given that all choices are encumbered in some way, I do not find Jacobs's approximation of freedom so deficient. It is, however, unusual for a woman writer to reveal this level of personal information. Tate explains how extreme Jacobs's strategy and the telling of it are: "The willful exchange of female sexual experience for the preservation of psychological autonomy and the assertion of political freedom were radical, indeed revolutionary acts for a woman, white or black, to execute, let alone to record in a public document" (*Domestic Allegories* 30). Indeed, Brent's choice shows that miscegenation could be used as a tool of resistance. Identifying one of the differences between the sentimental tradition and Jacobs's use of it, Jean Fagan Yellin observes, "Despite her language . . . [Jacobs] does not characterize herself conventionally as a passive female victim. On the contrary, she asserts that she was—even when young and a slave—an effective moral agent, and she takes full responsibility for her action" (273). Brent brilliantly exercises her choice in order to usurp Dr. Flint's control, defying his wishes and denying his desires.

A reader may anticipate what the text next provides: the heroine exhibits a moment of strong moral indignation. Conscious of her moral concessions, Brent rightfully indicts the institution of slavery as the cause of her shame. If slavery had been abolished, Brent reasons, she would have married the man of her choice, would have had a home, would have been protected by the laws, and would have retained her virtue (54). Instead, she enters into a sexual relationship with the sympathetic Mr. Sands, who later betrays her by not manumitting their children. She chooses Mr. Sands because he is the lesser of her known evils, but she *does choose him*. Of Brent's actions, Mary Helen Washington concludes, "Brent's deliberate and knowing choice to take a white lover and to bear two children by him in order to foil Dr. Flint's plans to make her his mistress is, in some ways, an act of emancipation" ("Meditations" 6). Brent hopes, as a part of her long-range strategy of resistance, that Sands will one day be able to buy and to manumit her and any children she may have by him.

Incidents proffers the climactic moment in which the heroine actually undertakes the act of self-definition. In passionate language, Brent laments her sad plight by proposing "a new definition of female morality grounded in her own experience" (Yellin 275):

> Pity me, and pardon me, O virtuous reader! You never knew what it is to be a slave; to be entirely unprotected by law or custom; to have the laws reduce you to the condition of a chattel, entirely subject to the will of another. . . . I know I did wrong. . . . Still, in looking back, calmly, . . . I feel that the slave woman ought not to be judged by the same standards as others. (56)

Understanding herself in relation to her world and the limitations of that world, Jacobs repeatedly asserts her human rights. With deliberation, Brent momentarily subverts and deflects Dr. Flint's intention to exploit her sexuality by removing herself from his grasp. She does so bodily in two ways: by reappropriating her sexuality as a weapon of resistance and by repossessing her body from his control.

Jacobs's narrative presents the heroine developing an awareness of her individual will. Linda Brent becomes increasingly aware of her right to choose one action over another action, and of her right to choose with or without explanation or declaration. Motherhood, as Brent knew, would occur as a result of her sexual encounters with her lover, Mr. Sands. Brent gives birth to a son, Benjamin, her "new tie to life" (58), and shortly thereafter to her daughter, Ellen, "another link to life" (76). Interestingly, while Linda Brent offers explanations concerning the conception and birth of her son, she offers no explanation, other than the obvious, for the birth of her daughter. One may conclude of this omission that Brent chooses, after the birth of her firstborn, to explore what Kristeva calls *jouissance*—blissfully erotic and sensual pleasure. In other words, if she begins her relations with Sands for a particular and singular reason—to deter Dr. Flint—what prompts her to continue? Narrative aporia serves as another tool of resistance against patriarchy's control of her sexuality. Her reticence, in this context, implies free will.

A measure of the magnitude of the dramatic conflict involved in *Incidents* may be seen in the complexity of the emotional stakes involved for the enslaved heroine who is a mother. The mother of two children at nineteen years of age, Linda Brent experiences the pleasures and dangers of motherhood. The enslaved Black mother, Brent explains, "may be an ignorant creature, degraded by the system that has brutalized her from childhood; but she has a mother's instincts, and is capable of feeling a mother's agonies" (16). Her son, she confides, took "deep root in [her] existence, though [his] cling-ing fondness excited a *mixture of love and pain*" (62; emphasis added). Since Dr. Flint, her antagonist, continues to seek control of Brent, she fears for her children and for herself as they all legally belong to Dr. Flint. They are, in other words, both the participants in the conflict as well as the prizes of the conflict.

Not wishing to succumb to her victimization, Brent attempts to secure her children's freedom through their White father, her lover Sands, but Dr. Flint quashes her plan by refusing to sell his legally sanctioned property. En-raged by her ability to thwart him and by his inability to possess her, Dr. Flint physically and verbally abuses Brent. His actions thus exacerbate the dramatic struggle. Dr. Flint seeks to tempt Brent into submission by offering her a home and by offering freedom for her and the children. She decides she would rather see her children killed than in his control under any circumstance, prefigur-ing several of the mother protagonists of the liberatory narrative. After rejecting his offer, Brent is dispatched from town to labor on his nearby plan-tation. The drama intensifies when Brent surreptitiously uses this new arrange-ment to further her plans for freedom. In a revealing passage, Brent identifies her primary concern: the untoward burden of motherhood on the enslaved mother. She explains, "I could have made my escape alone; but it was more for my helpless children than for myself that I longed for freedom. Though the boon would have been precious to me, above all price, I would not have taken it at the expense of leaving them in slavery" (89). Importantly, although they complicate her plans for escape, her children give her the inspiration and the courage necessary to secure their freedom. In this way, Brent is, accord-ing to Joanne Braxton, the "outraged mother" who "makes use of wit and in-telligence to overwhelm and defeat a more powerful foe" ("Redefinition" 385). Thus motherhood is the impetus, according to Jacobs, for the enslaved Black mother's determination and courage.

Jacobs resolves to free herself and her children no matter the cost. Em-ploying a strategy of resistance through concealment, Brent removes herself physically from the conflict so that Dr. Flint will be provoked into releasing his treacherous hold on her children. She first hides in the home of a sympa-thetic White woman and later in her grandmother's tiny garret, her "loop-hole of retreat" (114) where she remains for seven years, until she can escape to freedom. Valerie Smith explains,

> Jacobs's phrase, "the loophole of retreat," possesses an ambiguity of
> meaning that extends to the literal loophole as well. For if a loophole

signifies for Jacobs a place of withdrawal, it signifies in common
parlance an avenue of escape. ("Loopholes" 212)

The tables are more dramatically turned when she finds a way to manipulate
her oppressor economically. Eluding Dr. Flint, Brent forces him to spend a great
deal of money in pursuit of her. Her strategy, in turn, causes Dr. Flint, in need
of money, to sell her two children indirectly to their father. Step by step, she
moves closer to her dream of freeing her children: they are now owned by
their father, an improvement despite the fact that he does not exercise immediately his uncontested agency or moral authority to emancipate them.

Self-defined as a person capable of choosing a course of action, of defining her role in life, of reclaiming control over her environment through her
deliberate choice, Brent realizes that she alone possesses her self and thus resists all efforts to control or to subjugate her individual will. As Brent reveals,
"When [Dr. Flint] told me that I was made for his use, made to obey his command in *every* thing; that I was nothing but a slave, whose will must and should
surrender to his, never before had my puny arm felt half so strong" (18; emphasis in original). Brent, feeling empowered, resolves never to be conquered,
never to relinquish her self-defined worth as an individual. Brent's greatest
show of individuality grows out of her brave plans for escape. She relies upon
her free will, her volition, to make "a way out of no way."[9] Brent realizes that
some may consider her particular life as an enslaved Black woman a compara-
tively easy one as she was never overworked, never whipped, and never
branded; yet, she knows and shows that slavery, if not resisted, corrupts the
selfhood of even the least persecuted in bondage. Even after her escape to the
North, Brent maintains her righteous indignation toward the violation of her
personhood. Faced with racial discrimination in a Northern hotel, Brent, refusing to accept the definition of Other, rebukes the servants there who "ought
to be dissatisfied with *themselves*, for not having too much self-respect to submit to such treatment" (177; emphasis in original). Self-authorized, Brent acknowledges her own humanity and expects her humanity to be recognized by
others.

Because *Incidents* inscribes the awareness of individualism as directly related to the individual's link to her community, an examination of that self
in relation to the community is revealing. In African American culture, feminist individuality has little in common with the Anglo-American masculinist
concept of rugged individualism. For mainstream Anglo-America, individualism refers to the efforts by which the isolated individual advances. In African American female culture, the individual's efforts are a part of and supported
by the community. For example, while Brent enacts her escape, her commu-

nity helps in orchestrating its success. And Brent does not escape alone; she and another young enslaved woman, Fanny, sail to freedom together. Throughout Brent's trials, her community sustains her and assists her. Her relationship to her community undergirds the development of her self. With few exceptions, the community works for the betterment of the individual, as well as the community. Without her grandmother and her family, her enslaved community, and later her community of White women, Brent would not have been able to resist, nor escape her oppressor and her oppression. William L. Andrews explains, "*Incidents* unveils for us not just a private but a clandestine set of women's support networks, often interracial in their composition, which presided over perilous black female rites of passage in which the stakes were, quite literally, life and death" (254). Brent's community does indeed preside over her development from child to woman, and it also serves as a site of resistance as it protects Brent. Brent's grandmother, her brother, and her uncle all help the fugitive Brent by providing concealment and sustenance. In fact, one might argue that Brent's grandmother was a model of liberation for her. Of her grandmother's character, Brent writes,

> Although my grandmother was all in all to me, I feared her as well as
> loved her. I had been accustomed to look up to her with a respect
> bordering upon awe. I . . . felt shamefaced about telling her such
> impure things, especially as I knew her to be very strict on such
> subjects. Moreover, she was a woman of a high spirit. She was usually
> very quiet in her demeanor; but if her indignation was once roused, it
> was not very easily quelled. I had been told that she once chased a
> white gentleman with a loaded pistol, because he insulted one of her
> daughters. (28–29)

Other members of Brent's community help her to resist the indignities of enslavement. Earlier in her life, Brent petitions an influential White woman, a member of her community at large, to speak for her to Dr. Flint when her lover wants to marry her. Later, two White women collaborate with Brent and her community when they hide Brent during her initial escape from Dr. Flint. An enslaved woman, Betty, functions as a mediator between Brent and her family while she is in hiding. Neither is the community wholly women-centered. Brent's male relatives as well as male neighbors, such as Peter who escorts the masculinely disguised Brent to her "loophole of retreat" and to her getaway boat, also contribute to her successful escape. On the other hand, the enslaved community is not without its malignancies, such as the traitorous Jenny, who seeks to undermine Brent's attempts by betraying her. However, the community allows neither the outsiders nor its own members to destroy its communal responsibility to protect its members.

Not surprisingly, critics pay more attention to communalism than to individualism in Jacobs's narrative. At the end of the narrative, according to Joanne Braxton, Linda "celebrates the cooperation and collaboration of all the people, black and white, slave and free, who make her freedom possible. She celebrates her liberation and her children's as the fruit of a collective effort, not individual effort" (387). Valerie Smith carefully distinguishes Jacobs's narrative as not merely "the classic story of the triumph of the individual will; rather, it is more a story of a triumphant self-in-relation" ("Loopholes" 217). These are key characteristics of the female emancipatory narrative, and later, of the liberatory narrative. Cooperation, collaboration, and nurturing characterize the enslaved community, where the individual's achievement or success is not a solitary endeavor but a result of the communal efforts of many self-possessed, self-defined, volitional selves.

At the narrative's end, Linda Brent desires an unfettered freedom and a home of her own. Because her freedom is ultimately purchased and because she does not have her own domestic space, Brent concludes, "Reader, my story ends with freedom; not in the usual way, with marriage" (201). Of this juxtaposition, Carla Kaplan observes:

> By opposing freedom and marriage [Jacobs] undermines the nineteenth-century ideology of marriage as woman's "sacred absolute," the means of her personal fulfillment and the proper end of her life. By suggesting, moreover, that freedom does not have the "usual" meaning for black slave women that it has for free white women, she challenges us to think about freedom and agency as specific and contextual, not as abstract and universal. (93)

Jacobs may have been, in this regard, the first African American feminist theorist. Challenging us in her closing chapter to consider freedom and marriage as binary opposites, she draws attention to the fact that nineteenth-century marriages were inequitable property relationships, much like slavery. Furthermore, Jacobs theorizes about the concepts of freedom and agency in its "specific and contextual" application for enslaved Black women.

Jacobs's greatest literary legacy is that she provides a rubric—a liberatory one—for her literary daughters. Hers is the Black woman's story of the pursuit and the attainment of freedom. Borrowing some of the conventions of sentimental literature and of the male emancipatory narrative to create the female emancipatory narrative, Jacobs focuses on the issue of freedom—and how it is complicated in very specific ways for Black women. Through her narrative, Jacobs challenges a fundamental myth of American society: the idea of a universal American experience. This is most telling in her final assertions that her story ends not in the usual way with marriage and that she, nevertheless, still hopes for a home of her own. Freedom and agency, as Jacobs foreshadows, continue to be "specific and contextual" in the works of her literary daughters, in their liberatory narratives. Contemporary Black women writers respond directly to Jacobs's narrative. They do so, I offer, for the same reason that Jacobs wrote her narrative more than one hundred forty years ago: to raise the consciousness of Americans and to further the cause of a foundational and fundamental American principle—"liberty."

Chapter 2

Not Enough of the Past

Octavia E. Butler's *Kindred*

HAILE GERIMA'S 1993 FILM *Sankofa* confronts the legacies of slavery, highlighting the ways the past constructs the present, by cinematically transporting its viewers to that era of human bondage. Indeed, the word *sankofa* is an Akan word that means "one must return to the past in order to move forward." The film opens with the protagonist, a contemporary African American fashion model named Mona, on a high fashion shoot at Ghana's Cape Coast Castle, formerly a holding site for kidnapped Africans before their one-way departure through the "door of no return" to transatlantic slavery. It is obvious that Mona has forgotten her history as she happily poses for the photographer, seemingly detached from and oblivious to the implication of the historical context of her surroundings. Inside the castle, the spirits of the ancestors appear before her admonishing her to remember. Mona, along with the film's viewers, is then transported through time and space to a site of North American chattel slavery. This journey affords Mona, and the viewers, the opportunity to remember and to reclaim what she, and perhaps they, have forgotten or are in danger of forgetting: their "ancient properties" (*Tar Baby* 305).[1] The film's primary themes are the critical need for recovering and righting history, as well as the necessity of understanding the powerful connections between the past, present, and future.[2] Gerima's film inaugurated a cinematic trend in the 1990s of presenting the history of slavery from the perspective of the enslaved; it was followed, for example, by the movies *Amistad* and *Beloved*. In her fourth novel *Kindred* (1979), science fiction writer Octavia E. Butler likewise creates a dialectic between two specific historical moments in American history: the period of chattel slavery and the richly symbolic bicentennial year of 1976. When Mona, Gerima's protagonist, travels to the past in order to learn about the history she has forgotten or never knew, the audience does so as well. Likewise, when Butler's twentieth-century protagonist travels to antebellum Maryland, she learns how the past shaped and continues to shape the present. Butler's readers learn the same lesson.

Employing the device of time travel, like filmmaker Gerima, Butler offers—from a feminist perspective—a meditation on the nature of American freedom by creating a metaphoric Middle Passage between the nineteenth and twentieth centuries. In *Kindred*, a novel which has not yet received a great deal of critical attention, Butler offers a bridge between the past and the present through the time travels of her heroine, Edana (Dana) Franklin, a twentieth-century African American woman.[3] Dana's return to the past brings to mind the African's voyage of no return. "In her experience of being kidnapped in time and space," Robert Crossley writes, "Dana recapitulates the dreadful, disorienting, involuntary voyage of her ancestors" (xi). In *Kindred*, Butler certainly *signifies* on the nineteenth-century female emancipatory narrative, specifically Harriet Jacobs's *Incidents in the Life of a Slave Girl*. Examining the generic affinities between Butler's narrative and the emancipatory narratives, Sandra Y. Govan observes, "*Kindred* is so closely related to the experience disclosed in slave narratives that its plot structure follows the classic patterns with only the requisite changes to flesh out character, story, and action" ("Homage to Tradition" 89). While Govan is accurate in her observation, it seems to me that Butler does more than *signify* on the substance and structure of the emancipatory narrative in her revision. In what follows, I explain how Butler engages and revises the dominant themes of the nineteenth-century female emancipatory narrative—specifically, female sexuality, motherhood, individualism, and community—in order to interrogate the concept of freedom. In my reading, Butler's project in *Kindred* is to free her readers from a history that has been, as Dana concludes, "unusable."

In *Kindred*, Butler uses slavery as her site of memory, her *lieu de mémoire*, to deconstruct uninformed perceptions, like those of her childhood, concerning the nature of bondage, specifically Black women in bondage. When asked in an interview if much of her work dealt with the implications and legacies of slavery, Butler responded that it depended on the interviewer's definition of slavery. She explained,

> I hadn't understood why the slaves had not simply run away, because that's what I assumed I would have done. But when I was around thirteen we moved into a house with another house in the back, and in that other house lived people who beat their children. Not only could you hear the kids screaming, you could actually hear the blows landing. This was naturally terrifying to me, and I used to ask my mother if there wasn't something she could do or somebody we could call, like the police. My mother's attitude was that those children belonged to their parents and they had the right to do what they wanted to their own children. I realized that those kids had nowhere to go—they were about my age and younger, and if they had tried to run away they would have been sent right back to their parents, who would probably treat them a lot worse for having tried to run away. *That*, I realized, was slavery—human beings treated as if they were possessions. (McCafferty 56–57; emphasis in original)

In this lengthy passage, Butler reveals why she is careful about making assumptions concerning slavery because she realizes how naive definitions as well as explanations of slavery can be. Like Harriet Jacobs's fictional self Linda Brent, Dana embarks on a journey of self-possession and self-discovery when enslavement assures her that her future as property will be both unbearable and perilous. Dana's journey, unlike Brent's, takes her back and forth between her ancestral past of nineteenth-century antebellum slavery and her contemporary moment of 1976, highlighting how present the past truly is. Butler's use of the year 1976 as the contemporary setting—the year the United States celebrated two hundred years of freedom—reveals inherent contradictions in American history. This duality of setting forces the reader to consider how integral the past is in understanding the present and in constructing the future.

Butler's protagonist, Dana Franklin, a Black woman writer married to a White man, travels six times across time and space from her 1976 California home to the antebellum Maryland plantation of her ancestors. Although below the Mason-Dixon line, Maryland is often not remembered as a state of slavery, even though it is the birth state of the self-emancipated Frederick Douglass and Harriet Tubman, as well as the state from which they both escaped. By choosing the setting of Maryland, Butler reminds her readers of how widespread slavery was and that slavery was not confined to the deep South. Her choice of setting also allows Butler to dispel the notion of "deep South slavery" as the worst, when in fact, any type of slavery is barbaric and inhumane. Dana's first journey takes place on her twenty-sixth birthday, suggesting that Dana is experiencing a rebirth of sorts. How Dana travels through time is never explained in the text.[4] Of this phenomenon, Robert Crossley speculates that Butler's implied vehicle for time travel is "the vehicle that looms behind every American slave narrative, the grim death-ship of the Middle Passage from Africa to the slave markets of the New World" (xi). Conveniently, Crossley's choice of imagery—"the death ship"—does lend credence to the idea that Butler's liberatory narrative is a metaphoric Middle Passage designed to take its passengers from freedom, to bondage and, unlike the original passage, back to freedom. One may recall that California, admitted to the union in 1850, was largely untouched by nineteenth-century chattel slavery.

Why Dana travels, on the other hand, becomes quite clear. Whenever the life of her White ancestor Rufus Weylin, a great-great-grandfather, is in danger, Dana is summoned somehow to rescue him. Conversely, Dana is returned to the twentieth century when she herself perceives that her own life is in danger. Their familial "blood" tie inextricably binds Weylin and Dana. Rufus lives only because Dana saves his life again and again. By protecting him, Dana preserves her ancestry and herself: neither she nor her family would exist were Rufus not to survive to father her great-grandmother Hagar. Dana's mission as she articulates it, then, is "not only to insure the survival of one accident-prone small boy, but to insure [her] family's survival, [her] own birth" (Butler 29). It is only after Dana has fulfilled this responsibility in her past that she can have control over her own life in the present. Dana's struggle is compelling as she asserts her volition against the unseen forces which place her in slavery as well as against the obvious consequences of her enslavement. Ashraf Rushdy explains, "By becoming an agent capable of transforming history, Dana becomes to the same degree *subject to history*. . . . When she gambles against history . . . she can also lose to history; moreover, she endangers not only her own future, but also those who will not live to experience that future" (145; emphasis in original). Charged with this awesome responsibility—saving the lives of her ancestors and herself—Dana can be read as a heroic figure, even though her success is dependent upon the sexual enslavement of her great-great grandmother.

To examine the concept of freedom, Butler centers her narrative on the

most vulnerable: Black women in bondage.[5] To do so, Butler creates a deliberate doubling in the characters of Dana and Dana's ancestral grandmother,
Alice Greenwood, both enslaved in the nineteenth century. Of this doubling
Missy Dehn Kubitschek observes, "[t]o a certain extent, each woman feels the
other's choices as a critique of her own; each sees, in the distorting mirror of
the other, her own potential fate" (39). In other words, by establishing a dialogic relationship between the past and the present, Butler provides not only
a view of a free, twentieth-century Black woman's challenging experiences in
and unpredictable responses to nineteenth-century chattel slavery, but also,
as in the female emancipatory narrative, a window on the nineteenth-century
Black woman's life in slavery. This dialectic reveals how the past and the
present influence each other. By this I mean that the present is obviously more
self-conscious of the past, and the present is constructed usually either in agreement with or in opposition to that past. Not often considered, however, is
what Butler offers: that the past is shaped, or constructed, by the present as
to what we choose to remember as well as what we choose to forget, and by
the way we choose to interpret that which is remembered. Characterizing the
essential differences and similarities between Dana and Alice (regarding female sexuality, motherhood, individualism, and community) becomes the driv-
ing strategy of Butler's narrative.

In matters of sexuality, Butler portrays Dana as an empowered agent in
her contemporary environment. Dana acts of her own volition. Her twentieth-
century environment does not suppress, commodify, or abuse Dana's sexuality. Like Harriet Jacobs's Linda Brent, Dana embraces her right to choose her
sexual partner. Unlike Brent, her choice of Kevin, the White man she marries despite the misgivings of their respective families, is not subversive or coerced. Their relationship seems to be mutually satisfying, particularly if one
considers the emotional support they give to each other throughout Dana's
rationally unexplainable ordeal. Their metaphoric bond becomes literal: because he is touching her as she leaves for her third trip to the past, he travels
with her.

Butler offers two significant illustrations of Dana's erotic desires in her
sexual relationship with Kevin. The first instance occurs after Dana's first trip
to the nineteenth century. In a remembrance, Dana recalls her first date with
Kevin and the aftermath of that date: "Sometime during the early hours of
the next morning when we lay together, tired and content in my bed, I realized that I knew less about loneliness than I had thought—and much less than
I would know when he went away" (57). This retrospection suggests the mu-
tuality and compatibility of their nascent sexual and emotional relationship.

The second episode occurs when Kevin and Dana are reunited following Dana's sudden return to the present, leaving Kevin in the nineteenth century. The chronological differences between past and present in time travel are marked. When she returns to the past, they are still separated, as Kevin has left the Weylin plantation. Their separation lasts five years for Kevin; for Dana, it lasts eight days. After they safely return home, Dana initiates a sexual reunion with her husband despite the pain of her recently bullwhipped back, inflicted while in the past. Of their homecoming, Dana recollects that Kevin "was so careful, so fearful of hurting me. He did hurt me. . . . I had known he would, but it didn't matter. We were safe. He was home. . . . Eventually, we slept" (190). In this instance, sexual intercourse is an act of liberation, a way of confirming one's reality and grounding one's self in that reality. Dana is even willing to endure physical pain in order to reclaim the expression of her sexuality. Dana assumes complete control over her sexuality in her twentieth-century milieu. She enjoys sexual intercourse, unlike her foremother, Alice, whose sexuality produces trauma.

In contrast, when Dana travels to antebellum Maryland, the hegemony of slavery threatens to usurp her control of her sexuality. Vulnerability and victimization characterize the sexual experience of all enslaved Black women, without exception, in Butler's fictive world. Because she is separated from Kevin, the man for whom she has erotic desires and to whom she is married, Dana must suppress her sexual desires when she travels to the past. The appropriation and alternation of female sexuality by the institution of slavery and its agents are the first lessons that Dana, like Linda Brent, must learn: that the institution of slavery commodifies Black female sexuality in its attempt to perpetuate itself and to satisfy the lust of its agents. An example of the latter occurs during her second visit to the past, when Dana seeks refuge at the home of her ancestors, Alice's parents; a white patroller attempts to rape Dana, a stark reminder that she and all of her sisters in bondage are sexually vulnerable.

The violent episode that Dana witnesses between Alice's parents and the patrollers further exemplifies the distortions and contortions of black female sexuality. Butler uses this narrative passage to illustrate how invasive slavocracy was to its victims. Alice's mother was a freewoman; Alice's father was one of the Weylin enslaved men. As children born of Black women followed the condition of the mother, Alice was free. Because breeding enslaved Black men and women, considered livestock, equaled profit, Weylin disapproved of his enslaved Black men fathering free children, who would not be his property. Shortly before Dana's arrival at Alice's cabin, the patrollers, forerunners of the Ku Klux Klan, arrive to retrieve Weylin's property, dragging the naked couple from the cabin and beating Alice's father, who lacked a traveling pass. His capture serves as Dana's introduction to the realities of slavery. Dana remembers:

> I could literally smell his sweat, hear every ragged breath, every cry, every cut of the whip. I could see his body jerking, convulsing, straining against the rope as his screaming went on and on. My stomach heaved, and I had to force myself to say where I was and keep quiet. . . . I had seen people beaten on television and in the movies. I had seen the too-red blood substitute streaked across their backs and heard their well-rehearsed screams. But I hadn't lain nearby and smelled their sweat or heard them pleading and praying, shamed before their families and themselves. (36)

After they take away Alice's father, one of the patrollers, who had already physically assaulted Alice's mother, returns to rape her. Instead, he finds Dana and readily goes after her, hoping to satisfy his lechery. Although Dana successfully defends herself against this attempted act of violation, the possibilities for other and worse attacks exist, she realizes, at any juncture. Enslaved Black women were socially constructed as beasts of burden, or to use Zora Neale Hurston's oft-quoted phrase, "de mule[s] uh de world" (29). The standards of "true womanhood" for enslaved Black women, then, diametrically opposed those set by Anglo-Americans in their "cult of true womanhood." The most graphic example of sexual assault in *Kindred* occurs when Evan Fowler, the Weylins' overseer, viciously strikes Dana across her breasts to punish her for her failure to work efficiently in the field. This brutality inflicted on Dana's body signals how devalued she is as a woman, as a potential mother, as a human being.

Although Dana and Kevin enjoy a mutual, exclusive physical and emotional relationship, the nature of their relationship by necessity changes when Kevin time-travels with Dana to the Weylin plantation. With their marriage legally invalid in the nineteenth century, Dana and Kevin must pretend, in order to give validity to their close relationship, that they are master and servant rather than husband and wife. Even though Kevin opposes slavery and its ideals, he is implicated by his race. When Dana has to pretend that she is Kevin's sexual property, she realizes how easy it is for both of them to adhere to the constructions of nineteenth-century Black female sexuality and identity. Dana remarks, "I felt almost as though I really was doing something shameful, happily playing whore for my supposed owner. I went away feeling

uncomfortable, vaguely ashamed" (97). In light of the miscegenation visible
throughout the enslaved communities, it is ironic that Kevin and Dana are
assigned and expected to maintain separate sleeping quarters since it is clear,
by nineteenth-century standards, that Dana is Kevin's concubine. Some veneer of propriety, or rather a facade of hypocrisy, was then expected so that
licentious transgressors would not offend the bearers of true womanhood—
White women. Dana and Kevin, however, take matters into their own hands
by unobtrusively moving Dana to Kevin's room. Noticing their shared accom-
modations but pretending not to notice the enslaved children who physically
resemble her own husband, Margaret Weylin, the mistress of the plantation,
calls Dana a "filthy black whore" (93). Here Butler gestures toward the hy-
pocrisies of slavery, as well as to the way in which Black women became the
scapegoat for such practices. Dana bears the burden of misreading because she
is a Black woman without power in the system of patriarchy.

In ironic contrast to her supposedly inherent virtuous nature, Margaret
Weylin exhibits a strong physical attraction to Kevin. Dana's unobtrusive move
to Kevin's room is practical, in another sense, since Dana's departures are as
sudden as her arrivals; and the couple needs to be together if they are to return home together. Equally important, they are married. Sharing a bedroom
allows them some semblance of their contemporary normality; Dana and Kevin
do not want the institution of slavery to destroy them, individually or collectively. However, the institution of slavery does indeterminately and perhaps
irreparably affect Dana, Kevin, and their marriage as Dana makes five trips to
the past alone, her left arm severed during the final trip home. Kevin is left
behind in the past on one occasion during which he receives a mysterious
and unexplained injury, signified by a scar, to his head.[6] Not surprisingly, each
trip to the past necessarily changes the ways in which Dana and Kevin each
perceive their present lives, individually and with each other, as well as their
racial histories. At one point, for example, Dana realizes how useless, and sometimes dangerous, her twentieth-century knowledge is in the nineteenth century: "Nothing in my education or knowledge of the future had helped me to
escape" (177). After his own lengthy stay in the past, Kevin's personality
changes. He becomes introspective and less idealistic. Dana feared that "[i]f
he was stranded here for years, some part of this place would rub off on him"
(77). But remarkably, Kevin is able to stay true to his twentieth-century concept of freedom and equality as he participates in abolitionist work when he
is left in the past without Dana.

Another example of Dana's right to choose a course of action emerges
when she suppresses her sexuality in the nineteenth century. Although sepa-

rated, possibly permanently, from Kevin, Dana does not desire another man. When Sam, one of Weylin's enslaved men, shows a romantic interest in her, Dana adamantly declares that for her "one husband is enough" (230), belying the supposed lasciviousness of enslaved Black women. This episode allows Butler to show that enslaved Black women, as Harriet Jacobs shows as well, could make choices even in their deterministic world and that their own personal codes of morality were valid and intact. Rufus's final betrayal—his attempt to rape her—forces Dana to kill him in self-defense, thus severing their unique tie, for he has already, by then, fathered Dana's great-grandmother, Hagar. Dana cannot tolerate being violated by Rufus. Killing Rufus, instead of submitting to him as Alice does, is Dana's way of maintaining her self-esteem and psychic wholeness. For Dana, to submit to Rufus would be the same as accepting his definition of her as chattel, and this she cannot do. In other words, Dana refuses to relinquish her right to self-definition. That Dana continues to protect Rufus is a function of self-preservation. That Dana works to sustain the relationship between Rufus and Alice—so that Hagar may be born—is also a function of self-preservation. Although she could be labeled an enabler, it would be more accurate to indict the real culprit—slavery. Slavery as an institution and as a cultural practice obviates the personal interests and desires of its victims for the sake of its perpetuation—even those victims with a twentieth-century consciousness cannot alter its institutionalized power. Discussing the inevitable—killing Rufus—with Kevin before she is forced to do so, Dana offers this telling explanation of herself as a self-authorized human:

> "I'm not property, Kevin. I'm not a horse or a sack of wheat. If I have
> to seem to be property, if I have to accept limits on my freedom for
> Rufus's sake, then he also has to accept limits—on his behavior
> toward me. He has to leave me enough *control* of my own life to make
> living look better to me than killing and dying." (246; emphasis
> added)

It is noteworthy that Butler uses the word *control* because this is the essence of personal freedom—having command of one's thoughts, desires, and actions. Thus, when Rufus, grief-stricken over Alice's suicide, approaches Dana for sexual relations, he violates the limits of her personal freedom as well as the terms for their interaction as Dana had defined them. Recognizing the need to repossess herself in a moment of clear objectification, Dana stabs him to death.

The trait of vulnerability and the action of violation inextricably bind

Dana and her ancestor, Alice, in a common bond of sisterhood. Because they are blood relatives, Alice and Dana physically resemble each other, so much so that Rufus considers the two of them to be one woman (228). Consequently, Rufus has a complexly triangular relationship with Dana and Alice. "This triangle," Beverly Friend observes, "degenerates into an extraordinarily painful relationship, one compounded by rivalry, passion, guilt, love, lust, punishment, pride, power, and implacable hatred" (93). Rufus's conjoining of Dana and Alice might be interpreted as an example of the historically monolithic way of defining Black female identity, so pervasive in slavery because to acknowledge individuality or subjectivity would serve to eradicate slavery's very foundation. However perverse his love is, Rufus believes he loves both women, but in different ways. In her characterization of Rufus's complexity, Alice pointedly tells Dana, "He likes me in bed, and you out of bed . . . all that means we're two halves of the same woman" (229). One is led to believe—by the ways in which he tries to create a relationship apart from the act of sex with Alice—that Rufus does not want to force Alice; rather, idealistically, he desires that she give herself willingly to him. Juxtaposing the two, Butler further suggests that in a different time Rufus and Alice might have had a relationship like the one that Dana and Kevin share. As she is the "subaltern" of her society, Alice's desires are unmerited and unmediated by the institution of slavery which allows, sustains, and encourages the alteration and appropriation of enslaved Black women's sexuality by enslavers such as Rufus. Butler establishes this parallel relationship to highlight these differences.

Alice, Dana's freeborn ancestor, seems to possess an awareness of her individuality and of her free will when she rejects Rufus's sexual advances and chooses to "marry" Isaac, an enslaved man from a neighboring farm. Incensed by Alice's rejection of him and by her determination to choose her lover, Rufus rapes her. Rufus then mocks her choice: "She got so she'd rather have a buck nigger than me!" (123). Although powerless to protect or defend his wife legally, Isaac fights Rufus and seriously injures him. Shortly thereafter, Alice and Isaac attempt an escape to the North, knowing that Rufus will seek retribution against Isaac. Severely punished when captured, Alice forfeits her freedom as a result of her complicity in Isaac's escape attempt, and Isaac is sold South after he is mutilated: his ears are cut off. Rufus then buys Alice, or rather, he buys her body. In response to Dana's twentieth-century conviction that Alice's body is her own, Alice, a product of her circumscribed environment, resignedly answers, "Not mine, . . . Not mine, his. He paid for it, didn't he?" (167). Submitting her body but not her spirit (or, as Hortense J. Spillers would have it, submitting only her flesh), Alice posits her strategy of resistance: Rufus cannot buy her private self, her affections, or her desires.[7] To preserve her sense of self, Alice has to separate her body from her spirit. Because Alice does not and cannot desire Rufus in the way he wishes to be desired, this bifurcation results in an irreconcilable power struggle between Rufus and Alice.

After she recovers from the injuries she sustains during her capture, Alice has three choices: to go willingly to Rufus's room for sex, to be beaten into submission and then to have sex with him, or to run again from the plantation. Because each of these choices leads to devastating consequences, Alice provisionally chooses what might appear to be the least deadly: she goes to his room and seals her fate as his concubine. Yet Alice never completely accepts her sexual enslavement, often wishing she possessed the inner strength needed to murder Rufus. Butler reveals the cost to Alice's self: Alice "adjusted, became a quieter more subdued person. She didn't kill, but she seemed to die a little" (169). She never completely accepts her sexual enslavement. Though she seems outwardly accepting of her plight, in fact she is inwardly rebelling. Even after she bears four children by Rufus, she continues to plot her escape. Her continued acts of resistance lead ultimately to her death. Unlike Dana, Alice is both a product and a victim of slavery's deterministic environment; consequently, she cannot successfully enact strategies of resistance, as does Dana with limited success. Soon after her last child is born, Alice runs away again because she fears that she will "turn into just what people call [her]" (235). She fears that she will lose her sense of self and accept her position as sexual chattel.

Butler revises the theme of motherhood for the enslaved black woman in a novel way. Unlike Alice, Dana is not a biological mother; however, she does protect and nurture, as would a mother, her very own ancestors. She becomes, so to speak, her own ancestral mother. Because Dana has no children, her decisions and responses are not predicated on nor mediated by biological motherhood in the twentieth century. The perpetuation of her lineage, however, informs her decisions in both centuries. Additionally, Dana learns that her actions affect everyone on the plantation, family or not; therefore, the collective good of the enslaved community remains primary to Dana in the same way that a mother in similar circumstances might place the collective good of her family over her individual needs.[8] Butler most obviously and deliberately employs the theme of motherhood to underline Dana's role as a mother when Dana nurses Alice while Alice recovers from the severe dog bites she has sustained during her first thwarted escape. Reverting to a state of infancy induced by trauma, Alice calls Dana "Mama" (153) and looks to her for support and guidance. After her recovery, Alice's relationship with Dana becomes more sisterly in nature. Later in their relationship, Alice mockingly and insultingly predicts that Dana will one day become the "Mammy" of the plantation. By referring to Dana as "Mammy," Alice misinterprets both the archetype of the mammy as well as Dana's endeavors either to improve the enslaved community's conditions or to protect it through passive resistance. In this instance, Butler rewrites the stereotyped "Mammy" image, highlighting instead her quiet strength in making circumstances better for her family and her community and, so, revising the disparaging "Mammy" image as it has been employed historically.

Alice's journey of self-possession is thwarted by the institution of slavery and the experience of motherhood in slavery. Although a difficult task, Dana's charge—to keep Rufus alive until he fathers Hagar—is actually less complicated than Alice's mission, which is to continue to live in a state of bondage that offers little incentive to live. Because she is an enslaved woman who gives birth to enslaved children, Alice is not so lucky as Dana in exercising her volition. Butler shows how motherhood for enslaved Black women complicates their lives in ways that are fundamentally insurmountable. Of the four children born to Alice and Rufus, the first two children die in infancy due to improper medical treatment, about which Alice has no voice. Rufus uses the remaining two, as Alice explains, like "a bit in [her] mouth" (236). The children become objects that Rufus employs to control Alice's affection and sexual behavior toward him. While Alice loves her children, the institution of slavery constricts and circumscribes her love for them. Unable to own herself or her children, Alice lives in a liminal state, always vulnerable to Rufus's whims. Recollecting Dr. Flint's virulent threats to Linda Brent in *Incidents*, one remembers that his most potent threat was to sell her children.

Likewise in Butler's liberatory narrative, the same callous disregard for motherhood prevails. One enslaved mother's three young sons are brutishly sold to pay for the "new furniture, new china dishes, [and all of the other] fancy things" (95) that Margaret Weylin desires. For this and similar reasons, the enslaved Black mother reared her children one day at a time as their future together was indeterminate and unpredictable. Although Alice desires to escape North, she learns that she simply cannot run away—because of her children. Escaping alone is fraught with numerous difficulties, as both Alice and Dana painfully discover; with young children, physical escape is virtually impossible, as Linda Brent well knew when she chose to "escape" by hiding in her grandmother's garret for seven years. Alice, then, represses her own desires and submits to Rufus's desires. She seems to forsake her right to choose, that is, her right to self-possession. Not completely resigned, she hopes that her children will one day be free. She even secretly plants seeds of hope by naming her children Joseph and Hagar, the Biblical names of formerly enslaved persons in the Old Testament because "[i]n the Bible, people might be slaves for a while, but they didn't have to stay slaves" (234).[9]

The need to repossess the self in a moment of clear objectification inspires Alice to do so by drastic means. Rufus's final act of manipulation and intimidation—pretending that he has sold their children when they have only been sent from the plantation in order to remind Alice of his dominion over her—causes Alice to resolve, like Dana, that "killing and dying look better than living." However, Alice does not choose the way that Dana later chooses; she kills herself instead of her enemy. While Alice's suicide may be seen as an act of emotional weakness or an act of familial abnegation, it is not. Alice exercises her right to choose death—freedom of a different sort—over bondage.[10] She commits suicide, not because she can no longer bear to be in her untoward circumstance, but because she believes that she no longer has *reason* to live. Perhaps more importantly, the apparently powerless Alice is ultimately more powerful than Rufus inasmuch as she irreparably wounds him by dying and irrevocably escapes from her bondage without risk of recapture and return. In a final volitional act, Alice usurps Rufus's institutionally sanctioned power and opts to exercise her own personal power, which she does by removing herself permanently from him.

As a post-integrationist Black woman, Dana possesses a clear sense of her individuality. Strengthened by her racial pride, her personal responsibility, her free will, and her self-determination, Dana embraces her ability to define herself in both her past and her present. Choosing to define herself instead of accepting the definitions of others, she eschews familial and societal gender expectations in selecting her career as a writer. In her formative years, her aunt and uncle had encouraged Dana to pursue traditionally middle-class and stereotypically gender-specific occupations, such as a secretary, nurse, or teacher (56), white-collar occupations long considered to be respectable if not prestigious in the Black community. Attempting initially to satisfy her guardians, Dana enrolls in such classes but consciously chooses to discontinue them and to forge her own way despite financial repercussions. Consequently, she works for a while with a blue-collar temporary placement agency that she ironically refers to as "a slave market" (52). That expression is yet another example of how Butler reveals similarities between the past and the present, particularly in economic terms. This comparison between chattel slavery and the blue-collar temporary employment agency hinges upon class-based economic exploitation. Significantly though, she later becomes a secretary, a nurse, and a teacher to Rufus and to others in the past. That Dana finds in the past a need for the skills in each of the occupations that she rejected in her twentieth-century life highlights the limited, and some might say unchanged, economic possibilities for Black women. Likewise, that her present-day temp agency exploits its laborers recalls the economic structure of chattel slavery. Butler's fictive appraisal of traditionally female occupations offers real socio-economic commentary on how patriarchy shaped and continues to shape the lives of Black women in both centuries.

In her twentieth-century life, Dana is an individualistic and self-reliant Black woman, unlike her nineteenth-century counterpart. When Kevin offers to support her financially so that she can concentrate on her writing, Dana rejects his offer as she remembers, thinking of her aunt and uncle, that "even people who loved [her] could demand more of [her] than [she] could give—and expect their demands to be met simply because [she] owed them" (109). Abhorring secretarial work, Dana works "odd" jobs through the agency, jobs not typically identified as woman's work, to support herself while she writes. Dana rejects gender-specific societal expectations when they are forced upon her in the twentieth century. Her dislike of secretarial work also surfaces in her relationship with Kevin, her "kindred spirit" (57) who is also a writer. Kevin naively asks her at the beginning of their relationship to type a manuscript for him. The first time, she reluctantly consents out of a misplaced sense of duty; the second and third times, she categorically refuses. Being true to her sense of self, Dana chooses what she will and will not do. She refuses to accept roles that place her in a subordinate position. As a post-integration Black woman, she consciously nurtures her private self and freely creates herself in ways unimaginable as well as unavailable to her predecessors, as her trips to the past amply reveal. When she lives in the past, however, Dana learns firsthand why her foremothers were unable to resist overtly, with few exceptions, their enslavement and why they had to cloak their individuality. Alice's life, for example, is a cautionary tale for Dana.

For the nineteenth-century enslaved Black woman, few possibilities for self-definition existed, and, certainly, the improvisation of self was tantamount to a revolutionary act. Alice's life exemplifies the typical life of the enslaved Black woman for she has no uncompromising options. Even though Alice followed the condition of her "free" mother, who advises her to marry a "free" man, slavery still engulfs Alice and later her progeny.[11] After Alice's enslaved father was beaten and sold for simply visiting his family, her mother, speaking from her own experience, cautions Alice that "marrying a slave is almost as bad as being a slave" (156). Although she is freeborn, Alice forfeits her freedom

by assisting her enslaved lover's thwarted escape. Rufus purchases her because
of his complex feelings for her, but his overriding feelings are physical lust
and bodily possession. For Alice, her concubinage causes her a plethora of
emotional responses, all of which inform her perception of her personhood as
a unique subject: she hates that she cannot protect herself by slaying Rufus,
she loathes the fact that she recognizes and appreciates the relative advantages concubinage affords her, and she despises the possibility that she may
one day become inured to her odious condition. Tragically, the opportunity
for Alice's private self to develop or to find expression never materializes. This
lack of personal development is indicated most obviously in the doubling of
Dana and Alice, for Dana symbolically represents what Alice might have been
in a freer society.

Dana finds cooperation, collaboration, and nurturing in her ancestral
home. Dana's lack of community in her twentieth-century life may symbolize
the state of African American communities in post-integration years. During
slavery and later during segregation, homogeneous African American communities provided the necessary site for the conservation and perpetuation of
generational and cultural continuity. Perhaps symbolizing the many Africans
who crossed the Middle Passage, torn from family and country, Dana is literally an orphaned child. Moreover, she is estranged from her guardians, the
aunt and uncle who reared her, first by her ambition to be a writer and later
by her interracial marriage to Kevin, also an orphan. Other than the one cousin
whom Dana calls for assistance after one of her time travel returns, she mentions no other family. In fact when they marry, Dana and Kevin "go to Vegas
and pretend [they] haven't got relatives" (112). Neither does she have a community of friends. She mentions once a friend who gives her a wedding gift.
Because she has recently moved to a new and integrated neighborhood when
the time travels begins, she has no communal interaction. In her twentieth-
century milieu, then, there is little opportunity for the invoking of community
support. As suggested earlier, Butler may be critiquing the lack of post-
integration communal life for contemporary African Americans. However,
Dana learns, from her experience in the nineteenth century, the supreme importance of the African American community and earnestly invests herself
in its continuance.

In the nineteenth century, Dana learns to accept her communal responsibility although she is technically not one of Weylin's enslaved African
Americans. Dana is self-conscious about belonging, but her color—her sign—
guarantees her belonging. She feels compelled to find a useful niche for herself so that she can gain entrance into the enslaved community for

"everyone . . . will resent [her] if [she doesn't] work" (79). Dana later realizes the necessity of joining with the others through a collective endeavor where she is able to build relationships: "I need all the friends I can make here" (79). Always aware that she may return to the nineteenth century indefinitely, Dana consciously creates a place for herself in and accepts her responsibility to the enslaved community. At first, Dana's motivation to join with the community is utilitarian; her interest soon changes to one of true affection and affiliation. Sarah, the plantation's cook, her mute daughter Carrie, and Nigel, Carrie's husband, become Dana's extended family. Learning to cook under Sarah's tutelage, as daughters often do from their mothers, Dana takes an active part in the daily functions of the plantation. Of the interactions in the detached cookhouse, Dana reveals, "I liked to listen to [the enslaved] talk sometimes and fight my way through their accents to find out more about how they survived lives of slavery. Without knowing it, they prepared me to survive" (94). By word of mouth, the primary means of disseminating information for African Americans in the nineteenth century, the enslaved community's texts of survival empower Dana in the construction of her own liberation. And, by design, the reader is also empowered through Butler's words. In addition to her relationships with Alice, Sarah, and Carrie, Dana establishes close ties with other enslaved women such as Tess, a Black woman with whom she shares laundry duty. Reading Sarah's life as a text reveals to Dana, as well as to the reader, an often-misunderstood text of Black womanhood. Sarah seems accepting of her lot, and if she is, it is because she had lost so much and does not want to lose any more. The narrator explains, Sarah

> had done the safe thing—had accepted a life of slavery because she
> was afraid. She was the kind of woman who might have been called
> "mammy" in some other household. She was the kind of woman who
> would be held in contempt during the militant nineteen sixties. The
> house-nigger, the handkerchief-head, the female Uncle Tom—the
> frightened powerless woman who had already lost all she could stand
> to lose. (145)

Sarah's text changes the way Dana, and the reader, has been taught to think about Black women who were considered "mammy" figures. Sarah acts in order to better her family's and her community's lot. In Dana's nineteenth-century life, Black women play an important role in enlarging Dana's understanding of herself and of Black women.

As divisiveness exists in all communities, both Dana and Alice inspire envy in some enslaved women who feel that their own conditions may be worse than those of "the master's women" (229). This mode of thinking reveals how pervasively maligning the institution of slavery was, not only to the community but also to one's self-perception. Butler's narrator, by employing such resonant diction, also indicts patriarchal capitalism and the competition it still engenders. Through strategies of resistance, the community protects itself from those members who attempt to defy or to ignore their communal responsibilities. Dana's nineteenth-century family and friends protect and defend her. For example, Alice, Carrie, and Tess physically attack Liza, the jealous enslaved woman who reveals Dana's absence when Dana attempts her thwarted escape from the Weylin plantation. In reference to such incidents and to their effects on Dana, Robert Crossley observes that "one of the exciting features of Kindred is that so much of the novel is attentive . . . to [Dana's] complex social and psychological relationships with the community of black slaves she joins" (xvii). Indeed, the psychological explorations that Butler provides allow for a more comprehensive assessment of slavery's maligning influence on African American identity. Dana's official initiation into the enslaved community occurs during her fifth trip to the past. Participating in a corn husking party, Dana sincerely enjoys the camaraderie of the enslaved community, and not simply as an objective observer. The enslaved African Americans share "companionable laughter" (229) as they combine their collective energies to accomplish a common goal.

The perpetuation of the Black community is the most important responsibility its members have. While in the nineteenth century, Dana attempts, idealistically perhaps in light of her limited and infrequent trips, to improve the lives of the enslaved as much as she possibly can by resocializing Rufus's attitude toward the institution of slavery as well as toward African Americans. Dana is optimistic that she can, at the very least, keep the enslaved families together for as long as possible. Dana hopes that she will try "to plant a few ideas in [Rufus's] mind that would help both [her] and the people who would be his slaves in the years to come" during Rufus's formative years (68). Dana's goal remains unrealized until the death of the elder Weylin. Because she kept Rufus alive, none of the enslaved are sold when Tom Weylin dies. If Rufus had predeceased his father, the enslaved would have been sold without regard to familial bonds. Because of Dana, Rufus lives to inherit his property, and the enslaved families remain relatively intact. However, Dana cannot secure this effect permanently because she must return to her own historical time; indeed, seeking a permanent solution, she ultimately kills Rufus. After her final return home, during which she is horribly maimed through the amputation of her left arm in the unseen time travel apparatus, Dana and Kevin travel to Maryland to ascertain the fates of those she had diligently tried to help. They find, in an old newspaper clipping, the text they assume that Nigel constructed of Rufus's death, as well as the fateful notice announcing the sale of Rufus's property. All the enslaved, with the exception of Nigel, Carrie, Joseph, and Hagar, were listed for sale. Dana does not even get the satisfaction of knowing what happened to Hagar, other than she survived, except to know that Hagar, at some point, recorded the family's history in the family Bible. Feeling dejected by her inability to effect unalterably positive changes for all, Dana wonders why she had even traveled to Maryland in search of closure to her experience. While Dana heroically succeeds in protecting and perpetuating her immediate family, she fails to do the same for her extended family— all of the enslaved owned by the Weylin family. She ironically muses, "Why did I even come here? You'd think I would have had enough of the past" (264). Kevin's reply—"To try to understand. To touch solid evidence that those people existed. To reassure yourself that you're sane"—reveals the reason, I believe, why Octavia E. Butler constructs her liberatory narrative (264).

Arriving at this liberatory understanding, however, exacts a price from Dana: Rufus's grasp on her arm causes her arm to be left behind in the past when she returns to the present during her final trip. Freedom is not free; and the cost, in Dana's case, is much more than vigilance, to borrow from Frederick Douglass.[12] One must conclude from this highly symbolic occurrence that leaving the past behind is simply impossible as history has lingering effects on the present and the future. Having endured the psychological mutilation of slavery, she endures physical mutilation as well. While his injuries are not as severe as Dana's, Kevin does not escape unscathed. He has a scar on his forehead that he acquires while living in the nineteenth century. Their disfigurements— their texts of scarring—are significant:

> [t]heir wounds may help them to work together to recover and to rebuild their strength; or these different wounds may intensify the destructive power dynamics that perpetuate inequality and dominance, forcing Kevin and Dana to go their separate ways. . . . Both Dana and Kevin are implicated. Neither is innocent, morally superior, or passive. It is evident that the relationship between blacks and whites is mutually interactive. (Paulin 189)

Their disfigurements may also be read symbolically: both Black and White Americans have been scarred by the institution and legacy of slavery. That Dana and Kevin, both enlightened by their individual and shared experiences, are still together at the narrative's end suggests Butler's resolution of this complex issue. Their interracial relationship can be read as a metaphor for how America may be healed. Their relationship, in other words, represents what is necessary for Americans to do to alleviate the pain of our common history: they each must confront the past. That both races must join together in coming to terms with the past, I believe, is the rhetorical purpose of this metaphor because they both have an investment in the final outcome. After Dana's second trip to the past, she tells Kevin, "I need you here to come home to" (51). Kevin's reply sums up the reciprocal nature of their need: "Just keep coming home," he said finally. "I need you here too" (51). By highlighting our mutual need, Butler's liberatory narrative teaches that both Black and White Americans must confront their shared past of racism, must acknowledge the pain and the scars of that past, and must live together as kindred. Through the example of Dana and Kevin, Butler offers her readers on both sides of the color line not only the opportunity to understand slavery better, but the opportunity to explore possible collaborative solutions for contemporary race-related problems.

Kindred was written and published during a time when many gains had been made in civil rights, but many battles remained. Kindred's setting in the bicentennial year of 1976 brings to mind that many Black Americans may have felt it disingenuous to celebrate two hundred years of freedom given the legacy of slavery, Jim Crow, and segregation, perhaps with good reason. In 1968, the Kerner Commission's report examined the "extent of social and economic deprivation" (Verney 62) in Black America and concluded that America was "moving toward two societies, one black and one white—separate and unequal" (Levine 201).[13] One understands, then, why many of the objectives of the Civil Rights Movement were still subject to negotiation in the years following the report. Exploiting racial tensions, delaying integration, and opposing busing preoccupied much of 1970s politics.[14] Indicative of the times, President Richard M. Nixon (1969–1974) won the presidential campaign in 1968 by employing what has become known as the "Southern Strategy."[15] Nixon and his advisors rightly concluded that they could win the presidency by appealing to southern Whites with openly racial appeals. According to Kenneth O'Reilly, "Racism equaled opportunity in [Nixon's] calculus, a way to smash the New Deal coalition and realign the American political landscape now and forever to the Republican party's advantage" (279).

In terms of race relations, Nixon's presidency has been characterized by many as a period of "benign neglect." Many of its actions, however, could hardly be characterized as benign. For example, Nixon attempted in 1970 to block the renewal of the 1965 Voting Rights Act, fulfilling one of his promises to southern Whites that, if elected, he would counter civil rights legislation. He later authorized the petitioning of the federal courts to delay desegregation in Mississippi. "School desegregation emerged," O'Reilly explains, "as [the Nixon] administration's most important and enduring (anti-) civil rights crusade" (297). Nixon also opposed busing, refusing to enact any measure that would assist in the destruction of what he called "neighborhood schools" (meaning all-white) schools (O'Reilly 281). These are just a few of the many examples that shaped as well as reflected American sentiment concerning race relations in the 1970s. Nixon's successor, President Gerald R. Ford (1974–1977) continued in much the same vein. Nixon's 1972 war on drugs and crime, a mainstay of his campaign rhetoric, was overwhelmingly and disproportionately aimed at urban Blacks. In addition to new, tough measures on crime, then-FBI director J. Edgar Hoover's covert COINTELPRO, introduced in 1967 under the Johnson administration, was given full reign to "discredit and sabotage the efforts of suspected subversives," namely Civil Rights activists and Black Power groups (Verney 85). Ironically, one controversial yet seemingly positive civil rights remedy, affirmative action programs, began during the Nixon administration with his 1969 Philadelphia Plan which required companies with federal contracts "to increase . . . ethnic minority groups to [twenty-six] percent within four years" (Verney 87). While affirmative action policies certainly helped to economically empower Black America and certainly helped to integrate American society, the issue of affirmative action also "had the advantage of dividing Nixon's political opponents in the Democratic party" by creating what some White Americans considered unfair economic advantages for Black Americans (Verney 87). So what may have seemed an advance in terms of social policy may have been simply a shrewd political strategy. By and large, Nixon's agenda for the Black community amounted to less integration, more jails, and divisive racist rhetoric.

Prior to *Kindred*'s publication in 1979, affirmative action and equal opportunity laws were the primary civil rights issues during the Carter administration (1977–1981). Although President Jimmy Carter appointed a record number of African Americans to key positions in his administration, his presidency is not remembered for its strength in the field of civil rights. In 1978, Carter had the opportunity to defend affirmative action and chose not to do so. In a case that was ultimately decided by the U.S. Supreme Court, *Regents of the University of California v. Bakke*, the plaintiff challenged affirmative action policies on the grounds that they were unconstitutional. In advising the Supreme Court, Carter's White House attempted to "land in the comfortable middle and thereby appease all contending groups. The problem was that no contending group shared his definition of a middle where affirmative action programs were constitutional but rigid quota systems were unconstitutional" (O'Reilly 344). In the end, the Court's decision—race as a criterion for admission was not unconstitutional but quotas or "set asides" were—essentially gave Carter what he wanted, but it came with a hefty cost. Carter's lack of commitment to one side or the other led to his alienating large segments of both Black and White America. It is during such politicized and polarized cauldrons of race relations as these that Butler wrote her liberatory narrative.

Butler's choice to foreground miscegenation and interracial issues is an interesting one as this creates a trope of integration one may read as a strategy to assist American society in its ongoing struggle with race relations, such as I have sketched above. I am not suggesting that Butler offers miscegenation as a solution to race relations, or even that she is consciously responding to the political climate I have outlined, but rather, that she emphasizes the necessity of integrated collective engagement and coalition building across the color line as a way of solving some of our contemporary race problems. Butler's choice of science fiction works brilliantly in this regard as it allows readers to suspend their culturally constructed beliefs. To reveal the Black woman's story of slavery, even from the "safe" distance of the twentieth century, Butler selects a device—time travel—that serves to advance her exploration. In other words, Butler needed an inexplicable vehicle to assist her in presenting the inexplicable institution of slavery, its realities and its residuals.

By juxtaposing the past with the present through the vehicle of time-travel, Butler suggests that one can never have "enough of the past" as the past informs the present and ultimately the future. By revisiting the historical moment of chattel slavery and by engaging its indigenous literary form, Butler proffers, as Missy Dehn Kubitschek describes it, "a literal paradigm of coming to terms with a history of slavery and oppression [by] excavat[ing] history, then accumulating knowledge, and reinterpreting it from a forward-looking perspective" (51). Indeed, Butler does move beyond what we know of the enslaved Black woman's life by offering her meditation on the nature of Black womanhood in the present as well as in the historical past.[16] Butler further engages our narrative imaginations by amplifying our understanding of the condition of Black women in slavery as well as Black women in freedom. In her analysis of Kindred, Beverly Friend concludes that "[t]ransporting a contemporary heroine into the past serves neatly to highlight the contrast between current freedom and past oppression" (50). Perhaps it also highlights the contrast between past and current oppression. Butler's liberatory narrative reminds us that feminist issues are not new issues for Black women and are not unrelated to the construction of freedom. It also reminds us that history is not a static entity with little influence on the present. One must be true to the meaning of *sankofa* by returning to the past imaginatively as well as factually in order to live in the present and to move forward.

Chapter 3

History, Agency, and Subjectivity in Sherley Anne Williams's *Dessa Rose*

She saw the past as she talked, not as she had lived it but as she had come to understand it.

—*Dessa Rose*

Memory is the selection of images. Some are lucid, while others are imprinted indelibly on the brain. Each image is like a thread and each thread woven together to make a tapestry of intricate texture. The tapestry tells a story and the story is our past.

—*Eve's Bayou*

Novelists create not simply out of "memory" but out of memory modified, extended, transformed by social change.

—RALPH ELLISON

ALMOST ALL ASPECTS OF EIGHTEENTH- and nineteenth-century American history and society have been informed in one way or another by slavery, from America's 1776 Declaration of Independence and the writing of the Constitution through the Civil War and Reconstruction. Slavery built the American economy, shaped American jurisprudence, influenced the nation's westward expansion policies, and affected a number of presidential elections. In the twentieth century, slavery's cousin, Jim Crow segregation, continued to inform American culture and society. One contemporary cinematic representation of slavery's legacy may be seen in *The Long Walk Home* (1989), directed by Richard Pearce. Starring Whoopi Goldberg and Sissy Spacek, *The Long Walk Home* is set during the 1955 Montgomery bus boycott and is about women-centered activism. The movie depicts not just the politics of the time, but, more importantly, reveals the complexity of emotions for the female participants in the drama of integration. Goldberg's character, Odessa Cotter, is the maid of Spacek's character, Miriam Thompson. The two women have much in common, as they soon discover. Approximately the same age, they are both wives and mothers. Race, however, makes all the difference in their lives. One woman's labor is essential to the economic survival of her family, while the other is unemployed by choice. One is locked into a life of domestic servitude, with no hope of career advancement; the other lives a life of leisure and luxury. For Odessa, participating in the boycott means that she has a long walk to and from work unless she rides the bus or finds a ride, hence the movie's title. Not out of conviction but certainly out of compassion, Miriam chooses to drive Odessa during the boycott, even though she knows her racist, White Citizens Council-member husband would not approve were he to learn of her complicity in the boycott. Through her intimate, interpersonal interactions with Odessa, Miriam gains a greater understanding of the injustices and cruelties of racial discrimination. Miriam clearly has an authentic sense of justice, but she lives in a time and place where justice is prejudiced. Early in the movie before the boycott begins, Miriam demands and receives an apology for Odessa from a city policeman who evicted Odessa and her young White charge from the Whites-only park. Ironically, Miriam does not seem to understand her complicity in this instance, as she placed Odessa in the vulnerable situation by leaving her in the park alone. Miriam's race affords her the luxury to be unconcerned about where she can and cannot go. More importantly, when she is personally confronted by the discriminatory practices of the South, Miriam chooses to act. Miriam's growing racial awareness leads her to participate as a driver for the boycott, at great personal sacrifice. In order to make the changes that she makes, Miriam has to rethink her socially constructed ideas concerning race and its relationship to her daily life. What the film reveals about interpersonal race relations during the Civil Rights Movement is akin to what Sherley Anne Williams explores about slavery in her liberatory narrative, *Dessa Rose*, published a few years earlier in 1986. The movie's protagonists recognize what they have in common as women, and this recognition empowers them so that they join together as sisters to combat racism. Likewise, Williams's protagonists undergo a transformation born of their interpersonal relationship, forming a bond of interracial sisterhood. Thus Williams presents to her readers her feminist engagement with race, so that we can imaginatively consider what might have been in terms of interracial feminist coalitions during slavery as well as what should be in terms of interracial feminist coalitions now.

When asked why she "would want to probe that old scar" of slavery, Sherley Anne Williams responded, "Slavery . . . is more scab than scar on the nation's body. It's a wound that has not healed and, until the scab is removed, the festered flesh cut away, it cannot heal cleanly and completely" ("The Lion's History" 248). In *Dessa Rose*, Williams attempts to remove that scab on the body politic and to cleanse the wound. The main characters, Dessa Rose, the title character, and Ruth, have a relationship not unlike Pearce's Odessa and Miriam. Through their shared experiences, Dessa and Ruth undergo ideological shifts in their perceptions of the "other." In charting that dynamic, Williams provides for her readers an ideological liberation as they, too, experience, however vicariously, a transformative interrogation of received and accepted systems of belief concerning race.

Williams provides this opportunity through her elaboration of the familiar themes of the enslaved Black woman's life: female sexuality, motherhood, individualism, and community. By closely examining Williams's treatment of these themes, one finds that Williams constructs her protagonist Dessa Rose as an empowered agent who, like Jacobs's Linda Brent, overcomes what appear to be insurmountable odds. Dessa forcefully asserts her free will—her volition—within her deterministic and circumscribed environment in order to repossess her commodified self as an African American woman in the nineteenth century. Additionally, Williams's narrative is informed by Jacobs's emancipatory narrative, *Incidents*, in terms of its revelations concerning the enslaved Black woman's story and its continuing feminist thematics.

Williams's liberatory narrative is intertextual in the historical sense as well as in the literary sense. In the author's note, Williams recounts that while reading Angela Davis's seminal essay "Reflections on the Black Woman's Role in the Community of Slaves" (1971), she learned the sketchy details of a pregnant Black woman who in 1829 helped to lead a coffle uprising in the state of Kentucky. In pursuing Davis's source of this incident, reported in Herbert Aptheker's *American Negro Slave Revolts* (1943), Williams discovered the story of a White woman in North Carolina who allegedly gave refuge to a group of self-emancipated African Americans in 1830.[1] These two disparate historical texts of resistance became the pre-texts for a fictive occasion where the heroines of the incidents meet in *Dessa Rose*.[2] This fictive meeting affords Williams the opportunity to show that "slavery eliminated neither heroism nor love; it provided occasions for their expressions" (*Dessa Rose* x). Of this intertextual strategy, Patricia Maida observes, "By bringing the two women together, Williams creates a form of meta-history" (47). This conjoining of historical events highlights Williams's concern with one-sided representations of history.

How African Americans in history are represented is a motivating concern for Williams. In her author's note, Williams admits to "being outraged by a certain, critically acclaimed novel" (ix), namely William Styron's Pulitzer Prize-winning *The Confessions of Nat Turner* (1967; hereafter referred to as *Confessions*). Thus, in addition to the influences of nineteenth-century sources, a twentieth-century historical novel informs Williams's liberatory narrative. Styron's novel—which "travestied the as-told-to memoir of the slave revolt leader"—confirmed for Williams that "Afro-Americans, having survived by word of mouth—and made of that process a high art—remain at the mercy of literature and writing; often, these have betrayed us" (ix). Williams refers here to the reductive images and ridiculing representations of African Americans in American literature and culture in the nineteenth and twentieth centuries, of which Styron's depiction of Nat Turner and his rebellion of 1831 is but one example. Williams's enterprise, then, is to correct these discursive betrayals by reclaiming African American history, agency, and subjectivity in *Dessa Rose*.[3]

Why her author's note was written reveals much about the issues of interest to Williams in her first and only novel. Because *Dessa Rose* was so convincingly written, her editors feared that readers might think it was a true account. The issues of self-emancipation for Blacks, miscegenation between Black men and White women, and interracial friendships, as well as three-dimensional portrayals of African Americans seemed sufficiently threatening, even in the 1980s, for the editors to request a statement from Williams, making clear that her novel was indeed fiction. Williams recalls,

> I wrote the "Author's Statement" that opens *Dessa Rose* under protest;
> my editors seemed scared to death readers wouldn't know where fact
> ended and fiction began. Which in a way was precisely my point;
> white boys won prizes for doing just that and I didn't understand this
> sudden concern for "historical accuracy." . . . So I "authenticated" my
> own fiction and tried to subvert the convention. "History" is often no
> more than who holds the pen at a given point in time. ("The Lion's
> History" 257–258)

Signifying, in the Gatesian sense, on the practice of nineteenth-century White editors, such as Lydia Maria Child, who authenticated the veracity of nineteenth-century emancipatory narratives, Williams authenticates her own text by revealing her awareness of the complexity of historical veracity since history is a social construct. She writes in the "Author's Note," of *Dessa Rose*:

> This novel, then, is fiction; *all the characters, even the country they*

travel through, while based on fact, are inventions. And what is here is as
true as if I myself had lived it. Maybe it is only a metaphor, but I now
own a summer in the 19th century. (x; emphasis added)

By creating her fictional world, her *lieu de mémoire*, so powerfully and purposely, Williams calls into question the issues of historical representation and
historical veracity, thus creating insecurity among those for whom these issues are one-dimensional. In her note of assurance, Williams further problematizes the nature of truth in representation: it is and it is not, according to
one's perspective. That is why it was important to Williams to allow Dessa
the last word; hence, she provided a prefatory statement, not a coda. Williams's
point is that Dessa's truth is as true as any other character's in American history. More importantly, Williams reminds that all works of invention are the
products of imagination, and some imaginations reflect American racist and
patriarchal ideologies.

Recognizing that history is also a culturally constructed narrative, Williams corrects what she views as its betrayal by interrogating in her liberatory
narrative the White patriarchal hegemony that Styron represents. In doing
so, Williams deliberately writes against the so-called objective conventions
of the historical novel. Georg Lukács theorizes that the historical novel reflects and critiques the historical and material conditions of a particular historical reality. "What matters in the novel," Lukács writes,

> is fidelity in the reproduction of the material foundations of the life of
> a given period, its manners and the feelings and thoughts derived
> from these. This means . . . that the novel is much more closely bound
> to the specifically historical, individual moments of a period than is
> drama. But this never means being tied to any particular facts. On the
> contrary, the novelist must be at liberty to treat these as he likes . . . if
> he is to reproduce the much more complex and ramifying totality with
> historical faithfulness. (*The Historical Novel* 67)

The problem with Lukács's theory, as Williams's *Dessa Rose* reveals, is that
Lukács does not consider how perspective mediates the novelist's objectivity,
indeed mediates the novelist's understanding of reality and history and his or
her relationship to that history. In *Dessa Rose*, Williams revises Styron's revision of history, in which African Americans are either depicted in stereotypic
ways or silenced. She offers her readers the opportunity to consider the narratives of Black women and men as well as White women and men of the
nineteenth century and to see how those narratives intersect from a Black
woman's perspective. While she does make use of the Angela Davis, Herbert

Aptheker, and William Styron texts as well as others as her intertexts, Williams does not attempt, as Styron does, to recreate a specific historical figure or moment. Mae G. Henderson observes:

> [H]istorical fiction, as a genre, becomes, for Williams, a reconstitution based on other "nonofficial" sources of past experience—the oral and folk tradition. [Hers] is a process which shifts emphasis from the authority of the written, and closed, solipsistic text (i.e., the official record) to the oral, and open, collaborative text. ("Speaking" 653)

And, quite frankly, representations of Anglo-Americans by African Americans have not historically been used as sites of domination and misrepresentation. Styron—not unlike Thomas R. Gray, who recorded Nat Turner's narrative in 1831, and the other antecedent amanuenses who recorded the dictated narratives of enslaved African Americans—purports to enter the consciousness of Nat Turner to tell a story that cannot be a free story, to signify on William Andrews's work in this area.[4] In other words, Styron assumes the persona of a Black man, and in doing so, ignores most of the facts known about Turner in his construction of Turner as a historical figure. What, for example, was Styron's investment in portraying Turner as sexually attracted to both young White women and to young Black men when there was no evidence in Gray's narrative or in any historical record to support either possibility? Such appropriative acts in depicting the life of a cultural hero are problematic at best. As Donna Haisty explains,

> The real women who were the basis for Williams's novel . . . were not famous, and therein lies much of the reason why the response to [*Dessa Rose*] was nothing like the response to Styron's. Had Styron simply written a novel about a fictional slave leader, Black readers might still have taken offense at his presentation of slavery and might have disagreed with that fictional character's motivation, but there would not have been the sense that a White man, amid the Civil Rights turmoil of the late 1960s, was trying to take away the meaning of the life of a cultural hero. Styron took a hero and made him impotent; Williams . . . took little known . . . women and made them heroines—or at least made them live for a twentieth-century readership. (741)

Certainly, imaginative productions of historical figures and events are not required to limn the actual. Works of fiction are fictional. Writers are entitled to create freely, but they must be responsible in their creations and for their creations. I am not suggesting that the artist must conform to standards set by others. I am suggesting, though, that in matters of identity politics and representation, the artist, mindful that identity is always socially produced, should be aware of the hegemonic power inherent in representation and may be held accountable if his or her work reinscribes domination or silences another's subjectivity.[5]

For these reasons, Styron received a great deal of criticism from the African American community for his audacious portrayal of Nat Turner that had little grounding in historical fact; for example, his portrayal of Turner as not only a bloodthirsty murderer but also a religious fanatic who masturbatorily lusted after White women. A number of Black writers joined together to evaluate Styron's text as a cultural and social document.[6] In his introduction to *William Styron's Nat Turner: Ten Black Writers Respond* (1968), John Henrik Clarke writes,

> No event in recent years has touched and stirred the black intellectual community more than this book. [The contributors] are of the opinion, with a few notable exceptions, that the Nat Turner created by William Styron has little resemblance to the Virginia slave insurrectionist who is a hero to his people. This being so, then why did William Styron create *his* Nat Turner and ignore the most important historical facts relating to the real Nat Turner? These historical facts are far more dramatic than the imaginary scenes that were created for this novel. (vii; emphasis in original)

The trouble these writers (and many in the African American community) had with Styron's *Confessions* stems from the fact, as bell hooks reminds us, that "[f]rom slavery on, white supremacists have recognized that control over [representation] is central to the maintenance of any system of racial domination" (*Black Looks* 2). And therein lies the primary problem: many in the African American community felt that Styron, in his "meditation on history," reinscribed racist dominance in his reconstruction of Nat Turner and of African American history.

Engaging in what some have called "feminine discourse," an enterprise characteristically dialogic and relational, Williams responds to the calls and echoes in the narratives of both Jacobs and Styron. Writing in the late twentieth century, Williams breaks from the linearity of Jacobs's narrative by employing a circuitous narrative structure in which she, unlike Styron, allows the White male, the White female, and the Black female all to articulate their individual perceptions of reality. If Williams's creative enterprise is the engagement not only of the historical past but also of the reader's imagination in her revision of slavery, then Williams "pursues [the themes of] freedom and justice [to effect a] reconstruction of the American narrative imagination" (Callahan 263). Like Octavia E. Butler, Williams situates her liberatory narrative within the narrative frame of a prologue and an epilogue. Three sections comprise the body of *Dessa Rose.*[7] The titles of the sections are pertinent to the content of each section and to Williams's endeavors to present a panoramic view in her representation of history. "The Darky," the title of the first section, refers to an ungendered, racially pejorative focalization. This section, in which Dessa's voice emerges, is told from a White writer's, Adam Nehemiah's, point of view as he responds to Dessa's account. "The Wench," the title of the second section, implies a racist, gendered perspective. Significantly, this section is *omnisciently* rendered and treats primarily the relationship between Dessa and Ruth. Finally, the title of the third section, "The Negress," presented from Dessa's point of view, suggests a more dignified gender and racial representation.

In the setting of antebellum Southern slavery, Williams chronicles the persecution, exploitation, and victimization of her heroine, Dessa Rose, and more significantly, Dessa's journey of self-possession from slavery to freedom. The themes of bondage and freedom are complicated in Williams's depiction of her enslaved protagonist, Dessa Rose, who repossesses herself and then surprisingly continues to reside in the very site of bondage—the South. Beginning *in medias res*, the narrative quickly reveals the following: that Dessa Rose is pregnant, that her husband, Kaine, was killed by their master, that she attacked her master and mistress, and that she was brutally beaten and sold to a trader. These facts, revealed in the interviews with Dessa by a White writer, are to be included in his book, *The Roots of Rebellion in the Slave Population and Some Means of Eradicating Them.*[8] The events which place Dessa within Nehemiah's grasp are what Nehemiah desires to learn and to record. In her circuitous manner, Dessa tells of her participation in the uprising on the coffle of more than one hundred enslaved African Americans. Unable to continue running and unwilling to endanger her friends after the battle, the pregnant Dessa Rose is captured; some of the enslaved escape. While Octavia E. Butler's Dana is trapped in history, Dessa Rose is literally imprisoned, at the narrative's beginning, in a root cellar in Alabama, arguably a tropological reversal of Jacobs's "loophole of retreat," the garret. Significantly, Williams chooses an instance of live entombment, suggestive of how one can be buried, submerged even, by historical circumstance.

The theme of motherhood takes on a different meaning in Williams's liberatory narrative. While motherhood remains a source of inspiration, as in Jacobs's and Butler's narratives, motherhood is literally a lifesaver in Williams's narrative. Dessa's imminent maternity affects her punishment in that Dessa's sentence—death by hanging—is stayed until her baby can be born into slavery. Fate, however, mysteriously intervenes when Dessa's friends—three Black men named Nathan, Cully, and Harker—rescue her from the root cellar symbolically on the eve of the fourth of July, enabling her amazing second escape from slavery.[9] Here the narrative turns, as a tragic plot gives way to comic relief, widening its scope and foreshadowing its resolution. Fortuitously, the newly free group finds sanctuary at the plantation of Ruth Elizabeth Sutton, an isolated and lonely White woman whose gambling husband has apparently abandoned her and their two children, leaving them with no means of support.[10] Dessa, ridiculing the pretentiousness of the all-but-dispossessed Ruth when they first meet, marvels at the "[w]ay she was living up there in them two rooms like they was a mansion, making out like we was all her slaves. For all the world like we didn't know *who* we was or how *poor* she was" (176; emphasis in original). Here the self-emancipated Blacks join with other formerly enslaved Blacks to establish ultimately with Ruth what might be called a utopian community. Reciprocity marks the nature of this integrated community: the self-emancipated Blacks desperately need sanctuary, and Ruth desperately needs free labor. The community later decides to extend its collective efforts beyond the plantation setting by participating in a risky scheme in the marketplace which will benefit everyone financially. With Ruth's help, the self-emancipated African Americans parody the institution by selling each other back into slavery, collecting payment, and escaping again. In this endeavor, personal desires as well as communal responsibilities are resolved. The newly freed African Americans hope to earn the money needed to travel to the free West, and Ruth hopes to earn enough money to support herself and her children. Within this tragic-comic plot, Williams tightly weaves the liberatory themes of female sexuality, motherhood, individualism, and community.

As in the Ur-narrative, Jacobs's *Incidents*, a key feature of *Dessa Rose* is its depiction of the feminine volitional self. Of Dessa's "rememories" of her life, the narrator observes: "she saw the past as she talked, not as she had lived it but as she had come to understand it" (56). Through her narrative practices of flashbacks and stream of consciousness, Williams invites the reader to observe the dialogic dynamics of Dessa's repossession of self. For example, Dessa repossesses her self in a moment of clear objectification when her mistress accuses Dessa of being her master's concubine. After Dessa's husband, Kaine, is mortally wounded in a fight with the master Terrell Vaugham, pregnant Dessa attempts to kill her master but only succeeds in wounding him.[11] Seeking to understand why her husband would kill "the best gardener they ever ha[d]," (37) the mistress, aware of the sexual relations between enslaved Black women and White men, questions the paternity of Kaine's and Dessa's unborn child. The mistress, a miseducated reader of Dessa as text, thinks that the only reason for the altercation must have been Kaine's jealousy. Dessa recalls the mistress's promise when she erroneously deduces that Dessa's unborn child must be the master's child: "[If] Terrell live[s] . . . [he will live] knowing his slut and his bastid south in worser slavery than they ever thought" (37). Angered by the mistress's vile insinuations and verbal assault on her character, Dessa physically attacks her. For her insurgency, even though she is pregnant, Dessa is viciously punished: she is whipped on and around her genitalia, branded with the letter "R," placed in a sweatbox, and sold away from her family to a trader. Literally, this "writing" on her body alters Dessa as text since she is now marked with the consequences of her liberatory actions.

While Dessa is never assaulted by a White man verbally like Linda Brent or physically like Alice Greenwood, her sexuality—her erotic pleasure and desire—is nonetheless commodified and appropriated by the institution of slavery and its agents. Dessa first expresses her sexuality in her relationship with Kaine. In their relationship, Dessa receives love, affection, and nurturing. During their courtship, Kaine attempts to improve Dessa's work status from that of field worker to that of house servant because he resents that she must work harder than he does as gardener. Initiating his request through the unspoken chain of command, Kaine asks one of the mammies of the house, Aunt Lefonia, to ask the mistress of the plantation if Dessa can move to the house. Her reply reveals the peculiarly triangular relations between the master, the mistress, and the enslaved Black woman. Aunt Lefonia explains that Dessa is "too light for Mist's and not light enough for Masa. Mist's ascared Masa gon be likin the high-colored gals same as he did fo they was married so she don't 'low nothin' but dark uns up to the House, else ones too old for Masa to be beddin'" (10). Aware of her husband's past sexual inclinations, the mistress, as revealed in this passage, sought to control his sexual misconduct by removing what must be the objects of temptation—the Jezebels—from his immediate grasp. Although Williams provides no textual evidence to support the mistress's suspicions, the prevailing defamatory myth concerning the immorality of enslaved Black women indicts Dessa.

It is in her relationship with Kaine that Dessa becomes fully conscious of her own will to live. The narrative's prologue provides significant insight into the effects on Dessa of her awakening sexuality in her relationship with Kaine. In a flashback, Dessa remembers how Kaine made her feel more alive by stimulating her senses with his smell, his touches, and his kisses and how he

loved all of her—her taste, her hair, her nose, her mouth, and even her buttocks.[12] Desire filled her, then and in her memory, with the wish "[t]o be always in this moment, her body pressed to his, his warm in the bend of her
arm" (4). "These moments," explains Farah Jasmine Griffin, "of remembered
touching, pleasure, affirmation, playfulness and laughter are not in and of
themselves acts of resistance, but they are acts of nurturing and sustenance
that become resources for resistance" (529). In other words, these healthy relations engender a healthy concept of the self, a necessity for resistance. Later
at Sutton's Glen, after Dessa and Harker, her "thunder and lightning" (209),
are intimate, she remembers Kaine as "sunshine [and] song" (209). Employing the imagery of nature, Williams suggests that deeply intimate and interpersonal relations between Black men and women, however altered and
commodified by the institution of slavery, existed and were natural.

Unlike Linda Brent and Dana Franklin who do not have relationships
with Black men, Dessa possesses a meaningful relationship with Kaine, a relationship significant to her developing personal and racial consciousness as
well as to her developing sexuality. Soon after Dessa and Kaine are married,
Dessa becomes pregnant. The narrator problematizes parenthood to illuminate the complexities inherent in this condition for both enslaved African
American men and women. Kaine, keenly perceptive of the horrid affronts
and atrocities endemic to and perpetrated by the institution of slavery, refuses
to increase the coffers of slavocracy with his progeny. He wants Dessa to abort
their baby. Perhaps Kaine feels so strongly because his own mother was sold
"when he little bit and he never know her face" (33). Having attempted to
escape several times, Kaine has resigned himself to his condition of bondage
by the time he meets Dessa, but he enacts his own strategy of resistance by
refusing to increase his master's stock with his seed. If they can find "a place
without no whites," Kaine tells Dessa, "we can have us babies then" (47). Unwilling to compromise his position, Kaine asks Dessa to see Aunt Lefonia about
performing the abortion. Although she understands the precarious nature of
parenting for enslaved parents—that the child is bred to be sold "cause [Masa]
know we can always make another one"—Dessa refuses to destroy the life that
she and Kaine created (45). Dessa is reminded of the reality of her life as an
enslaved woman when she realizes that even if she does save her baby from
Kaine and Aunt Lefonia, she cannot save her child from its owner, the master.

In matters of sexuality, Williams, unlike Jacobs in the Ur-narrative, uses
her liberatory narrative to reveal the covert strategies by which the enslaved
community resisted the enslavers' commodification of the Black woman's body.
For enslaved Black women, Elizabeth Meese explains, "Revolutionary acts be-

gin with the body, the slaves' control over the (re)production of slavery through their control over reproduction itself, or a woman's decision to think through her body as well as her mind" (140). The termination of pregnancy is one such revolutionary act of resistance, although it could not be used frequently for fear of detection. The use of contraception is another example of the enslaved community's resistance to the alteration and appropriation of the Black woman's sexuality and of the Black family. Using conjure or "roots," the enslaved community developed a means of preventing conception. The narrator reveals the use of contraception as Dessa recounts an episode in which Vaugham, the master, pairs Dessa's sister, Carrie Mae, a physically small woman, with an unusually large man, Tarver, for the purposes of breeding. Fearful that Carrie would have difficulty birthing what could be a large baby, Mammie Hattie, an older enslaved woman, performs a mysterious rite which prevents Tarver's "seed from touchin Carrie Mae" (11). Consequently, Tarver and Carrie Mae are reassigned new breeding partners, due to their inability to conceive.

That a representative of patriarchy's racist and sexist practices, Adam Nehemiah, has the opportunity to speak with Dessa is directly related to another aspect of the commodification of her sexuality—her pregnancy. Nehemiah, considering "the darky's pregnancy a stroke of luck" (23), rushes to Alabama to interview Dessa, the surviving insurgent, for his book. Having written one successful book on the plantation management of enslaved African Americans, *The Masters' Complete Guide to Dealing with Slaves and Other Dependents*, Nehemiah concludes that writing about the institution of slavery is the way that he, too, can profit from the exploitation and commodification of African Americans without actually owning any human himself. This arrangement suggests the complexity of Nehemiah's psychological makeup. His reasons for not participating in slavery through direct ownership are not rooted in righteous principles. Unlike his Calvinist father, who owned African Americans but abhorred slavery, Nehemiah abhors the enslaved *and* the institution yet seeks to profit just the same. He views his participation in the sordid mess as a rung above the others, although the ends are the same. In Dessa's situation, while the White enslavers expect to sell the child born of the imprisoned and doomed Dessa, Nehemiah expects to sell her words for his own economic gain. Thus, *Roots*, his work in progress, will he hopes guarantee his entrance into the aristocratic southern planters' society he desires to join.[13]

Thinking himself qualified by virtue of his race and gender to record and to interpret Dessa's story, Nehemiah, another miseducated reader of Dessa as text, thinks that all he must do is simply ask his questions and record her responses. In other words, he believes that she will openly reveal herself to him, and he will *know* her. "It is no accident," Mary Kemp Davis observes, "that Adam Nehemiah . . . bears the name of that archetypal namer, Adam, whose 'first recorded activity' was the giving of names" (547). He soon, however, becomes frustrated and annoyed as Dessa "answers questions in a random manner, a loquacious, roundabout fashion—if, indeed, she can be brought to answer" (16). She does not intentionally answer in this manner to annoy him: "She couldn't always follow the white man's questions; often he seemed to put a lot of unnecessary words between his why and what he wanted to know" (54). More importantly, Nehemiah is incapable of attending to what Dessa says because he has already defined her as the Other—"a darky and a female at that" (16). In this way, his misinterpretation of Dessa symbolizes the misinterpretations of Black female subjectivity that have existed and continue to exist in White American society. This misinterpretation seems necessary to Nehemiah's construction of self. When Dessa eludes him for the final time at the novel's ending, Nehemiah is depicted as a broken and demented man, requiring Dessa's "function as other . . . for the constitution of his own identity as a 'masterful' speaking subject" (Meese 142). In this way, Williams adroitly shows how intertwined and interdependent White and Black identities are.

The most graphic example of the sexual assaults on enslaved Black women is literally and symbolically etched on and around Dessa's genitalia. Unable to read the truth of Dessa's story, Nehemiah and Ruth, both miseducated readers, conclude that Dessa's scars "bespoke a history of misconduct" (13). Because they do not know her story, they both believe that she surely provoked her mistress by enticingly "making up to the master" (145) as they subscribe to the dominant culture's prevailing notions of Black womanhood. Instead of bullwhipping her back for attempting to kill her master and mistress, which would impair her retail value, Dessa is whipped around and on her pubic area, a hidden punishment that leaves thick, ropy, keloidal scars that looked like, Williams writes, "a mutilated cat face. Scar tissue plowed through [Dessa's] pubic region so no hair would ever grow there again" (166). Ironically, Dessa's scars do indeed bespeak a history of misconduct: the centuries old misconduct of White enslavers and other beneficiaries of slavery toward African Americans and their bodies. Clearly, the ideological tenets of the nineteenth-century's "cult of true womanhood" do not inform the enslavers' racist and sexist treatment of enslaved Black women.

Mindful of the racism inherent in the construction of womanhood for the nineteenth-century White woman, Williams critiques this construction by employing irony and inversions. The strongest critiques of the differences between Black and White womanhood occur at the narrative's beginning and also when the newly freed African Americans plan their scheme of selling themselves into slavery, escaping with the profit, and then returning to the group. In the first instance, when Dessa remembers Kaine's murder, she ironically concludes, "Was I white, I might woulda fainted when Emmalina told me Masa done gone upside Kaine head" (9). If she were White, Dessa would not have been the property of a master who was authorized to punish his "property" in any way he chose. Dessa is also referring to the expected internalized and institutionalized differences in the emotional and psychological responses of nineteenth-century Black women and White women. On the surface, one could read Dessa's observation as commenting on the supposed frailty of White womanhood. White women, embodying the tenets of the "cult of true womanhood" have, Dessa implies, the "luxury" of abdicating responsibility—of fainting—because White patriarchal rule valorizes the White male as the caretaker of all responsibilities. Because of her race, Dessa enjoys no such accommodation. The second instance occurs when Ruth and Nathan, a formerly enslaved man, are discovered in bed together by Dessa.[14] The Black occupants of Sutton's Glen, Ruth's plantation, exhibit various responses to this anomaly as they discuss this perilous sexual relationship. One of the young men, Ned, who obviously has accepted the constructed stereotypic role of enslaved Black women as beasts of burden, accuses the Black women of disliking Nathan and Ruth's unconventional relationship because they are jealous that "don't nobody want no old mule[s]" like them (198). Ned's use of bestial imagery serves to emphasize the age-old and current binary oppositions concerning Black and White women—ugly versus beautiful, sexual versus chaste, bestial versus angelic. Enslaved Black women are only seen, in Ned's way of thinking, as beasts of burden and breeders of stock.

Unlike Harriet Jacobs, who pled for the inclusion of Black women in a morally protective cult of true womanhood, Williams critiques the bankrupt notion of Anglo-American "true womanhood" by imploding that construct in her characterization of Ruth Elizabeth Sutton, who learns to look at Black people and see, not deviance, but only color (*Dessa Rose* 184). Michele Wallace accurately characterizes Ruth as having "no revolutionary or abolitionist intentions in providing a refuge for slave runaways—she has stumbled accidentally into the situation" (143). While this is true, it does not erase the fact that Ruth chooses to participate and that she *allows* the situation to change her. It is, perhaps, more powerful that Ruth is not drawn in heroic proportions. Through her willingness to interact with and to learn from the self-emancipated African Americans, Ruth learns to acknowledge their humanity and, consequently, her own; she also learns to see them and herself as self-authorized subjects. In Jacobs's narrative, White women do figure prominently by offering covert assistance to Linda Brent in her struggle for freedom, but Williams's Ruth exceeds previous images of White women in their role as agents and subjects. In addition to providing sanctuary for the newly free community, Ruth cares for the ill Dessa, breastfeeds Dessa's infant son, and loves a Black man.

Perhaps the most suppressed text of the nineteenth century concerned the sexuality of the White woman. Quiet as it's kept, mutually desirous sexual relations between White women and Black men existed in the nineteenth century.[15] Williams's Ruth and Nathan represent one such relationship. Initially, Nathan seems to seduce Ruth in order to secure her participation in their scheme; however, it is later revealed that they indeed share a genuine affection for each other as they continue their physical relationship well after the scheme begins. They even contemplate making their relationship a permanent one. Barely recovering from the shock of seeing Nathan and Ruth in bed together and from the shock of confronting the taboo topic of White female sexuality, Dessa is further amazed to learn of the sexual vulnerability and victimization of White women. During their scam on the road, Ruth is sexually assaulted by her overnight host, Mr. Oscar. After helping Ruth to thwart Mr. Oscar's attempts in a comedic scene that involved overpowering him with pillows, Dessa is astonished to realize that White women are as sexually vulnerable as she and her Black sisters are. Of the relationship between Dessa and Ruth, Nicole King concludes that

> Williams allows her two women protagonists not only to appear
> differently from what the conventional stereotypes would have led the
> reader to expect but also allows them actively to refigure their roles
> and identities. As characters, each is able to understand the other in
> terms other than those offered by the white patriarchal power
> structure. (359–360)

Thus, motherhood and sexual vulnerability become the two sites of commonality for Dessa and Ruth in their bond of sisterhood. Could this narrative have been written before the feminist movement of the1970s? Probably not. Although the differences between White feminism and Black feminism have always existed, it was during this time that the disparate agendas of those on both sides of the color line became more prominent. Williams, it seems, is offering possible solutions to those divisions in her narrative.

Motherhood empowers the African American woman in *Dessa Rose* as it does in *Incidents*. As with Linda Brent, motherhood motivates Dessa to exercise her volition in freeing herself. When Kaine asks Dessa to have an abortion, Dessa suggests that they escape to freedom instead. But having attempted to run several times, Kaine dismisses her suggestion as futile. What Dessa and Kaine would have done is impossible to know because he is murdered before they can act. Her impending motherhood, however, continues to motivate Dessa. After she is sold to the trader, she continues her plan to free herself and her child, and she almost actualizes her dream of freedom in the coffle uprising. While imprisoned in the root cellar after her capture, she despondently contemplates how tragic it is to have come so close to freedom only to fail. Thoughts of her unborn child preoccupy Dessa's mind:

> To be spared until she birthed the baby . . . the baby . . . Could she but
> do it again, . . . she would go to Aunt Lefonia if that would bring her a
> minute, real and true, with Kaine. But to let their baby go now, now. . . .
> She would swallow her tongue; that's what Mamma Hattie said the
> first women had done, strangling on their own flesh rather than be
> wrenched from their homes. . . . She would ask Jemina for a knife. . . .
> She would take the cord and loop it around the baby's neck. (62)

These fragmented thoughts, delivered in free indirect speech, represent the fragmentation of the self by the institution of slavery. In spite of her pain, however, Dessa continues to author her own text—to exercise her volition—by continuing to plan, however desperately, the direction of her life.

Like Jacobs and Butler, Williams depicts the institution of motherhood for the enslaved Black woman as callously disrespected and the experience of it as viciously abusive by slavocracy and its agents. Dessa's own mother, Rose, gave birth to ten children; she had only one daughter left after Dessa was sold. In addition to Dessa, each of the four formerly enslaved women at Sutton's Glen—Milly, Flora, Janet, and Ada—had horrific experiences with the enslavers's institution of motherhood. When Ned refers to the Black women as mules, Dessa considers the ironic validity of his statement. After all, Milly, Dessa recalls, gave birth to

> seventeen children in eighteen years and seen them all taken from her
> as she weaned them, been put outdoors herself when she went two
> years without starting another child. . . . Flora [escaped from slavery]
> so she could keep her babies to herself. Janet was mistreated cause she
> was barren; Ada's master had belly-rubbed with her, then wanted to
> use her daughter [his granddaughter]. . . . Oh, we was mules all right.
> What else would peoples use like they used us? (198–199)

Williams provides, in this brief passage, a cataloging of the sadistic ways in which Black women were abused specifically in terms of motherhood and sexuality. In the case of Dessa, however, fate gives her a second chance at freedom as well as a chance at motherhood when she is rescued from her death sentence by Nathan, Cully, and Harker, her fellow freedom seekers. The fact that Dessa actually gives birth to her son during her escape is symbolic of her good fortune; she and her baby are rescued in the nick of time. Due to her physical illness after her escape and her child's birth, the community, including Ruth, cares for the baby. In a reversal of the mammy role, Ruth, who has a toddler, breastfeeds the baby for the infirm Dessa. Not without reservations because of the inherent risks, Dessa consents to participate in the money-making scheme, for she hopes to secure her son's continued freedom and future through her efforts. Once again motherhood is the impetus for action for the Black mother in bondage.

In addition to the dream of freedom that he gives to Dessa, Kaine also gives her the ability to perceive herself as an individual who can exercise her free will. Before Dessa meets Kaine, Dessa's mother, having lost much to slavery and only wanting to protect what was left, cautions Dessa that exhibiting individualistic tendencies is dangerous because attention "ain't never got a nigga nothing but trouble" (78). Kaine, however, refuses to allow slavocracy to suppress his individuality. The specific details of the fight between Kaine and the master are unknown. But what is known is that the master breaks Kaine's cherished banjo, an instrument Kaine had been taught how to make and to play by an African man, a man whose "home be his; it don't be belongs to no white folks" (33). Even Dessa wonders why it happened: "Kaine could have made another banjo. . . . Why," Dessa thinks, "when they had life, had made life with their bodies—? The question gnawed at her like lye" (63). What the banjo represents to Kaine sheds light on why Kaine rebelled. It symbolizes his ancestral home—his homeland where Blacks are self-ruled. Of his metaphysical dilemma, Kaine philosophically concludes that there are two lists, both written by the White man: White man *can* and Black man *cannot*. The reader discerns, as does Dessa, that the fight was related to the destruction of the banjo, engendering in Kaine the need to exercise the limits of his personal freedom. In doing so, Kaine removes the racially assigned negation from his list of institutionally sanctioned proscriptions by exhibiting his volition. From Kaine, then, Dessa learns the act of self-definition. When asked by Nehemiah why she killed White men during the insurrection, Dessa, not sarcastically but with conviction, responds, "I kill white mens cause the same reason Masa kill Kaine. *Cause I can*" (13; emphasis added). Continuing to define herself, Dessa later corrects Ruth's mispronunciation of her name by saying, "my name Dessa, Dessa Rose. Ain't no O to it" (256; emphasis in original). Not surprisingly, Adam Nehemiah, too, mispronounces her name as if he is entitled to name her what he chooses. Later in the narrative, Dessa ridicules Nehemiah's arrogant attempt to read her life's story when he "didn't even not know how to call [her] name—talking about Odessa" (247).

As revealed in the epilogue, Dessa realizes the ultimate act of self-definition by dictating her story—her liberatory narrative—to one of her grandchildren so that they will know how "we paid for [the] children's place in the world again, and again" (260).[16] With this act, Dessa, according to Mae G. Henderson, "moves from intervention to appropriation and revision of the dominant discourse. As the author of her own story, Dessa writes herself into the dominant discourse and, in the process, transforms it" ("Speaking" 35). That Dessa is an omniscient narrator as well as a first-person narrator breaks with traditional convention and allows Dessa to tell her story as well as the stories of Nehemiah and Ruth from her own racial and gendered perspective. In other words, Williams not only allows Dessa to use her voice, she allows her to wrest narrative control from those traditionally in control.

Vivid memories of familial and communal nurturing, however, sustain her in her quest for self-definition. "Always, whether her eyes were open or closed," Dessa remembers, "Kaine walked with her, or mammy. Jeeter tugged at her head-rag or Carrie Mae frowned her down about some little foolishness. Aunt Lefonia, Martha—They sat with her in the cellar" (51). Before she is sold, Dessa has a happy life with her family and friends. Like Butler, Williams presents the camaraderie of the enslaved community in the scene of a corn husking party where the members turn their usually tedious work into a carnival-like atmosphere. Dessa recalls:

> [a] corn husking was not, strictly speaking, work. Master provided music and food . . . and invited the masters of neighboring plantations to bring their people to the husking. . . . The food, the music, the competition over who would be the corn general, over which side would finish shucking its pile of corn first, all these made you want to come. (77)

Dessa recreates this spirit of community on the coffle. Nathan and Cully become kindred spirits with Dessa. They take care of Dessa, recently out of the sweatbox and weak from her punishments, by providing her with extra food and by helping her to walk on the coffle. When Nathan decides to escape, he plans to take only Dessa and Cully. Exercising her communal responsibility,

Dessa insists that he offer the opportunity for freedom to everyone. As with Linda Brent's escape to the North, communal cooperation, collaboration, and nurturing guarantee the relative success of the coffle uprising. Although "[n]othing went as planned," (60) two men on the coffle, Elijah and Nathan, seize the opportune moment created by the guard, who leaves the irons unsecured when, in order to rape her, he releases the mulatto woman, Linda, from the chain.[17] Dessa earns the name "devil woman" and "she-devil" because of her ferocity in the ensuing fight.[18] Dessa's commitment to the continuance of her community ultimately compels her to "force Nathan and Cully to abandon her" (59) when she realizes that her condition endangers their freedom. Later in the root cellar, Dessa finds comfort in the thought that perhaps one of the formerly enslaved did escape. These depictions of tenderness between Black women and men, absent from traditional historiography of slavery and historical fiction, are yet another example of how Williams attempts to correct the historical betrayal of Blacks by Whites in fiction and in "non-fictional" writing (ix).

Dessa creates a community at Sutton's Glen with her guardian angels (Nathan, Cully, and Harker) who emancipated her from the root cellar. These kindred spirits establish their community as they join their collective efforts with other newly freed African Americans to forge a life in freedom. The scheme to earn the money needed to travel to the free West requires the cooperation of the entire community, including Ruth, or "Rufel," as she was nicknamed by her mammy. In their scam, McDowell contends, the community turns

> the "authoritative" texts of slavery back on themselves. They use all
> the recognizable signs of those texts but strip them of their meaning
> and power. These escaped slaves contrive to repeatedly sell them-
> selves back into slavery only to escape again. They exploit Southern
> law and custom and faithfully enact the narrow roles [the law] assigns
> slaves and women. Dessa plays the "Mammy"; Rufel, the "Mistress";
> and Nathan, her "Nigger driver." ("Negotiating" 158)

In other words, they plan to profit economically by signifying on the institution of slavery so that they can be economically enfranchised instead of economically disenfranchised.

Another example of how the identities of Black women are subsumed by stereotypes occurs when Ruth and Dessa argue over Mammy's true identity. For Ruth, the recently deceased Dorcas, who had been her mammy and had cared for her since she was a teenager, was simply Mammy to her.[19] For Ruth, "[n]othing in the days and weeks since Mammy's death had filled the silence where her voice used to live" (118). For Dessa Rose, her biological mother Rose was Mammy. While remembering the pride Mammy took in her physical appearance, Ruth suddenly realizes that she knows very little about Mammy, a woman she loved. Selfishly, Ruth had never considered Mammy's individuality, or even Mammy's personhood or humanity, but had objectified Mammy as an agent, devoid of humanity, whose only desire was to satisfy Ruth's needs. Ruth never considered whether or not Mammy had children, whether or not she had dreams of her own, whether she had wanted to be free or had despised her enslaved condition. Dorcas, like her namesake in the Bible, is brought to life by the evocation of her name. Sensing Ruth's insensitivity to and objectification of Mammy, Dessa angrily tells Ruth, "You don't even know mammy" (124). Dessa vehemently dislikes Ruth's casual attitude toward Mammy, who represents all Black women to Dessa, and so she confronts her. Realizing that they are thinking and talking about different women, each comes to understand that their argument is symbolic. Their exchange forces Ruth to consider Mammy's individuality as well as what was stolen from her; Ruth can no longer simply objectify Mammy. Conversely, Dessa removes her own mother as well as herself from Ruth's objectifying gaze by providing a litany of her mother's life. Dessa shouts at Ruth, "Her name was Rose[. . . .] That's a flower so red it look black. When mammy was a girl they named her that count of her skin—smooth black [. . . .] Mammy gave birth to ten chi'ren that come in the world living. . . . Oh, I pray God mammy stil got Carrie Mae left" (125–27). In this act of commemoration, Dessa memorializes her own mother, historicizes her personal past, and reasserts her individuality.

In this and other characterizations of Dessa, Williams depicts the integral relationship of the enslaved Black woman to her family and community. What is innovative about Williams's depiction is that this community is an integrated one. I believe that Dessa and Ruth learn to do more than tolerate each other in the end and that they are not color-blind; through their unifying experiences they create a new model of relating, rooted in difference. "Institutionalized rejection of difference," Audre Lorde theorized,

> is an absolute necessity in a profit economy which needs outsiders as surplus people. As members of such an economy, we have *all* been programmed to respond to human differences between us with fear and loathing and to handle that difference in one of three ways: ignore it, and if that is not possible, copy it if we think it is dominant, or destroy it if we think it subordinate. But we have no patterns for relating across our human differences as equals. As a result, those differences have been misnamed and misused in the service of separation and confusion. (115; emphasis in original)

Lorde's words are instructive, as slavery was undeniably a "profit economy" that capitalized on difference. Williams's liberatory narrative provides a way of "relating across our human differences as equals" in the examples of Dessa and Ruth.

Although the success of the moneymaking scheme is predicated on the co-operation of a White woman who "was everything [Dessa] feared and hated," (182) Dessa reluctantly agrees to participate in the risky plan. In the course of their collective endeavor, Ruth and Dessa, like Miriam and Odessa in *The Long Walk Home*, overcoming their respective preconceptions about the other, recognize their shared gendered vulnerability and bond of sisterhood. The newly free community is "able in an adventure as exciting as any in American lore," Barbara Christian concludes, "to free themselves and go West" ("'Somebody'" 339–340). Their story is as American as apple pie. After the community successfully escapes to the West, Dessa and her family live in an integrated community. All is not perfect, as racism still exists, but they are free. Ruth and her children leave their native South and go East. What becomes of her or if she continues her integrated life we do not know. What we do know is that Williams offers her readers the paradigm of an integrated community to highlight the symbiotic relationship between African Americans and Anglo-Americans, because after all it is *the American narrative of slavery* that still haunts all Americans.

In constructing her liberatory narrative, Williams subverts the dominant discourse of patriarchy by revising disturbing narrative voices like Styron's in *The Confessions of Nat Turner*. In his author's note, Styron characterizes his novel as "a meditation on history," as if history were a singular narrative. Aware of history's multiplicities, Williams attempts in *Dessa Rose* "to apprehend that other history"—the history of African Americans who have "no place in the American past [where they] could go and be free" (x). The ending of Williams's liberatory narrative resists closure, appropriately symbolizing the open-endedness of history. As McDowell concludes, *Dessa Rose* negotiates "the past and the present to reveal, not surprisingly, that they are not at all discrete" ("Negotiating" 147). Employing the oral tradition, Dessa narrates her own life story, dictating it to her grandchild, whom she asks to read back what she has written for Dessa's approval, so that her grandchildren and the future generations will know. Her story cautions her progeny, as well as all who read it, to read resistantly the received narratives of history, race, and gender. By doing so, one is able to return to the past and perhaps to see it anew. Healing the wounds of slavery involves revisiting that past and reconsidering one's relationship with that past, as Dessa does. "Because Williams's commitment is to model healing from slavery's legacy," Ann Trapasso notes, "the novel sustains a delicate balance between representing the horrors and demystifying them" (219). Through that balance, Williams shows how one can remember even an oppressive past and not be buried by the remembrance, particularly if one is willing to take "the long walk" necessary to write one's own liberatory narrative.

The Metaphysics of Black Female Identity in Toni Morrison's *Beloved*

Chapter 4

*Freeing yourself was one thing; claiming ownership of
that freed self was another.*

—*Beloved*

I feel, therefore I can be free.

—AUDRE LORDE

"You got to be a spirit. You can't be no ghost."

—*Bulworth*

BULWORTH (1998), a movie written, directed, and produced by Warren Beatty, is a satire on contemporary politics as well as a commentary on contemporary race relations. The protagonist, Senator Jay Bulworth, is a White liberal with great existential angst. The movie's opening montage features pictures of Bulworth and 1960s political leaders, all once committed to social justice and equality. Once upon a time, Bulworth, played by Beatty, had himself been a committed public servant. Bulworth is now disillusioned by his meaningless political career and vacuous personal life. Deciding to end his miserable life, he accepts a bribe—a ten-million dollar insurance policy—from a lobbyist and then arranges for someone to kill him. Faced with imminent death, Bulworth becomes (refreshingly to some, annoyingly to others) liberated; he becomes what he wishes he still had the courage to be—committed, honest, and idealistic. Taking freedom of speech to a new level, Bulworth begins to reveal his free self in his political speeches, decrying greedy corporations, racial and gender inequalities, opportunistic foreign policies, class disparities, and dishonest politicians. Not surprisingly, race plays a significant role in

Beatty's illumination of the inequities and corruptions inherent in American democracy.

Bulworth is particularly forthcoming about the role of race and the insidiousness of racism in politics. With nothing to lose, Bulworth is also less guarded in his relationships, seeking and accepting companionship from members of the Black community. Life becomes so much better that Bulworth changes his mind about dying and tries to cancel the contract on his life. As fate would have it, he cannot. Complicating matters further, Bulworth falls in love in his liberated state. His love interest, Nina, is a young, race-conscious Black woman played by Halle Berry. After partying together in a South Central club and spending time together on his campaign reelection trail, Nina seems genuinely concerned for him and hides him at her family's home in South Central from the danger he fears. His immersion in the Black community and its culture changes him fundamentally and profoundly. In an example of identity as performance, Bulworth assumes many of the tropes of Blackness, including urban dress, that is, tennis shoes, baggy pants, gold chains, and sunshades, and he raps his speeches. Now wanting to live, he is unable to stop the contract on his life. As they grow closer, Nina confesses that she is the hired killer. Because of their relationship (and perhaps because the situation is resolved that initially forced her to take the job), she cannot kill Bulworth. With the hit now canceled, Bulworth leaves his hiding place to return to his life. But after his metamorphosis, who is he? The audience is not sure whether he will continue his new life or return to his former self. Unbeknownst to Bulworth, an insurance company executive has also hired a hit man to kill Bulworth because of the danger he presents in his liberated state. As he emerges from safety with his love interest by his side, Bulworth is assassinated.

Bulworth's solution to his problems had been to end his life; ironically, he has to lose his life in order to find the value of it. Throughout the movie, a *griot*, played by poet and playwright Amiri Baraka, gives Bulworth an alternative to death by admonishing him to "be a spirit. You can't be no ghost."[1] The griot exhorts Bulworth to awaken from his dead state, that is, his life of disillusionment as a cynical "ghost," and to become a "spirit" alive with the ability to promote change. Although Bulworth does not understand the griot, this is essentially what he does after he places the hit on himself. In the context of *Bulworth*, "ghosts" wander with no sense of purpose; they are truly dead. But a "spirit" has a purpose; they are the repositories of memory. As such, spirits represent the past. In a diasporic world view, Barbara Christian writes, "[S]pirits are everywhere, are naturally in the world, and are not ghosts in the horror-genre sense of that term" ("Beloved, She's Ours" 43).[2] Linking the past and the present, Christian continues, spirits are crucial because "continuity, not only of genes but also of active remembering, is critical to a West African's sense of her or his own personal being and, beyond that, of the beingness of the group" ("Beloved, She's Ours" 44). But because Bulworth does not understand the griot's admonition, perhaps due to cultural differences, he never embraces his past, never identifies its usability. He succumbs still a ghost. At its center, *Bulworth* is primarily concerned with metaphysical issues: What is the nature of existence? What role does free will play in existence and in the choices we make? What is the nature of freedom? Is one ever really free?

In her fifth novel, *Beloved* (1987), Toni Morrison grapples with these same issues, relying upon the concept of incorporeality as well. In *Beloved*, which has received a great deal of critical attention, Morrison returns to the historical moment of chattel slavery and challenges traditional ways of theorizing both bondage and freedom in the context of Black womanhood.[3] In doing so, Morrison proposes a paradigm of metaphysical liberation: she shows that freeing the soul requires the individual to take a journey, both physical and metaphysical, in which one confronts one's past. Morrison's character, Beloved, has often been described by critics as a ghost, but I read her as a spirit who serves as the repository of memory and thus uses those memories to promote change in the narrative's other characters.[4] In this vein, Orquidea Riberio explains,

> Instead of reviving the past, memory is the resurrected past—the surrogate presence of Beloved—that slowly summons memory in its wake. The novel is structured by a series of flashbacks and repetitions with variations which succeed in bridging the shattered generations by repeating meaningful and multi-layered images. This narrative strategy helps with the healing process. Beloved emerges in the flesh to challenge a continuous process of forgetting, refusal, and evasion. (163)

Morrison further reveals the complexities of the newly free Black woman's attempt to construct a whole sense of self and community in a racialized society while still dealing with the memories of slavery. Through Beloved, the narrative's characters—and perhaps the readers—are empowered to confront the metaphysical dilemmas of their personal and collective pasts in terms of slavery, effecting a liberation from the historical pain and shame of slavery.

Morrison's *Beloved* is based upon a singular historical incident, the life of Margaret Garner, an enslaved Black woman who, after escaping slavery, killed her young daughter when her enslavers arrived to return her family to slavery. Unlike Williams's *Dessa Rose* (in which she melds two disparate historical incidents to create her liberatory narrative), *Beloved* probes each of the feminist themes and presents the interior life of a formerly enslaved Black woman who successfully escapes from bondage to live in freedom.[5] While the antecedent text, Jacobs's *Incidents*, understandably centers its focus on the immediate effects of chattel slavery on the life of the enslaved Black woman, the focus of *Beloved*, as is characteristic of the liberatory narrative, centers on the incessant and lingering effects of slavery on the newly free Black woman. Moving beyond the Black woman's physical condition of bondage, Morrison interrogates the dominant feminist themes as they continue to inform the life of a self-emancipated nineteenth-century Black woman, Sethe Suggs, the protagonist of *Beloved*.

In ways reminiscent of Butler's juxtaposition of past and present in *Kindred* and Williams's juxtaposition of bondage and freedom in *Dessa Rose*, Morrison shows through her non-linear narrative how the past may unconsciously impose on or intersect with the present. To put it another way, Morrison allows the past to weave, as Melissa Walker observes, "into the primary story so continually and subtly that the tyranny of that past impinges on the experience of the linear narrative just as the characters have felt it interfere with their lives" (15). By doing so, Morrison challenges her readers to participate imaginatively in the creation of the narrative's significance. Drawing upon the story of Margaret Garner, Morrison engages her readers' literary imaginations and historical knowledge of female sexuality, motherhood, individualism, and community as she constructs Sethe, an empowered woman capable of exerting her free will to alter her destiny despite her restrictive environment.[6] Brian Finney explains, "Part of [Morrison's] narrative strategy, then, is to position the reader within the text in such a way as to invite participation in the (re)construction of the story, one which is usually complicated by an achronological ordering of events" (21). In this process, Morrison's readers are asked to rethink what they think they know, not only about slavery, but about psychic phenomena and existence itself. That Morrison asks this level of participation from the reader is not surprising as she describes her writing as "expect[ing], demand[ing] participatory reading. . . . It's not just about telling the story; it's about involving the reader" (*Black Women Writers* 125).

Like Williams, who employs the narrative strategies necessary to render multiple subject positions in *Dessa Rose*, Morrison uses a polyvocal approach in her liberatory narrative; she produces a symphony of voices through her use of interior monologues, streams of consciousness, flashbacks, and ambiguously shifting narrative points of view. If Williams breaks from the linearly rendered emancipatory narrative to challenge traditional historiographies of slavery, Morrison intensifies this strategy to reveal the rich interiority of African American life as she situates her narrative completely within the African American community, telling its story from the inside out. Morrison peoples her liberatory narrative primarily with African Americans, with Anglo-Americans playing only supporting roles. "In her re-visioning of the history of slavery," Karla Holloway offers, "Morrison proposes a paradigm of that history that privileges the vision of its victims and that denies the closure of death as a way of side-stepping any of that tragedy" (523). Through her narrative techniques, Morrison presents a full range of experiences directly related to the dominant and dynamic themes of the formerly enslaved Black woman's life. The reader's expectations are initially disrupted by the narrative's *in medias res* beginning and by the vivid personification of place, 124 Bluestone Road, the narrative hook that centers each of the novel's three sections.[7] The house is described vividly and specifically as "spiteful" (3), "loud" (169), and "quiet" (239). Of her strategy, Morrison explains:

> The reader is snatched, yanked, thrown into an environment completely foreign, and I want it as the first stroke of the shared experience that might be possible between the reader and the novel's population. Snatched just as the slaves were from one place to another, from any place to another, without preparation and without defense. . . . And the house into which this snatching—this kidnapping—propels one, changes from spiteful to loud to quiet, as the sounds in the body of the ship itself may have changed. ("Unspeakable Things" 396)

To effect these goals, the novel features a complex of vignettes recalling exploitations of Black female sexuality, abuses and misuses of motherhood, explorations of the self, and interrogations of community.

Identifying the eighteenth- and nineteenth-century autobiographical impulses of enslaved Blacks as central to her cultural heritage, Morrison engages in a type of "literary archeology" when she describes those early writings as "the site of memory" that inspires her "to extend, fill in and complement slave autobiographical narratives" in her own work ("The Site of Memory" 120). Additionally, slavery—Morrison's *lieu de mémoire*—has been traditionally and historically rendered and examined along non-intersecting gender lines. In constructing *Beloved*, Morrison confronts the counterproductive bifurcation of the Black man's narrative and the Black woman's narrative: "[Paul D] wants to put his story next to [Sethe's]" (273). Indeed, their individual narratives are both independent and dependent. Morrison presents both narratives, creating an intensely intertextual relationship that highlights how essential one is to the other. Certainly, Morrison is primarily concerned with the free Black woman's story after slavery, but she constructs, unlike Jacobs, that story as relational to the free Black man's story after slavery. Constructing her liberatory narrative in this way, Morrison allows her readers, both men and women, to participate in their own liberatory event. *Beloved* "reminds us," Dana Heller asserts, "that true 'freedom,' for the post-Civil War black family, was no freedom from the southern plantation, nor freedom by means of an emancipation proclamation" (116). Morrison accomplishes this reminder by evoking historical and literary imperatives embedded in both stories.[8]

The action of *Beloved* revolves around Sethe Suggs, the formerly enslaved Black woman who embarks on a journey of self-possession. While Morrison juxtaposes incidents that occur elsewhere between the years of 1796 and 1874, the narrative's primary setting is Cincinnati, Ohio, between the years of 1855 and 1874, with flashbacks to Kentucky in the years before 1855. The narrative proper opens in 1874 at Sethe's home, 124 Bluestone Road, where "there had been no visitors of any sort and certainly no friends" for eighteen years (12). Tomb-like, the house has no back door, is enclosed by a fence, and contains two rooms downstairs and two rooms upstairs with windows in the ceiling, not in the walls. The placement of the windows as well as the singular front entrance/exit suggest a claustrophobic containment from which all the characters suffer.[9] Sethe's immurement in 124 Bluestone revisits Linda Brent's in the garret, Dana Franklin's in the nineteenth century, and Dessa Rose's in the root cellar. For the liberatory narratives, these claustrophobic climes may also represent the stagnant and oppressive nature of the past, unexamined and uninterrogated.

The troubled Sethe, whose "future was a matter of keeping the past at bay" (42), lives at 124 Bluestone with her only remaining child, Denver, and with the spirit of the young daughter whom Sethe murdered eighteen years ago. Emancipating herself eighteen years earlier while six months pregnant with Denver, her fourth child, Sethe escaped from the enslaving state of Kentucky to the free state of Ohio. The plantation from which Sethe had escaped, the ironically named Sweet Home, is a setting that critiques the idea of "benevolent slavery." There, Mr. Garner, a "good" White owner, had encouraged the five enslaved Black men—Paul A Garner, Paul F Garner, Sixo, Halle

Suggs, and Paul D Garner—to be "men" despite the fact that society ordinarily classified enslaved Black men as either animals or perpetual children. Mr. Garner granted his "men" a degree of latitude in their psychological, mental, and emotional development. For example, he allowed Halle to work for someone else on Sundays, for five years, his only day of rest, so that he could earn the money to purchase his mother, Baby Suggs, out of slavery. The enslaved men were men only at Sweet Home and only by Mr. Garner's permission. The narrator explains philosophically, "Everything rested on Garner being alive. Without his life each of theirs fell to pieces. Now ain't that slavery or what is it?" (220). Flesh being flesh, Mr. Garner dies, and Schoolteacher, a relative of Mrs. Garner, turns what had once been a bearable situation into an unbearable one.[10] He is so named by the enslaved community because of his ethnographic interest in them; he uses his voyeuristic gaze to strip them of the bit of humanity they had been able to retain in the dehumanization of slavery. "Through Schoolteacher," Linda Krumholz posits, "Morrison demonstrates that discourse, definitions, and historical methods are neither arbitrary nor objective; they are the tools in a system of power relations" (113). In addition to making their physical conditions worse, he performs demeaning scientific examinations on the enslaved men and women—for example, comparing their human attributes with their animal attributes—which he records ironically with the ink that Sethe makes.[11] Anne Goldman explains this episode of physical and psychological domination: "By appropriating her milk/ink for himself, then, the 'master' at once covers over the fact that the materials which make his writing possible are not produced by him and simultaneously reassures himself of his master(y) over the woman who does produce them" (325). Thus, Sethe's own labor is used as a tool of her oppressive degradation, a fact that fills her with shame. Although she had no choice in this appropriation, she still feels that she has been complicit in her own dehumanization. For Sethe, freedom is choice.

Realizing after Schoolteacher's arrival that their family would soon be splintered, Sethe and her husband, Halle, plan their escape to freedom. Before they can achieve their freedom, however, Schoolteacher's young nephews sexually assault the pregnant Sethe by forcibly taking her milk. Because Sethe speaks of the horrific act to the sickly Mrs. Garner, the boys brutally whip Sethe, planting what is later vividly described as "a chokecherry tree" in her back. Having sent her three young children ahead of her to their free grandmother's house in Ohio, Sethe escapes Sweet Home without the absent Halle. Fate sends Amy Denver, an equally unprotected White woman, like Ruth in Williams's *Dessa Rose*, to assist in Sethe's successful escape and in the delivery of the baby, Denver, who miraculously lives. Reunited with her children in Ohio, Sethe enjoys being free and being a part of a community for twenty-eight days before Schoolteacher, under the auspices of the Fugitive Slave Act of 1850, arrives to reclaim Sethe and her children. Determined that neither she nor her children would return to slavery, Sethe impulsively enacts a murder-suicide plan. After she kills her "crawling already?" baby and attempts to kill the other three children, she is stopped. Schoolteacher, convinced that she is criminally insane, returns to Kentucky without her and the remaining children. Thereafter troubled by her murderous action, Sethe daily fights with her past and her rememories of her past. Sethe's community ostracizes her, and Baby Suggs abandons all hope. As the narrative begins, Paul D, "the last of the Sweet Home men," (72) arrives at 124 Bluestone Road, and his arrival brings to flesh the spirit of Beloved, the murdered baby so named after the only words that Sethe remembers from the baby's graveside service.

In Morrison's liberatory narrative, as in the Ur-narrative, the enslaved Black woman's sexuality is subject to exploitation and commodification by White patriarchal hegemony. The social consequence of her participation in conjugal relations is not procreation; it is a profitable procreative function for the power base. Like Anne Goldman, I, too, am collapsing maternity and sexuality because "the exploitation of the black woman as sexual object and as worker are conflated because of her position as reproducer for the [enslaved] labor force" (318). When Schoolteacher tells Halle to discontinue his work outside of Sweet Home while his sons are young, Sethe realizes that Halle will never be able to buy the children out of slavery without the money from the outside work and that Schoolteacher does not intend to sell them to Halle. In any case, Sethe's children are commodified and, as commodities, they will ultimately be taken from her. Thus, her sexuality as an enslaved woman is exploited by the hegemony. It is her realization of this appropriation that inspires Sethe to secure her family's freedom. After all, Sethe knows that Baby Suggs, Halle's mother, had borne eight children by six different fathers and that Baby had seen only one child, Halle, reach adulthood. More personally, Sethe's own mother had not seen Sethe reach adulthood. Before Sethe can enact the escape plan, she becomes pregnant with her fourth child, an occurrence that complicates the escape; but the enslaved men and women, intent on possessing themselves, incorporate her pregnancy into the plan by leaving before she is due to deliver.

Completely unprotected, enslaved Black women and their bodies were subject to all kinds of sexual and physical abuses. In slavery, Hortense J. Spillers explains, "the customary lexis of sexuality, including 'reproduction,' 'motherhood,' 'pleasure,' and 'desire,' are thrown into unrelieved crisis" ("Mama's Baby" 473). Not only is her sexuality exploited by slavery's beneficiaries, Sethe is physically battered, sexually assaulted, and psychically scarred. Sethe's assault in the barn by Schoolteacher's nephews is just one example of the vulnerability of Black women. Halle and Sethe had planned to meet there just prior to their escape. Sethe went to the barn at the appointed time, and the nephews followed her. One nephew held Sethe down, while the other sucked the milk from her breast with "their book-reading teacher watching and writing it up" (70). The assault holds triple horrors: she is milked as if she were an animal; the nutrition intended for her children is profanely appropriated; and Schoolteacher records the event as a part of his ethnographic research. Sethe recounts,

> [T]hey had me down and took it. Milk that belonged to my baby. Nan
> had to nurse whitebabies and me too because Ma'am was in the rice.
> The little whitebabies got it first and I got what was left. Or none.
> There was no nursing milk to call my own. I know what it is like to be
> without milk that belongs to you. (200)

This brutal experience lives in Sethe's memory long after the traumatic event; for Sethe, the violation itself goes far beyond its immediate horrors. It also has historical import and generational meaning. Because her own enslaved mother had not been allowed to mother her, let alone nurse her, Sethe took great pride and pleasure in being able to mother—and to breast-feed—her own babies.

A new horror presents itself when Paul D arrives at 124 Bluestone. Paul D reveals that Halle witnessed Sethe's violation in the barn. Unbeknownst to Sethe, Halle was in the barn rafters when Sethe was assaulted by the nephews. Unable to protect her from the brutish and obscene profanation of motherhood, womanhood, and personhood because to do so would have meant certain death for him, Halle was last seen, Paul D reports, sitting beside the milk churn with butter and clabber on his face "because the milk they took was on his mind" (70). His inability to protect his wife led to a mental breakdown. "All I knew," Paul D says when he reveals this information to Sethe, "was that something broke him. Not a one of them years of Saturdays, Sundays and nighttime extra never touched him. But whatever he saw go on in that barn that day broke him like a twig" (68). This news convinces Sethe that she will never again see Halle as he would be too humiliated, if he ever recovered, to face her. Contemplating the possibility of peacefulness in madness, Sethe thinks how nice it would have been if she and Halle had been able to go crazy together—to play in the butter, made from milk, together. But the realities and demands of motherhood preclude for Sethe the luxury of madness; she is pregnant when she runs, and she is responsible for three young children, one needing her milk.

Sexual exploitation for the nineteenth-century Black woman does not cease with the end of slavery: the interlocking factors of racism and sexism continue to engender a nexus of sexual and economic exploitation. Nor does Sethe's successful escape from slavery save her from all exploitation of her sexuality. After she is released from jail for the murder of her baby girl, Sethe desires to place a grave marker at the child's grave. As the baby had not yet been named, Sethe wishes to have the stone engraved with the only words she remembers, the words she feels most appropriate, from the graveside services: "Dearly Beloved" (5). Because Sethe is unable to pay for the engraving, the engraver lewdly offers, "you got ten minutes I'll do it for free" (5). Morrison provides a sensational description of Sethe's recollection of "rutting among the headstones with the engraver, his young son looking on" (5). Accepting his offer, Sethe views her acquiescence to the engraver's lust as an act of penance; she hopes the act would absolve some of the guilt she feels about killing her child, but "those ten minutes she spent pressed up against dawn-colored stone studded with star chips, *her knees wide open as the grave, were longer than life,*" and they did not grant her absolution (5; emphasis added). The lascivious engraver engraves only the second word—*Beloved*—in exchange for Sethe's ten minutes. Afterwards, she wonders if another humiliating ten minutes, a half hour at most, would have purchased the entire sentiment. As Sethe is a free but disenfranchised Black woman, her body remains a commodity for the marketplace.

As a result of her horrifying experiences, Sethe represses her sexuality from the time of her escape until Paul D's arrival. Because of their shared past, however, Sethe allows herself to feel sensual again. She feels safe with him because she knows that he knows. She is relieved, when she and Paul D make love for the first time, that the responsibility of her breasts—symbolizing her sexuality—is "in somebody else's hands," not her own and certainly not in slavery's hands (18). Sethe's sexual enjoyment, however, is short-lived. Before Sethe realizes who the young, mysterious visiting woman is, Beloved enacts her own strategy to aid Sethe and Paul in confronting the past they have tried to forget with Sethe beating back the past and Paul D hiding his self-described "tin heart." Sethe and Paul's relationship is a distraction, with its emphasis on the present, if they are to face their past. Beloved separates Sethe and Paul D so that they each may be transformed through a confrontation of their individual psychic and metaphysic dilemmas. Beloved forces Paul D to move into the storage house by causing him to feel uncomfortable in Sethe's house and then seduces him in order to drive him, guilt-ridden, away from Sethe. Beloved's plan is successful as it does cause a temporary break in their relationship. This break allows both Sethe and Paul D to face the pain of their former lives. Sethe, unaware of the affair, reconciles with Paul D, inviting him to return to her bed. But he must leave again in order for Beloved's work as a spirit to be complete. The past inserts itself between Sethe and Paul D when he hears the story of Sethe's bloody act from Stamp Paid.

Morrison peoples her liberatory narrative with many Black women, besides Sethe, who suffered from the inhumane appropriation of their sexuality during their enslavement. Sethe's mother-in-law, Baby Suggs, "coupl[ed] with a straw boss for four months in exchange for keeping her third child, a boy, with her—only to have him traded for lumber in the spring of the next year and to find herself pregnant by the man who promised not to and did" (23). Ella, the woman who meets Sethe on the free side of the Ohio River, spent her puberty "in a house where she was shared by father and son, whom she called 'the lowest yet.' It was 'the lowest yet' who gave her a disgust for sex and against whom she measured all atrocities" (256). Similarly, Beloved is rumored, by those who do not know who she is, to be a girl who, like Ella, had been sexually abused by White men. Even Beloved reveals a tale of sexual violation from the other side, during the Middle Passage, where "dead men lay on top of her. . . . [and g]hosts without skin stuck their fingers in her and said beloved in the dark and bitch in the light" (241). Vashti, the wife of the Underground Railroad ferrier Stamp Paid—born Joshua—had been taken from her husband, sexually used by her White owner, and then returned to Joshua. Lady Jones, Denver's schoolteacher, is herself the product of White male licentiousness—with her "[g]ray eyes and yellow wooly hair, every strand of which she hated—though whether it was the color or the texture even she didn't know" (247). Lady Jones's hatred highlights the peculiar psychological dilemma of miscegenation on the African American psyche. Lady could hate the color—blonde—as it represented the odiousness of her European ancestry. The wooly texture of her hair signals the foundation on which racial slavery was built: the abjection of the African American body. Abjection and self-loathing are just two of the negative psychological responses to slavery that enslaved and formerly enslaved African Americans suffered.

Alongside such symptoms of derangement, Morrison weaves into her novel the Ur-text of sexual assault for Black women: rapes that took place during the Middle Passage. These dehumanizing assaults on enslaved Black women, as documented by historians such as Deborah White, began on the transatlantic trip, and Morrison recovers this history. Sethe's mother, an African woman who survived the Middle Passage, was sexually assaulted multiple times by the crew on the ship that transported her to America as well as during her time on an unspecified Caribbean island. Impregnated several times by the traders who found it advantageous to satisfy their lust and to increase their profits with their own seed, Sethe's mother enacted her own strategy of resistance by throwing "them all away. . . . The one from the crew she threw away on the island. The others from more whites she also threw away. Without names, she threw them" (62). Morrison does not, however, limit her examples of sexually victimized women to enslaved Black women. Even Amy Denver, the runaway White indentured girl who helps Sethe to deliver Denver, suspects that her former master, Mister Buddy, may be her father. Her situation is analogous to that of many enslaved mulatto children in bondage, such as Linda Brent's children and Alice Greenwood's children, all of them the property of their White father/masters.

Motherhood is, as we have seen, a theme closely related to sexual exploitation for enslaved Black women. Sethe continues to suffer from the enslavers' institution of motherhood well after she is free. Both Morrison's Sethe and Williams's Dessa Rose share similar maternal experiences imposed upon them by the enslavers. Sethe and Dessa, both bearing the scars of brutal beatings inflicted upon them while pregnant, escape from their hostile environments and give birth during their respective escapes. Sethe has no experience as a daughter and no model of motherhood.[12] Arriving alone at Sweet Home at the age of thirteen, Sethe barely knew her own mother when they lived on the same plantation for they were separated within a few weeks of her birth, a common practice on southern plantations. Enslaved Black mothers rarely cared for their own children and were expected to return to work as soon as possible after delivering. In many cases, one enslaved Black mother breastfed the enslaved community's infants (and in many cases the master's children as well); and even if the enslaved mother was allowed time to breast-feed, the enslaved children's daycare, if any, generally consisted of an elderly or a mutilated enslaved woman no longer capable of working. In *Beloved*, Nan, a one-armed woman who traveled with Sethe's mother on the ship, cared for Sethe and the other children whose mothers worked the rice fields. Sethe only remembers that her mother wore a cloth hat in the fields and that she was branded with the sign of the cross under her breast; Sethe last sees her mother hanging from a tree in punishment for an unspecified act of rebellion. Sethe reflects, "I wonder what they was doing when they was caught. Running, you think? No. Not that. Because she was my ma'am and nobody's ma'am would run off and leave her daughter, would she?" (203). Certainly, Linda Brent does not. But motherhood, even for the enslaved mother, is not a monolithic entity. Sethe wants to believe that her mother was not caught trying to escape without her, and it is possible that she was lynched for an act unrelated to escape. But if Sethe's mother was escaping without Sethe, then the notion of the enslaved mother as self-sacrificing is exploded. This is yet another example of how Morrison brilliantly complicates these feminist themes to show the nuanced properties of constructions like motherhood.

Sethe's impetus to seek freedom for herself and her family occurs when she perceives the future dangers for her enslaved children. Her reward lasts twenty-eight days, one full cycle of the moon. Sethe, for the first time, knows true freedom; she enjoys her children and herself. Later, recounting her newfound maternal joys as well as her newfound sense of self to Paul D, Sethe explains,

> I did it. I got us all out. . . . It was a kind of selfishness I never knew
> nothing about before. It felt good. Good and right. I was big, Paul D,
> and deep and wide and when I stretched out my arms all my children
> could get in between. I was *that* wide. Look like I loved em more after
> I got here. Or maybe I couldn't love em proper in Kentucky because
> they wasn't mine to love. But when I got [to Cincinnati], when I
> jumped down off that wagon—there wasn't nobody in the world I
> couldn't love if I wanted to. (162; emphasis in original)

Sethe's attempts to alter her destiny seem to be successful when she safely arrives at her mother-in-law's home where her children had been sent ahead of her. The sudden arrival of Schoolteacher, however, threatens the defenseless Sethe and provokes her to protect her newly won liberty and her children's freedom, instinctively and immediately. Unwilling to relinquish her newly acquired access to her selfhood, Sethe enacts her own radical strategy of resistance. Recognizing Schoolteacher's approaching hat, Sethe seeks to "put [her] babies where they'd be safe" (164) by killing them. Thereafter, she planned to kill herself so that they could all be together with her mother. Although she tries to kill all four of her children, she only succeeds in killing the "crawlin' already?" baby girl, which she does by cutting her throat with a handsaw. The two older boys are injured, and Stamp Paid prevents Sethe from crushing the baby Denver's skull. Sethe refuses to allow her children to live as property. She cannot accept "[t]hat anybody white could take your whole self for anything that came to mind. Not just work, kill, or maim you, but dirty you. Dirty you so bad you couldn't like yourself anymore" (151). Like Jacobs's Linda Brent,

Sethe exercises her right to choose her children's fates as well as her own. But as Jennifer Fitzgerald argues, "Slavery severed Sethe's bond with her mother before she had developed a separate identity; consequently, her sense of self and of the boundaries to that self is dangerously weak" (677). Sethe's attempt to secure her children's freedom by murder plunges her and those around her into an existential quandary and the reader into an ethical one. Is she free to kill her children in order to save them? The morality of her action does not concern Sethe; she is concerned only with protecting her children from the immoral terrors of Schoolteacher and of slavery.

The institution and the experience of motherhood, tainted by slavocracy, irreversibly overrule the whole of Sethe's existence. Before Paul D knows of Sethe's crime, he attempts to assuage the guilt he feels about his sexual relationship with Beloved by confessing to Sethe. Unable to confess, however, he asks Sethe instead to have his child. Rafael Perez-Torres asserts that "[t]he reason Paul D wants a child is . . . the excuse of a child might be, he reasons, what it takes to cause a rift between Sethe and Beloved" (700). This may be true, but I believe that he does so to reaffirm his manhood in a conventional way because the spirit Beloved causes him to question his masculinity—"[a] grown man fixed by a girl" (127). The thought of having another baby, revealingly, frightens Sethe. She thinks, "Needing to be good enough, alert enough, strong enough, that caring—again. Having to stay alive just that much longer. O Lord, she thought, deliver me. Unless carefree, motherlove was a killer" (132). But Morrison seems to be asking: When is motherhood carefree? Motherhood, for Sethe, is a constant vicissitude of competing passions and emotions. Her word choice is double edged: for Sethe, a mother is a killer, and being a mother can kill. Even the rootless and long motherless Paul D recognizes the risk: for a "used-to-be slave woman to love anything that much was dangerous, especially if it was her children she had settled on to love" (45). Most of Sethe's traumas, produced by slavery, reside in the construct of motherhood: she is prevented from knowing her mother, she watches her mother murdered; she is beaten while she is pregnant; she gives birth in slavery and while escaping; and she murders her daughter to save her.

Because Baby Suggs becomes a surrogate mother to Sethe, her text of motherhood, although not a discourse of resistance, is significant. Having borne eight children by six men, Baby Suggs eventually loses all of her children. Pondering her experience of motherhood, Baby Suggs recalls the birth of her last child, Halle:

> The last of her children, whom she barely glanced at when he was
> born because it wasn't worth the trouble to try to learn features you

would never see change into adulthood anyway. Seven times she had
done that: held a little foot; examined the fat fingertips with her
own—fingers she never saw become the male or female hands a
mother would recognize anywhere. She didn't know to this day what
their permanent teeth looked like; or how they held their heads when
they walked. . . . All seven were gone or dead. What would be the
point of looking too hard at that youngest one? (139)

What Baby Suggs learns, then, seems to formulate a syllogism of motherhood:
as a mother, to love is to lose, to lose is to suffer; therefore, to love is to suffer.
What Baby Suggs "called the nastiness of life was the shock she received upon
learning that nobody stopped playing checkers just because the pieces included
her children" (23). Unlike Sethe, Baby Suggs chooses to accept her inability
to change her circumstance and to turn her energies, once free, to spreading
a message of love to her community. The paradoxical nature of Sethe's decision to save her children by killing them, however, so confounds Baby Suggs
that she is stunned by the act and by her response: she lays down both her
"sword and shield" (86). Unable to "approve or condemn Sethe's rough choice"
(180), Baby Suggs abandons all hope and takes to her bed to contemplate
color, the very entity that has determined her life. After Sethe's action, known
as "the Misery," Baby Suggs is unable to heed her own advice because "[t]hose
white things have taken all [she] had or dreamed . . . and broke [her] heart-
strings too. There is no bad luck in the world but whitefolks" (89). For Krumholz, "Baby Suggs represents an epistemological and discursive philosophy that
shapes Morrison's work, in which morality is not preset in black and white
categories of good and evil" (112). Baby Suggs's decision to ponder color may
be read in at least two ways: either she wishes to examine that aspect of her
reality which so conditioned her life, or she chooses to spend the last part of
her life peacefully, examining aesthetic beauty as an escape from "the Misery." While Trudier Harris reads Baby Suggs's surrender as a return "to the passive, acquiescent role that defined her character during slavery and indeed
makes her a slave to life," I read her surrender as yet another powerful testimony to the corruption of slavery (148). That slavery and its aftermath caused
even Baby Suggs to quit suggests how pervasively pernicious is the institution.

A key feature of *Beloved*, as is characteristic of the liberatory narrative, is
the development and assertion of the volitional self. Sethe, the only young
Black woman at Sweet Home, does not have a community of women from
which to learn the basics about mothering. She does, however, have the memories of a mother who died as a result of an act of resistance and who "threw
away" the offspring born of her repeated violators. The impressionable Sethe

reads her mother's life as a discourse of resistance. In the short time they are together, Sethe learns from her mother the value of the self. Spillers explains, "If the child's humanity is mirrored initially in the eyes of its mother, or the maternal function, then we might be able to guess that the social subject grasps the whole dynamic of resemblance and kinship by way of the same source" ("Mama's Baby" 472). As a child, Sethe seeks to differentiate herself; she learns to identify her mother—the woman who belonged to her—by the cloth hat that she wears among the scores of straw hatted other women in the rice field. Her mother also shows Sethe the symbol—the brand—under her breast that sets her apart from all others. Sethe recalls this conversation with her unnamed mother:

> She said, 'This is your ma'am. This,' and she pointed. 'I am the only one got this mark now. The rest dead. If something happens to me and you can't tell me by my face, you can know me by this mark.' Scared me so. All I could think of was how important this was and how I needed to have something important to say back. . . . 'Yes, Ma'am,' I said. 'But how will you know me? . . . Mark me, too,' I said. (61)

This conversation is significant to Sethe's psychic development in as much as it is here that Sethe learns of her mother's and her own marked individuality.

For Sethe, freedom is making choices. Indeed, Sethe refuses to accept the enslavers' dictum that the "definitions belong to the definers—not the defined" (190). After arriving at Sweet Home, Sethe exercises her free will by *choosing* one of the Sweet Home men as her husband. One may recall that in *Kindred* Alice chose Isaac before her choice was expropriated by Rufus and that Williams's Dessa found great value in Kaine's choosing her. Before she will marry Halle, however, Sethe decides that she must have, like Mrs. Garner, a wedding dress. Even though the dress is made of pilfered and incongruent materials, Sethe's act bespeaks her craving for self-definition. If she is to be a bride, she wishes to look like her concept of a bride. Characterizing Sethe's marked determination, Paul D describes Sethe as "the one with iron eyes and backbone to match" (9). Another example of Sethe's volition is manifest in her habit of bringing flowers with her to her work at Sweet Home. She had, the narrator reveals,

> to bring a fistful of salsify into *Mrs. Garner's kitchen* every day just to be able to work in it, feel like some part of it was hers, because she wanted to love the work she did, to take the ugly out of it, and the only way she could feel at home on Sweet Home was if she picked some pretty growing thing and took it with her. (22; emphasis added)

With so much of her life beyond her control, Sethe needed to have control over locating her self in her environment, in her work, in order to feel that she belonged. All of these instances lead to Sethe's perceptions of her personal uniqueness, and subsequently, to her drive to repossess herself and her children from slavery. She later ruefully recollects her attempt to assert her selfhood at Sweet Home: "As though a handful of myrtle stuck in the handle of a pressing iron propped against the door in a whitewoman's kitchen could make it hers" (23). At 124 Bluestone, Sethe accepts the responsibility of her personhood and acknowledges the realities of her life: "I got a tree on my back and a haint in my house, and nothing in between but the daughter I am holding in my arms. No more running—from nothing. . . . I took one journey and I paid the ticket" (15). Sethe's stance is not one of hopefulness; rather, she is resolved to her fate.

Sethe's assertion of selfhood begins in her formative years and is the result of her mother's brief influence. Baby Suggs, on the other hand, contemplates her individual self only after she is in Ohio, away from the evils of slavery. It is as if she cannot have a sense of self as long as she is chattel. Morrison writes, "But suddenly [Baby] saw her hands and thought with a clarity as simple as it was dazzling, 'These hands belong to me. These my hands.' Next she felt a knocking in her chest and discovered something else new: her own heartbeat" (141). It is significant that, as Valerie Smith observes, "[w]hen Baby Suggs is finally free, the change in her status is recorded in terms of physical sensations; she claims ownership of her hands and heart" because these are the two body parts that have not been depleted by slavery ("Circling the Subject" 348). It is as if Baby Suggs is reborn. During the ride with Mr. Garner to her new home in Ohio eighteen years earlier, Baby Suggs asks him why he calls her Jenny. Replying that Jenny was the name on her sales ticket, Mr. Garner asks, "Ain't that your name? What you call yourself?" (142). Baby Suggs's reply—"I don't call myself nothing"—is indicative of the dehumanizing effects of slavery on the psyche of its victims. One of the greatest atrocities inflicted on enslaved African Americans by the institution of slavery was its devastating effect on the African American's self-conception. Suddenly aware of the harm done to her, Baby Suggs examines her own life and laments.

> [T]he sadness was at her center, the desolated center where the self
> that was no self made its home. Sad as it was that she did not know
> where her children were buried or what they looked like if alive, fact
> was she knew more about them than she knew about herself, having
> never had the map to discover what she was like. (140)

Perhaps the example of Sethe's relentless claim to her selfhood prompts Baby

Suggs to define herself and to accept her mission. Deciding to use the one organ—her heart—that slavery had not depleted, Baby Suggs "offered up . . . her great big heart" (87). As an "unchurched preacher," Baby Suggs, holy, preached a message of loving one's self. In the Clearing, she shared with the community the lesson she learned: "that the only grace they could have was the grace they could imagine. . . . [l]ove your heart. For this is the prize" (88–89). But this prize changes for Baby Suggs, holy, after Sethe's desperate act.

As seen in the Ur-narrative, a good relationship between the enslaved woman and her community is critical, and this continues in freedom. Not only does Sethe lack communal support at Sweet Home in Kentucky, unfortunately she also lacks communal support later in Ohio after "the Misery." Because Sethe was so young when she left her first plantation and because Sweet Home was a small plantation, Sethe's interaction with any community was limited. As the only enslaved woman at Sweet Home, Sethe has no community of sisters; but the Sweet Home men are her brothers, especially Sixo, the African.[13] Because Sethe had no women to learn from or talk to about child rearing, she felt uncertain and insecure about her ability to mother her children. Explaining to Paul D the need she had in her youth for other women, Sethe recalls, "I wish I'd a known more, but, like I say, there wasn't anybody to talk to. Woman, I mean. So I tried to recollect what I'd seen back where I was before Sweet Home. . . . It's hard, you know what I mean? by yourself and no woman to help you get through" (160). Once she escapes, however, Sethe has, for a short time, a loving and nurturing community. The narrator describes Sethe's twenty-eight days of communal living as

> days of healing, ease and real-talk. Days of company: knowing the names of forty, fifty other Negroes, their views, habits; where they had been and what done; of feeling their fun and sorrow along with her own, which made it better. One taught her the alphabet; another a stitch. All taught her how it felt to wake up at dawn and *decide* what to do with the day. . . . Bit by bit, at 124 and in the Clearing, along with the others, she had claimed herself. (95; emphasis in original)

Clearly, however, claiming one's self in a commodity-driven society is not a one-time act, and bringing together the physically and psychologically battered formerly commodified African Americans does not ensure unity.

The community's cooperative, collaborative, and nurturing aspects are short-lived. The mainstays of slavery—divisiveness, inhumanity, alienation—prevail over the community of newly free citizens who, in the process of organizing themselves in an atmosphere of freedom, succumb to insecurity and jealousy. The journey from psychological mutilation to psychological whole-ness is a complex one, and Morrison paints a panoramic view of that journey. Visiting Baby Suggs soon after Sethe's arrival, Stamp Paid decides to bring the reunited Suggs family a token of thanksgiving. He brings spectacular black-berries: "Just one of the berries and you felt anointed" (136). The celebratory dinner begins innocently; Baby Suggs cooks the pies, Sethe suggests the chick-ens, and Stamp thinks fish would be satisfying. Friends are invited, and the food grows. In a scene reminiscent of the New Testament's miracle of the loaves and fishes, the ninety people eat, laugh, and drink merrily through the night. Of the community's subsequent response to the party, Morrison reveals a heartbreaking degree of spitefulness:

> 124, rocking with laughter, goodwill and food for ninety, made them angry. Too much, they thought. Where does she get it all, Baby Suggs, holy? Why is she and hers always the center of things? . . . Loaves and fishes were His power—they did not belong to an ex-slave who had probably never carried one hundred pounds to the scale, or picked okra with a baby on her back. Who had never been lashed by a ten-year-old whiteboy as God knows they had. Who had not escaped slavery—had, in fact, been *bought out* of it by a doting son and *driven* to the Ohio River in a wagon. . . . It made them furious. They swallowed baking soda, the morning after, to calm the stomach violence caused by the bounty, the reckless generosity on display at 124. Whispered to each other in the yards about fat rats, doom and uncalled-for pride. (137; emphasis in original)

Although Baby Suggs, Sethe, Stamp Paid, and everyone in the community had good reason to celebrate and to be proud, they are unused to having the occasion and the freedom to do so. Additionally, Baby Suggs, holy, forgot that "she didn't approve of extra. 'Everything depends on knowing how much,' she [had] said, and 'Good is knowing when to stop'" (87). While the occupants of 124 may have overstepped themselves, the community fails in its commu-nal responsibility to protect its members. The community allows their envy and spite to destroy its members as well as itself. Because they are spiteful, no one alerts Baby Suggs and her family to the arrival of the strange White men, who must surely be enslavers. This betrayal is yet another reason for Baby Suggs to retreat to her bed: "to belong to a community of other free Negroes—to love and be loved by them, to counsel and be counseled, protect and be pro-tected, feed and be fed—and then to have that community step back and hold itself at a distance—well, it could wear out even a Baby Suggs, holy" (177).

Not only do Sethe's murderous act and the violation of her yard cause Baby's despair, the community's "meanness" (157) contributes to her loss of faith.

The community, however, is given the opportunity to redeem itself. Denver seeks communal support when she realizes that she has to save her mother from Beloved, who has forced Sethe to confront her past. But because one cannot live only in the past, Denver, representing the present and the future, functions to force Sethe to reconcile the past and present. After not warning Sethe, the community continues to shun her, ashamed of its neglectful spite. Not only do her action and her pride offend the community, the community realizes its complicity in the crime. Unable to forgive themselves, the community refuses to forgive Sethe. Consequently, Denver, ostracized with her mother, is afraid to leave the yard. In order to save her mother and herself from the past because the past cannot overtake—cannot dominate—the present, Denver leaves the yard and asks the community for help. As Denver stands terrified of venturing into the unknown, the ancestral voice of Baby Suggs inspires Denver, reminding her of her legacy:

> 'You mean I never told you nothing about Carolina? About your
> daddy? You don't remember nothing about how come I walk the way I
> do and about your mother's feet, not to speak of her back? I never told
> you all that? Is that why you can't walk down the steps? My Jesus My.'
> But you said there was no defense.
> 'There ain't.'
> Then what do I do?
> 'Know it, and go on out the yard. Go on.' (244)

Taking a chance, Denver seeks help from the women of the community, and they respond with generosity and kindness. Discovering through Denver who it is visiting at 124, Ella convinces the others "that rescue was in order" because "the past [was] something to leave behind" (256). But one never leaves the past behind; the past is always present. One must face the past and learn from it.

Beloved, the spirit who represents that past, symbolizes the uncontrollable psychic forces breaking loose and asserting themselves in the psyches of the characters. Thus, Beloved has multiple interpretations: she becomes the means by which Sethe and Paul D may become whole; she provides Sethe with the opportunity to confront her rememories of the past; she empowers Denver to take responsibility not only for herself but for her mother; she continues Baby Suggs's affirmation of good through Denver; and she allows the supporting cast of characters, particularly Stamp Paid and Ella, to atone for the sin of resigning from their communal responsibilities. She is an instrument of self-examination, too, for Morrison's readers.

At the end of the novel, Ella and twenty-nine other women walk to 124 Bluestone to face the past embodied in the spirit of Beloved. The reader stands outside 124 Bluestone along with them. Outside the house, Ella, recalling the baby she had delivered by "the lowest yet," hollered, and "instantly the kneelers and the standers joined her. They stopped praying and took a step back to the beginning. In the beginning there were no words. In the beginning was the sound, and they all knew what that sound sounded like" (259). The sound created in response to Ella's call affects Sethe, who is, in this moment, reliving the day that Schoolteacher came into the yard. This time, Sethe, holding an ice pick, instead of turning on her own flesh, attacks her innocent land-lord, Mr. Bodwin, whom she mistakes for an intruder. Ella, Denver, and the other women intercept Sethe before she can harm Mr. Bodwin. Having brought the community together, the spirit Beloved vanishes. As Mae G. Henderson explains, "In a scene of collective re-enactment, the women of the community intervene at a critical juncture, to save not Beloved, but Sethe. Thus, by revising her [spontaneous] actions, Sethe is able to preserve the community, and the community, in turn, is able to protect one of its own" ("Beloved" 81). It is a liberatory moment. Sethe does more, it seems to me, than preserve the community; she redeems it, to paraphrase Morrison, with their holding hands holding hers.

In Beloved, published in 1987, Morrison seems to be writing against forgetfulness when we consider the retreats and reversals in civil rights legislation alive in the 1980s. If the 1970s may be characterized as unsympathetic, then the 1980s may be characterized as retrograde. Affirmative action goals, or quotas, remained a major issue during the two terms of President Ronald W. Reagan (1981–1989). Like Nixon, Reagan played to the fears of White America in terms of busing, public housing, welfare programs, and civil rights. Reagan set the tone of his administration when he opened his campaign in Philadelphia, Mississippi, the home of the murderers of civil rights activists Michael Schwerner, James Chaney, and Andrew Goodman, with the words, "I believe in states' rights" (O'Reilly 350). Using the rhetoric of a color-blind society, Reagan advanced his assault on affirmative action polices. Opposing reverse discriminatory practices as they affected White males seemed the primary objective of the Reagan years. Kevern Verney writes, "William Bradford Reynolds, Assistant Attorney General for Civil Rights in the Justice Department, became a leading adviser in the Reagan administration. Reynolds tried to remove or weaken affirmative action programmes, championing 'individual opportunity over group entitlements'" (95).

A friend of corporate America, Reagan attacked not only civil rights legislation but also social programs for the economically disadvantaged. "So with black unemployment at [fourteen] percent on the day he took office and the black poverty rate at [thirty-six] percent some eighteen months into the first term," Kenneth O'Reilly relates, Reagan "called the inner-city homeless . . . 'homeless, you might say, by choice'" (358). Welfare under Reagan's helm was further racialized, giving cultural currency to the term "welfare queen." Reagan also opposed the extension of the Voting Rights Act of 1965 and, like Nixon and Ford, "sought without success to substitute a weaker measure for the protection of black voting rights" (Sirgo 89). Reagan's Supreme Court nominations were equally indicative of his ideologies. Sandra Day O'Connor (appointed in 1981), William Rehnquist (elevated to chief justice in 1986), Antonin Scalia (appointed in 1986), and Anthony Kennedy (appointed in 1988) were all politically conservative, particularly Rehnquist and Scalia. All and all, during the Reagan years, America was not, for its Black citizens, a "shining city on a hill." It was against this political backdrop of the 1980s, fraught with reversals in policies and attitudes, that *Beloved* appeared. I offer that Morrison writes against the possibility of contemporary disenfranchisement by reminding her readers of the "peculiar institution" that underpins so much of American politics, society, and culture and also by cautioning her readers of how institutionalized bondage occurs and operates.

Morrison's liberatory narrative reveals to an unprecedented degree the inner life of the newly free Black woman as she tests the limits of her personal freedom in freedom. Jacobs's path-breaking *Incidents* is critically applauded, I believe, not only for its literary genius, but for its successful depiction of the enslaved Black woman's resilience and resistance in slavery. However, because of its nineteenth-century audience's sensibilities, *Incidents* does not—could not—reveal the offending truths that the contemporary liberatory narratives, particularly *Beloved*, reveal. *Beloved* does more, though, than simply illuminate the past. The past should be a spirit, not a ghost. It should have a role in the present, as Beloved does, because it *is* a part of the present. Through her characters, Morrison forces her readers to face the difficult and emotional journeys involved in remembering slavery and to rethink what they know about their own existence in the context of a history of bondage, because the past must not be "disremembered and unaccounted for" (*Beloved* 274). Neither should it overtake the present. If we are to heal from slavery's wounds and if we are to learn history's lessons, the past, as *Bulworth*'s griot admonishes, has "to be a spirit. [I]t can't be no ghost."

Chapter 5

J. California Cooper's *Family*

Of (Absent?) Mothers, (Motherless?) Daughters, and (Interracial?) Relations

HISTORY. LIVED, NOT WRITTEN, is such a thing not to understand always, but to marvel over.

—*Family*

What tangled skeins are the genealogies of slavery!

—HARRIET A. JACOBS

Narrative has never been merely entertainment for me. It is, I believe, one of the principal ways in which we absorb knowledge.

—TONI MORRISON

IN THE CLOSING years of the twentieth century, two non-fiction books captured the public's literary imagination—Edward Ball's *Slaves in the Family* (1998) and Henry Wiencek's *The Hairstons: An American Family in Black and White* (1999). Meticulously researched, both books examine a seldom acknowledged aspect of American society and social history: the complex genealogical relations created through miscegenation during slavery. From their late twentieth-century perspective, Ball and Wiencek, both White, foreground the humanity of the enslaved and their enslavers while humanizing, as personal histories can do, the institution of slavery. Both books received a great deal of critical attention: Ball's won the National Book Award and Wiencek's garnered the National Book Critics Circle Award. In his book, Wiencek asks readers to re-examine what they know about interpersonal and interracial relationships during and after slavery through the story of a distinctly American family—the Hairstons—a biracial family created in slavery and divided by race. Writing about members of the Hairston family on both sides of the color line, Wiencek reveals "the legacy of slavery, and how that legacy has been passed into our own time" (xix). Ball does likewise but in a more subjective way: he researched his own family's involvement in trading enslaved Africans as well as in enslaving African Americans. The Ball family of South Carolina owned more than four thousand African Americans between 1698 and 1865. Of his odyssey into his personal history, Ball observes, "To contemplate slavery—which for most Americans is a mysterious, distant event—was a bit like doing psychoanalysis on myself" (13). It is noteworthy that Ball uses the word *psychoanalysis* to describe the process he undertook in writing his personal history, considering that the treatment of psychoanalysis is undergone, presumably, for liberatory purposes. J. California Cooper in her first novel, *Family* (1991), affords her readers the same promise of deliverance from the neurosis of racial prejudice as they consider "[w]hat tangled skeins are the genealogies of slavery" (Jacobs 78). Cooper's fictional *Family*, like the historical narratives of Ball and Wiencek, deepens our understanding of the complex American family created during slavery and, in so doing, provides for readers the opportunity to experience a release from the lingering psychological residuals of slavery that continue to affect all members of the American family with links to the crucible of slavery.[1]

Family, as a theme, is of central importance to the master narrative of American social history. Indeed, family remains one of the key institutions of American society. Created by the enslavers' lust and greed, miscegenation, according to Cooper, created a vast human family of epic proportions and epic struggles. Her narrator philosophically poses: "[I]f from one woman all these different colors and nationalities could come into being, what must the whole world be full of?!" (230). Cooper's *lieu de mémoire*, then, is a narrative by one enslaved woman's spirit but centers on the whole complex of human relations endemic to the institution of chattel slavery where indeterminacies abound, as gestured toward in this chapter's title. As depicted by Cooper, mothers are not really absent, daughters are not really motherless, and relations are more than interracial. In her depiction, Cooper does not simply create a new female myth, as Elizabeth Beaulieu observes in one of the few critical essays devoted to *Family*; rather, she presents the repressed "historiography" of enslaved Black women.[2] If enslaved families were primarily matriarchal, as traditional American historiography concludes, Cooper identifies the cause as White patriarchy's sexual abuse and exploitation of enslaved Black women that perverted the institution of family for enslaved men and women, denying them opportunity for unmolested interpersonal relations. To accomplish this sort of exploration, Cooper shifts attention away from the sort of information available in our recorded history, the disempowering master narrative we already have, to a history lived and experienced but ignored, the empowering public (not synonymous with dominant) narrative we need.

Like the nineteenth-century female emancipatory narrative, *Family* is written in the first person from the perspective of the enslaved. Unlike the antecedent narrative, however, it is written exclusively in vernacular English, and the narrator is not the protagonist. Always, the principal protagonist, is the daughter of Clora, the narrator. While Clora dies early in her own narrative, she continues as a disembodied narrator and loving mother. In this way, Cooper counters the reductive assumption about enslaved mothers that slavery created: that enslaved Black mothers are "not mothers; they are 'natally dead,' with no obligation to their offspring" (*Playing in the Dark* 21). Clora's obligation to her daughter transcends death. Even in death, she continues her loving concern for her children. Certainly in this way, Cooper defines freedom in opposition to physical bondage, but she also defines it in opposition to the past and its discourses. The sense of historical continuity present throughout her narrative indicates that society cannot escape its history, but must instead face that history. An emotionally charged narrative, *Family* reminds us that all members of the American family have not always been treated as "family" and certainly have not always been rendered or read through the lens of racial and gender equality. Cooper's narrative establishes that equality as a matter of fact.

History is narrative. History can only be recorded and transmitted through a type of narration: oral, written, or visual. For example, singing the National Anthem may be considered oral history, reading the Constitution of the United States a type of written history, or viewing the Washington Monument a kind of visual history. I maintain that the liberatory narrative seeks to disrupt the malignancies of the master narrative and its singular perspective. History, as the liberatory narratives remind us, is composed of multiple story lines. Although each of the liberatory narratives examined herein is different in its structure, substance, and strategy, all of them engage the same historical moment through the use of multiple intertexts and interpretations.

History is a matter of memory: *who* is allowed to remember determines *what* is remembered. What is remembered as well as what is not remembered informs and influences both the present and the future. Such has been the case with chattel slavery in North America. Generally, the narratives of those who have been or are disenfranchised are silenced or erased. Moreover, in the United States, highly selective memory has been the usual practice as it relates to the historical moment of slavery. In recent years, individuals from a number of disciplines have recognized the therapeutic value of correcting the public narrative of history for those who have been marginalized, misrepresented, or disempowered. We now know traumatic events, personal or collective, can be made more psychologically manageable through the telling. Historian Gerda Lerner explains that an "aspect of history-making, namely, its function in the healing of pathology is recognized and ritualized by most systems of psychology" (199). Not only can one remake history by recounting one's personal history, one can also begin to heal from the trauma of one's history by inserting it into the public narrative as evidence, as remembrance, or as correction.[3] This is important, Lerner explains, because history satisfies these basic human needs: (1) history is memory and a source of personal identity; (2) history is collective immortality; (3) history is cultural tradition; and (4) history is explanation (116). If these needs are not met, one is without a discourse of memory, identity, and culture. The liberatory narrative functions as a discourse of memory because the legacies of slavery continue to inform American culture, as well as racial and national identities, both individually and collectively.

In her 1993 Nobel Prize lecture, laureate Toni Morrison explored the intersection between personal history and collective history, calling attention to the interlocking nature and instructional value of history, narrative, and knowledge. Before recounting her meditation on language, Morrison asserted that narrative "is one of the principal ways in which we absorb knowledge" (*Nobel Lecture* 7). In telling her story of a blind, elderly, Black woman, Morrison uses the well-known phrase "once upon a time" to begin her meta-narrative on the power of language, engaging her audience's literary imaginations with this most familiar phrase. Cooper seems to agree with Morrison's strategy: she, too, relies upon "once upon a time" and uses the phrase to begin her own narrative of personal and collective history, where "[h]istory don't repeat itself, people repeat themselves" (229). In this way, she too engages the reader's literary imagination, and in asking the reader to contemplate the fabric of history and knowledge, she also asks the reader to consider who or what is privileged in the construction of historical knowledge.

Cooper's narrative challenges, as is characteristic of the liberatory narrative, how history has been written and received in American society by focusing on the fundamentally personal—the family. Cooper prefaces her liberatory narrative with a creational myth in which the dramatic action is transacted between mother and child—the Earth Mother and the Earth Child. This cosmogonic perspective places women-centered issues in prominent view. The Earth Mother's question—"When does a tree bear fruit that is not its own?"—calls to mind the symbolic image of the family tree and posits the connection between the earth and all of its inhabitants, the family of humankind. The Earth Mother's query alerts the reader that Cooper's version of creation is not the usual narrative—that there may be times when the tree bears fruit it does not *claim* as its own, as was the case during slavery. Reminding the reader of the multiplicity of events and perspectives, Cooper observes that "[t]ime is so forever that . . . you can say 'Once upon a time' thousands of times in one life" (1). Rendering her narrative as a near-omniscient oral history, Cooper liberates her work from the conventions and constraints of written, empirical history in order to portray more affectively and, I argue, more effectively the culture and legacy of slavery.

Setting her narrative in the unspecified South, Cooper establishes early in *Family* her interest in narrative and history, but she challenges conventional assumptions regarding their relation to time and space. In her world view, the history of humankind is tantamount to a narrative of miscegenation. In the beginning, according to Clora, the narrator of special spiritual powers, an Afro-Greek man and an Afro-Italian man met along the Nile River. They traveled together to the Afro-Italian man's home in Africa where the Afro-Greek man fell in love with and married the Afro-Italian man's sister. The couple "moved farther down into Africa to live. They had children. After many years, their children had children. And so on and so on. Came the time when the slave catchers came. . . . These children had children by their owners and others. Portuguese, Spanish, English, Italian, French, Irish, Scottish, others. Men from lands all over the world" (2). The world's races and lineages, according to Cooper, are intertwined to the point where they are really no longer distinguishable from one another, though they may be labeled "Portuguese, Spanish, English, Italian, French, Irish, Scottish," according to where they eventually lived. Cooper eliminates the binary of races as opposing or contrasting groups by interweaving the races, much as miscegenation did, to the point where they are virtually indiscernible to the human eye. Cooper offers, then, an alternative model of the origins of humankind and universalizes the experiences of individuals of mixed parentage by tying them genetically to the heritage of all the world's races.

Like Morrison in *Beloved*, Cooper relies upon the device of incorporeality to design her liberatory narrative. Unlike Morrison's spirit, who dissolves the boundaries of past and present by becoming flesh and who provokes those who have repressed the memories of enslavement to confront those rememories, Cooper's spirit remains bodiless as she narrates across time and space, dissolving those boundaries to show, as Butler's time travel does, the fluidity of such boundaries. Clora, the narrator of *Family*, dies early in the narrative, becoming the disembodied and omniscient narrative voice—the narrative spirit, if you will—who bears witness to racism's wide sweep well into the twentieth century. In her incorporeal state, Clora is not bound by time or space; thus, she is free to observe generations of her family, splintered and scattered by the institution of slavery. Clora is able to work through the trauma of her life by telling her story. Because of her unique, omniscient perspective, Clora recounts events that both preceded and succeeded her earthly existence. Through her unusual narrative voice, Cooper challenges both time and space by stripping her narrative of the familiar in order to highlight the *familial*. Clora establishes a relationship to her free-born reader when she asserts her own free humanity clearly and early in the narrative. She will not accept the definitions of herself attempted by others: "Some people say we was born slaves . . . but I don't blive that. I say I was born a free human being, but I was made a slave right after" (3). With such rhetorical designs, Cooper draws in her readership and engages her readers' imaginations in her liberatory project.

Employing these innovations, Cooper offers a liberation from the boundaries of race, time, and space, boundaries that are perpetuated by our own investment in those boundaries. More specifically, Clora is able in death to do what she could not do in life: keep her children, particularly her daughter Always, the narrative's protagonist, under her watchful eye. As Clora's ability to mother and to nurture her children is usurped by slavery, death does not alter their relationship. After dying, Clora reveals, "I didn't go nowhere. . . . I was watching cause I wasn't in with my body. I was at a distance, yet I was close" (35–36). Her view is so encompassing that she sees well into the twentieth century with its "wars and famine, depressions and recessions, union fights, labor horrors, poverty worse, look like, then some slavery. For all colors this time" (229). Describing her new state of being Clora explains, "This dead-but-not-gone thing was *not like being a ghost*. . . . I seem to know all kinds of different knowledge floatin round in space. I couldn't touch nothin, but could think . . . and I could move" (37; emphasis added). Clora is not, as she says, a ghost; she is a spirit, like Morrison's Beloved, who bears witness to a personal and communal history, allowing others to listen and to learn.

While all of the feminist thematics are present in *Family*, Cooper's primary focus, it seems, is on enslaved Black mothers and their daughters. As Harriet Jacobs reveals in her narrative, motherhood is paradoxically both a confining and liberating site for enslaved Black women. Even though the enslaved mother, Jacobs writes, "knows there is no security for her children" (56), she remains "resolved that out of the darkness of [slavery] a brighter dawn should rise for them" (85). This is true as well in *Family*, even for mothers who choose death as a means to freedom. As Laura Doyle theorizes,

> In the race-bounded economy the mother is a maker and marker of
> boundaries, a generator of liminality. . . . She is forced across a border,
> or she is prohibited from crossing a border; in either case her function
> is to reproduce, through offspring, the life of that border. (27)

The border that Cooper's narrator-mother is forced across is an unusual one for even raced mothers. Cooper's use of the disembodied mother figure is a fascinating strategy, signaling that motherhood is not a fixed and static identity. Cooper's mother figure continues to mother, although from a different sphere of existence. In this vein, one may wonder how the construct of motherhood could ever be considered fixed and static if enslaved Black mothers and free White mothers had such different experiences? In Cooper's narrative, enslaved Black mothers sometimes choose strategies of resistance and empowerment, such as murder and suicide, that are unconventional, questionable, and in some cases, counter-productive, but they do so to exert their agency within an institution that seeks to eradicate the Black woman's power and sense of self.

As in each of the liberatory narratives examined so far, the conflicts of exploited female sexuality and motherhood dominate the lives of enslaved Black women in *Family*. Black female sexuality, in the hands of White enslavers, is a site of violence, exploitation, and commodification. In *Family*, as in *Incidents*, *Kindred*, and *Beloved*, Black women are sexually assaulted frequently and habitually by White men. Fammy, Clora's mother, is the concubine of the master, or as Cooper calls him, the "Master of the Land." Fammy is the mother of nine children, all sold from her, by the Master. Clora is her only child of choice, like *Beloved*'s Sethe, born as a result of her relationship with a neighboring Black man; thus, Fammy is able to keep Clora—unlike the other children who were "all sold when they got to be bout three years old by the Mistress of the Land cause they was too white and lookin like the Master of the Land. That, and the money" (4). In this regard, Cooper asks us to consider how White personal and economic desires find expression on the Black body. Fammy lives an exhausting and dehumanizing life: "All day she belonged to the Mistress for the work in the big house, and in the nights he chose, she blonged to the Master" (6). The final insult for Fammy occurs when she is assigned to have sexual relations with the master's son. Realizing the generational implications—that she cannot protect her daughter from a future of similar concubinage, among other assaults—Fammy chooses to resist outwardly and violently.

In *Family*, as in *Incidents* and *Kindred*, sexual assault becomes the impetus to freeing one's self. Fammy determines to repossess herself from her oppressors. That she kills the master and herself after obeying his order to have sexual relations with his son suggests that this final act of degradation convinces her finally that her life as chattel was unbearable, unlivable. Returning from the son, Fammy stabs the master with a pitchfork when he, continuing his surveillance of her, inquires about the encounter. Not killing him instantly, she finds a knife and finishes the job. Knowing that killing a White man yields certain death, Fammy then kills herself in an act of supreme volition, even though she realizes that the consequences of her actions will be visited on her daughter. Unlike Butler's Alice or Williams's Dessa, Fammy chooses *against* staying alive for her child's sake. Leaving her daughter Clora alone and vulnerable, Fammy knows that she could not protect her even if she were to remain alive. One might argue that killing the master might conceivably help Clora in some future context because *he* would not have control of her life and destiny. However, capitalism, the infrastructure of slavery, validated the conveyance of property from generation to generation through inheritance, and therefore, his son would become her owner. Most importantly, though, Fammy bequeaths to her daughter a powerful legacy of self-emancipation and self-possession, one we are told she learned from *her* mother: "Grandmother had killed herself rather than stay in slavery and keep on bringing more babies into the world to be made more slaves or whatever anybody wanted them to be" (5).

Ironically, Clora, like her mother before her, reaches a point where she too can no longer endure her life as chattel. After bearing four children by her new owner, the deceased master's son, Clora devises her own strategy of liberation when she realizes that as chattel she can no longer protect her children. One day, as Clora worked in the "big house," the mistress struck Clora with her hand and attacked her with the fireplace poker after noticing the resemblance between Clora's baby and her husband. Cooper writes, "Mistress leaped at me and commenced to slappin me with her hands first, then a poker that was kept by the fireplace" (31). After the mistress turns her wrath on the baby, Clora, protecting her baby, took the poker from the mistress because, as Jacobs wrote, the enslaved mother "may be an ignorant creature, degraded by the system that had brutalized her from childhood, but she has mother's instincts and is capable of feeling a mother's agonies" (16). It is at this point, realizing that her impudence will cost her, that Clora decides to kill herself and her children: "They would have no mother, worthless even as she was to them, they needed me for whatever I *could* do for em" (34; emphasis added). She does not want her children to witness her severe punishment, and she does not want to leave them unprotected after her own death. Before killing herself, Clora looks at nature and sees herself in relation to the universe. Cooper, establishing here a dialectic between the natural world and the world the enslavers made, writes:

> [Clora] looked out over them beautiful fields, up into that beautiful
> sky so full of soft white clouds and the sun so warm and good to shine
> down on the earth. I saw them tall beautiful trees, weavin and wavin
> in the winds that come from all crost the earth. I saw birds. Birds what
> was free to fly off or stay, whatever they wanted . . . free. Better off
> than me and my slave sisters and brothers. (33)

Continuing, Clora observes that a multitude of animals—birds, snakes, bugs, and even mosquitoes—are free, but she is not.[4] Her observation highlights that the enslavement of humans is indeed *unnatural*. Thus, she poisons herself *and* her children. Inexplicably, the children survive, and Clora dies, leaving her four children motherless. The irony of life expressed here is that an enslaved mother cannot protect her children from their destiny, try as she might.

Cooper portrays sexual relations between enslaving White men and enslaved Black women, such as those that drove three generations—Fammy, her mother, and indirectly Clora—to suicide, as non-consensual, as coerced. Clora is forced to be the sexual partner of the "Young Master of the Land" when she is twelve years old. Of her violation, Clora confides, "I hated [the Young Master of the Land]. I never felt love with or bout him. And the men I coulda loved freely, knew I was hisn so they stayed away from me. . . . I just hated him. Not only for ownin my body, but for blockin my mind, lettin my heart dry and shrivel up cause it didn't have nothin to do but hate him" (21–22). Not only did this assault have a detrimental effect upon the psyche of the enslaved woman, her children also suffered. Clora recalls that when the master came to her for sexual intercourse, Always, her daughter, "would lay under that bed and not make a sound. Sometimes, when he left, she would be sleep with her thumb in her mouth like I used to be" (26). One imagines a child trying to comfort herself as she witnesses unspeakable brutality.

Generational sexual abuse and its consequences, then, are portrayed in *Family*. Always, Clora's daughter, is, like her mother and grandmother, the victim of sexual assault. After she is purchased away from her home and her siblings, Doak Butler, her new owner, rapes Always before they arrive at his plantation. The narrator describes what his power over her means to him: "She was beautiful . . . and she was his, his slave, his body to do with as he liked, at any time, or any place, and none to say nay" (85). Because Always becomes pregnant as a result of the en route assault and because Doak's new wife, Sue, gets pregnant soon after her arrival, Always and Sue deliver their babies, both by Doak, on the same day. Cooper presents an alternative text of White womanhood in the character of Sue, who, perhaps due to her own humble origins, is not the stereotypical mistress.[5] Sue, like Williams's Ruth, allows herself to question the texts she has received from her society concerning Black womanhood as she has great difficulty reconciling her perceptions of Always, a woman she considers a friend, with those reductive texts. Of Sue's dilemma and her sympathy, the narrator comments that, even so Sue did not offer freedom to Always or her baby; she "just felt a little pity. That's all" (109). Querying Always about the paternity of her baby, Sue believes Always when she answers that she does not know where the father is. Always, in fact, really does not know where Doak is at that very moment. Thus, Always misleads Sue into believing that Doak is not the father. While this subterfuge could be born of embarrassment or of respect for Sue, it more than likely is an act of self-preservation as Always might suffer if Sue voiced her displeasure or disdain to Doak.

Cooper characterizes the relationship between White mistresses and enslaved Black women, then, as immensely complex because of the sexual politics that validated White male licentiousness. If enslaving husbands were sexually active with enslaved Black women, their wives were likely to abuse not only the enslaved women but also their husbands' children by the enslaved women. Unable to assign blame to the rightful party in these cases because of their own lack of power, White mistresses exerted what power they had over the victims directly. This attitude was so pervasive that it extended to the mothers of enslavers as well: when a young Clora becomes pregnant by her owner, his mother calls her a "twelve-year-old slut" (16). White women, according to Clora, would accuse Black women of being sex fiends and of seducing their husbands, "[j]ust like [the black women] wasn't slaves or that they had made them babies all by their own selves . . . or forced them white men!" (6). Wisely, Clora recognizes the gendered-subject position she shares with the mistress, noting that "the Master of the Land was Master of us both, and all of us, in this thing and she was captured in a net just like I, as a slave, in this net of time" (32). These family relations and interactions are indeed complex. In the plantation South, according to Catherine Clinton,

> the refinement of patriarchy resulted in a system of "penarchy"—a
> system whereby the males of the elite use sexual terrorism to control
> women of all classes and races. . . . Women of their own class are
> judged by the dominate males by one system of standards and those of
> the subordinate group of another. Within the slave-owning South,
> white women were placed on the pedestal while black women were
> put on the auction block. (208)

The point remains—objectified they both were.

As Williams does in *Dessa Rose*, Cooper illuminates a little-discussed aspect of the nineteenth century traditionally hidden in discourses of slavery—the sexual relations between White women and Black men. Loretta, Always's half-sister and Doak's second wife, has a sexual relationship with Sephus, Always's son and Loretta's own nephew. When Sephus miraculously returns to the Butler plantation years after he is sold, Loretta seduces him because he reminds her of Sun (her half-brother), to whom she was also strongly attracted. Of these "tangled skeins" the narrator points out, "if we all done come from Adam and Eve, we done always been relatives anyway" (162). With Doak now dead, Loretta's unwed pregnancy is inappropriate, in terms of nineteenth-century morality. That she is pregnant by a Black man makes her fall more egregious.[6] Doubly fallen from her pedestal of true womanhood, Loretta tries to hide her pregnancy, but cannot hide it from Always. Thus, Loretta gives birth to Always's first grandchild and her own niece. Not wanting anyone to know of her transgressions, both moral and racial, Loretta asks Always to raise her daughter. Always agrees, but not without reminding Loretta of Always's own past of scattered siblings and children, a past in which Loretta's family played a part: "you be so lucky, so blessed . . . able . . . to keep your baby. I wish I coulda kept mine. I wish I coulda kept my mama too" (167). Always symbolically names the baby Apple because she is born of the forbidden fruit, just as Butler's Alice symbolically names her babies.

Motherhood for the enslaved Black women, in addition to being a site of exploitation and commodification, is characterized as a generational dilemma. Fammy's status as mother contributes to her decision to kill her rapist-master, after bearing nine children by him who are sold. Clora bears six children by her master: Always and her sister are sold, two die in infancy, one emancipates himself, and the youngest dies accidentally at the age of five. Clora's daughter, Always, bears five children by her master; all except one are sold. Cooper gives us not only enslaved mothers' stories, she also provides enslaved daughters' stories. For example, Clora remembers that she and her mother

> wasn't together too much cept in the nights and some most of them
> the Master of the Land came in and pushed me over and out the bed.
> I'd lay there on the floor with my eyes closed, sucking my thumbs til
> he was gone. Then she be mine again. I would rock her to sleep and
> myself too. I cried cause she cried. We was both tired of the life we
> was livin. I wasn't nothin but a baby-child but I was still tired of
> things I didn't even know what name to call em. (4)

Seldom considered are the effects that the sexual abuse endured by their mothers had on the children of enslaved women, as we see in Cooper's narrative.

Motherhood, for the enslaved Black woman, elicits a range of emotions. Like Linda Brent at her daughter's birth, Clora mourns her daughter's birth as she imagines her dismal future:

> I would look at her through *tears and love* cause I knew SOMEBODY
> had already decided what her life was to be. How far she could go in
> life . . . in anything . . . for as long as she drew breath on this earth.
> THEY had done decided she would never go to school, never learn to
> read and count, never be married in the right way in front of the Lord
> and man, never be in love cause she don't know how long fore they be
> sellin her man-love . . . *just never nothin she wanted.* (17–18; emphasis
> added)

Ironically, the same feeling of helplessness exists after Clora kills herself: "This bein here and not bein here all at the same time was a hard thing to be. I couldn't help nobody or nothin! It is surely hard thing to be. And not know why . . . or even how. I only knew I couldn't help my babies. None" (80). Another example of her helplessness as a mother occurs when two of her babies died while Clora, leaving them unsupervised, worked. One died from sunburn, the other from a poisonous bite. Clora remembers, "I cried, oh how I cried. You don't want them to grow to be slaves, but you do want your children to grow up" (25). This lament is the essence of the enslaved mother's feelings concerning motherhood. Prior to her desperate act, Clora thought of escaping, but she "would look out crost the world far as [she] could see and [she] didn't know nothin bout what was out there or whichever way freedom might be" (27). More importantly, though, she reveals, "I couldn't run off anyway. My children was too small and I couldn't leave em" (28). In death, Clora is transfigured to the vantage point of a seer, although she is still powerless to help her children.

With the separation of families so prevalent, it is not surprising that other mothers existed in the enslaved community to provide motherly care and affection to the children in need. For example, when Fammy kills the master and herself, Miz Elliz takes the young Clora into her "shack," although she fears for her own safety (for helping Clora) and for Clora's (because of her mother's violence). With no remaining family, Clora, then, is raised by Miz Elliz. After Clora's suicide, Miz Elliz also takes care of Clora's four children, just as she took care of Clora after her mother's death. Knowing that they missed having her and perhaps to assuage her sorrow for leaving them, Clora compliments Miz Elliz's mothering: she "did teach them manners tho and tried to tell them ways to stay 'way from white folks trouble" (41). Standards of familial flexibility and necessity are personified in the character of Miz Elliz.

In a scene reminiscent of a scene in *Dessa Rose*, Cooper explores the issue of motherhood and naming. "Mammy," the word used by Whites to describe Black mothers, is seen as pejorative because the mammy figure is erroneously thought of as a Black woman whose sole joy is to love and to nurture her oppressors.[7] When Loretta refers to Sun's mother, Clora, as mammy, Sun corrects her: "My mama wasn't no mammy. She was my mother" (44). Loretta's reply—that she thought Black mothers were called "mammy"—reminds the reader of Morrison's observation that "definitions belong to the definers" (*Beloved* 190) and of Williams's insistence on reading Black mothers in their proper context without the glare of semantic shackles. Sun corrects her saying, "No, mam, that what white folks call em. We call our mother, mama" (45). In this exchange, Cooper critiques the way in which texts of slavery as well as Black women as texts have been misread by others.

In spite of all the institutionalized deterrents, exercising one's agency in sexual matters remains fundamental to the enslaved woman's sense of self. Like Jacobs's Linda Brent, Williams's Dessa Rose, and Sethe's mother in *Beloved*, Fammy, Clora's mother, chooses to have a baby by a man of her choice. As Linda Brent knew, "There is something akin to freedom in having a lover who has no control over you, except that which he gains by kindness and attachment" (55). In this same spirit, Fammy chose a Black man as her lover "so she could have a brown baby" (4). As relations between Black men and women were subject to surveillance, Fammy "wouldn't tell who [Clora's] daddy was so they wouldn't hurt him or sell him cause they hadn't been let to do no lovin together. She said they was in love but that wasn't lowed. They didn't get to be in love no-more tho cause she was watched hard" (4). Clora also reveals that Fammy's mother, Clora's grandmother, killed herself rather than be enslaved and continue to have children who were enslaved. Such choices, however, are not without complications or consequences.

In addition to echoing Jacobs's narrative, Cooper brings to mind a nineteenth-century Anglo-American discourse of slavery, Mark Twain's *Pudd'nhead Wilson* (1892), in her construction of Always as mother.[8] Always's plan to switch the two babies fathered by Doak, born on the same day to his wife and to Always, revisits the plan Twain's Roxy enacts by switching her son with the master's son. In this way, Cooper problematizes, as Twain did in his novella, the construction of American identity. But in the context of her narrative about family, Cooper's switching of the babies offers keen indictment, from a contemporary perspective, on the ways in which families were constituted during slavery, on the sexual assaults sanctioned by slavocracy, and on the enslaved mother's sacrifices for her children. Always gives her birth child a chance to live freely. The two boys grow up thinking they are what they are not: the boys are good friends as children but as they grow older, Doak Jr., who was born Black, feels and acts superior to Soon, who was born White. Cooper thus shows how one's environment shapes one's attitude and one's outcome. Years later, Always reaps the benefit of the switch. She forces Doak Jr., by confessing the secret of his birth, to buy some property for her with the money she has saved through the years. Always offers not to tell "nobody you is my own son. I will move crost the road a way, you don't have to see me no mo. You just do the legal papers for me. That's all I's askin" (199). She needs him to handle the legalities because she cannot as a Black woman. He does so, not out of affection but out of fear that he will be exposed. Thus, Always subverts not only the racial constructs of the society, but the economic and legal constructs as well.

If exercising one's agency is an expression of one's individuality, then eradicating one's individuality with a group identity and a myriad of stereotypes should eliminate one's agency. As the liberatory narratives show, this was not the case for all enslaved Black women. Clora explains what it meant to be enslaved, materially as well as psychologically:

> Diggin in ground hard and full of weeds, snakes, and scorpions. To pull and drag things that strip the hands of flesh, make them to bleed. To never look up and say "Tomorrow . . . I can rest. This even, I can rest." To bury hands to the shoulders in hot water boiling over a fire, filled with lye soap, to wash another person's dirt, for no pay and no thanks. To cook and serve, sick or well, serve people that don't care how you feel, never think of what is in your mind, in your heart. (55)

Cooper imbricates the reader into the weave of her narrative with the rhetoric of direct address, calling the reader "you," in order to reveal the pain-filled life of the enslaved:

> But it is so hard to explain to anybody how each minute, each hour, each day had to be lived. Yes, you was fed, and clothed of a sort, you had a place to sleep. But count your own life and see, even with these important things taken care of, how much more there is to life. Would you exchange freedom for these small things given to you? No . . . not given . . . well paid for. (52)

Just as the sexual exploitation of enslaved women affects not only the enslaved woman but also her children, the denial of selfhood has generational implications. Clora remembers that her mother "[d]idn't have her own self no time. A somebody with a mind will surely go crazy like that cause no matter what you think, it don't count for nothin. She didn't have nothin of her own but me, and I blonged to them too" (6). Perhaps because of her mother's example, Clora accepts her humanity; she thinks for herself, and she does not accept the definition of others.

Cooper rightly suggests that seeing one's self and knowing one's self are indeed relational. Most of the enslaved community had little idea of what they themselves looked like, unless they had access to the "big house" where they might see their reflections. Without her mother, orphaned Always is subjected to greater abuse by both the mistress and her mother-in-law as she works in the "big house." Ironically, these women in a different context would be known by their familial relations to Always as her stepmother and her grandmother. Always saw, because of her access to mirrors in the "big house," that she was as White-looking as the White people around her. She wonders why, then, her life was filled with trauma, abuse, and loss at the hands of people who looked like her. With this realization, "Always got mad and stayed mad from then on" (41). If blackness is so immutably definable, then "looking" White proves in a plantation society that the notion of family has been travestied in some way.

After she is sold to Doak Butler, Always works diligently to establish her own home and community at this site of oppression. Cooper foreshadows that this task will be a difficult one, for the Butler plantation is arid, dismal, and desolate, where even "[t]he trees looked mean and broodin" (89). Taken from her home and the siblings she raised, Always vows to destroy the Butlers and their land. Her community, like Sethe's at Sweet Home, is a small one: there is only one Black woman, Poon. Eventually, Doak's handicapped brother,

Jason, also becomes a part of her community. Poon's nineteen children, all sold away, had been the means of purchasing most of the land. Native Americans are also a part of Always's community, and she learns a great deal about the land and agriculture from them.

Denied access to other motivations, hate motivates Always to plan for her future. She, like Harriet Jacobs before her, wants both freedom and a home of her own. Ever industrious, she renovates an old chicken house and starts cultivating the land, seeing its potential richness. Realizing that they "can't slave [her] wishin none," Always sets into motion her own plan of economic enfranchisement—a garden from which she will sell produce (111). Not able to enact all of her plans without help, Always enlists Poon's help in community building. Reminding her that if something happened to Poon's charge, Master Jason, she would be back in the field. Always advises Poon to protect herself by improving her own economic standing. Resistant to the changes Always advocates, Poon does not understand the source of Always's desire because Poon has been so destroyed by her enslavement. Poon is afraid of change as she perceives her situation as better than before: "You ain't gonna get me killed. . . . Well leave me be. I'm doin alright. I got my own house now. I don't have to tend to Masr Doak's bed, just Masr Jason" (115–116).

During the Civil War, Always provides safe haven to the self-emancipating Blacks on their way North. With freedom pending, Always sees herself and positions herself as a self-authorized individual. She tells her mistress, "I don't have to do nothing but die, Miz Loretta" (169). When word of freedom finally reaches Always, "realization crept slowly, and silently into every piece of her body that had been a slave for all its life" (173). The feeling of freedom feels alien. It may be an inalienable right, but if it has been withheld, one has to learn to be free: "This freedom thing was movin out like water, through her mind and body" (174). Replying to Loretta's pronouncement, in which she attempts to reinscribe domination, that the Butlers will no longer provide for her in freedom, Always says, "You never did take care a me. All us slaves took care you'll. And we never did blong to you, you just kep us, by whippin and killins" (175). This assertion symbolizes the beginning of Always's move from object relations to subject relations.

The land represents many things to Always, but most of all, it represents her home. The land rejuvenates her; it is where she has labored and where she has built her community. In order to claim ownership to the land so that she can establish her home land, Always has to redefine the terms of ownership in this capitalist construct. Calling upon God for strength, Always explains,

"All my babies you done give me . . . been sold by this master to buy
this land. This land I hold here in my hand. If that don't make it
mine, Lord, what do? What make it his? Thems? Cause he own
me? . . . My tears done run down on it. My sweat done built it up.
Done fed us all. Don't that make it mine too, Lord? I hurt all over my
body cause of this land, Lord. My feelins is used up over this land,
Lord. This land is part of my body. My root is deep in this ground."
(201)

Always has two specific reasons for her claim to the Butler plantation: as the
site of her enslavement, she feels that she has contributed her labor, including her children, to its acquisition and development. Moreover, Always feels
connected to the land because she "lived here, slaved here, give birth here,
cried here, died a thousand times here, buried in loneliness here. Worked,
worked, worked here. Lost her children here. Here" (191–192). Always, like
Williams's Ruth, employs cooperative economics in building her community.
She retains the help of newly freed African Americans to help her build her
community in freedom. She in turn allows them to stay on her property for a
small payment. What she establishes is a fair system of sharecropping. In addition to her vegetable and fruit business, she rents carriages for transporta-
tion. She understands that the land provides economic freedom which makes
physical freedom possible.

Marriage becomes a trope that signals not only the enactment of freedom after emancipation but the attainment of middle-class standing for the
formerly enslaved in *Family*. Always makes wedding plans with Tim, a neighboring Black man with whom she falls in love. After building their home,
Always and Tim have a wedding, presided over by a minister and followed by
a honeymoon. They even agree not to have sexual relations until they are
married. Clora comments to the reader, "Magine! Two slaves in a real house.
THEIR house! Picked each other out to love. And DID IT! Never before in
either of each life had they ever been able to make such a *choice*" (207; emphasis added). In these ways, the formerly enslaved begin to participate in
middle-class ideologies, mores, and customs. These ideologies become a part
of how the formerly enslaved creates a new, post-slavery identity.

Romantic love, as Williams and Morrison also show, can be redemptive
for the formerly enslaved, scarred both physically and psychologically. Commenting on Tim's scarred back, Always suggests using her "special linment"
(207). Tim replies, "Yo special linment is love. You done already rubbed me
all over my heart and soul. My body be awright now" (207). Always confesses
that "'[m]os my scars is in my mind. Can't see em clear. . . . You done soothed

my scars with your love and kindness and goodness" (207). Their subsequent lovemaking is gentle, consensual, playful, and loving. Always learns, as Jacobs's Linda Brent also knew, that "there ain't nothin, NOTHIN, like you wantin somebody and them wantin you. . . . Just really nothin like makin love to somebody you love, when you BOTH want to and you together doin it" (211). And through her physical relationship with her husband, Always has, like her grandmother Fammy had wanted, a baby with a Black man. The birth of her son, Master More, is surrounded with a number of firsts for Always, even though he is not her first child. In addition to his birth in her own home, she is attended by a midwife for the first time. It is also the "first time she could look up at its daddy, hold his hand, and wait for their child of love to be born" (211). As many newly emancipated African Americans did, Always and Tim choose their last name symbolically: they select the name "More" because they hope to have more of the good that life has to offer.

But more of the good is not what Always gets. Because Clora's view is long, we witness the failures of Reconstruction. As was the case for many African Americans, Reconstruction did not secure Always's enfranchisement as an American citizen. Doak Jr. steals from Always most of the land that Always had earned, although she kept his secret, and the Ku Klux Klan kills Tim as he is defending their home. Doak Jr. even helps the Klan terrorize Always on the condition that they not kill her. Remembering but still resenting that she is his mother, he is insecure about how others will perceive him racially if he does not participate in the sanctioned mob violence. The other children of Clora who passed as White are the ones not subject to the same tumultuous turmoil that Always is. I do not believe that Cooper is advocating passing as a solution as this would be too simplistic; rather, I believe that Cooper is using passing as another indicator of the interracial relations created in slavery that give rise to her holistic construct of family.

The indeterminacy of race and family relations is indeed prominent in Cooper's narrative and purposefully so. Her narrative strategies are informed by this indeterminacy. Cooper weaves the reader, whomever she or he may be in the spectrum of color, into the narrative so as to include the reader in her construction of family. Of passing, a situation created by miscegenation but typically considered only in relation to African American existence, Clora wonders, "Maybe a whole lot of other whitelookin men and women are free that way too, and they don't know it. Who knows? Maybe they do know it" (226). Cooper, like Butler, examines interracial family relations during slavery. However, Cooper's narrator, unlike Butler's narrator, has a conversation with the reader in which she broadens the concept of family. Through her insistence on seeing race as the human race and on showing what happened when we have not done so, Cooper offers in her narrative a liberation from the boundaries of race, time, and space, boundaries that are perpetuated, she maintains, by our own investment in them. Cooper asks her readers to consider whether the circumstances and effects of chattel slavery are as immutable as they may have been presented. In the manner characteristic of liberatory narratives, Cooper challenges how history has been written and received in American society, but she accomplishes this in a new way: Cooper, like Ball and Wiencek, focuses on the personal feelings and interactions of the members of a far-reaching, extended American family.

Chapter 6

The Economies of Bondage and Freedom in Lorene Cary's *The Price of a Child*

*"But what I'm learning . . . is that being free costs dear.
Now, mind, it's not that I won't pay. I'm just trying to
find out what all it's gonna cost this time."*
—*The Price of a Child*

The price of liberty is eternal vigilance.
—FREDERICK DOUGLASS

*If I am a part of the American house, and I am, it is
because my ancestors paid*—striving to make it my
home—*so unimaginable a price.*
—JAMES BALDWIN

As a nation, our collective memory of slavery is often felt, but seldom vocalized. Perhaps no other issue in our shared history has been as pervasive, controversial, and divisive as the issue of slavery, yet when it comes to addressing this period in history, Americans have been (and still are) strangely reticent. Its legacies can be felt in all aspects of American life and yet, as a nation, we resist confronting those legacies. When asked to consider the legacy of slavery in the form of public policy, the nation and its leaders have consistently refused. Many have wondered and still wonder, Would a discussion of slavery and its impact on contemporary race relations move society forward? A few have attempted to bring this paradox to the public consciousness. As mentioned previously, Representative Tony Hall (D–Ohio) proposed in 1997 that Congress, on behalf of the nation, apologize to African Americans whose ancestors suffered under slavery. His proposal was not the first congressional resolution to address the issue of slavery in recent years. In every legislative session since 1989, Representative John Conyers Jr. (D–Michigan) has proposed legislation that addresses the issues of slavery, discrimination, and reparations.[1] The 1999 version of Conyers's *Commission to Study Reparation Proposals for African-Americans Act* asks Congress:

> To acknowledge the fundamental injustice, cruelty, brutality, and inhumanity of slavery in the United States and the 13 American colonies between 1619 and 1865 and to establish a commission to examine the institution of slavery, subsequent de jure and de facto racial and economic discrimination against African Americans, the impact of these forces on living African Americans, to make recommendations to the Congress on appropriate remedies, and for other purposes. (H.R. 40)

His resolution has never received substantial support, nor has it ever reached the House floor. Conyers's proposed bill simply asks for the establishment of a federal commission to examine what slavery has meant and means in American society, and this commission's final report would include recommendations to Congress. While some argue that such a study would unnecessarily reopen the wounds of the past, many others argue that the past's wounds were never closed. The primary questions for the commission and for Congress would be: Should the United States government issue a formal apology for sanctioning slavery, and Is a debt owed to the descendants of enslaved African Americans?

In recent years, apologies for wrongs abound.[2] In 1990, Congress apologized to uranium miners contaminated in the 1940s by nuclear testing in Nevada. In 1993, Congress apologized to native Hawaiians for the United States government's role in helping to overthrow the Hawaiian government in the nineteenth century. In 1997, British Prime Minister Tony Blair apologized for England's role in the Irish Potato Famine of 1845–1851. In 1995, Pope John Paul II offered an apology for the violence of the sixteenth-century Counter-Reformation and, in 1999, he apologized for all human rights violations sanctioned by the Catholic church, although in listing the violations, he failed to name slavery specifically. In 1997, President Bill Clinton apologized for the United States government's role in the Tuskegee syphilis study where Black men were infected with the disease, left untreated, and subsequently studied. And in 2000, the nation's largest health insurer, Aetna, apologized for issuing life insurance policies to enslavers insuring the lives of enslaved African Americans in the 1850s. Many domestic and foreign precedents for apologies, then, have been set for the United States government to apologize for sla-very, should it choose to do so. Often coupled with the apology issue is the more controversial issue of economic reparations and, I believe, this is one of the primary reasons an apology has not yet been offered. Indeed, the reticence to apologize is tied to the complex nature of reparations. Quite simply, if the United States government admits liability by apologizing, then the govern-ment would be liable legally and economically. If reparations were in order, determining what is fair, just, and appropriate would be the next hurdle.

The idea of reparations for African Americans is not a new idea. Many have heard the phrase "forty acres and a mule." This original reparations pack-age was created by General William T. Sherman on January 16, 1865. Thou-sands of newly liberated and displaced African Americans followed the Union Army through Georgia after the Civil War's end. With the War Department's approval, Sherman issued Special Field Order Number Fifteen, setting aside confiscated Confederate lands along the Georgia and South Carolina coasts for Black resettlement. Each family was to receive forty acres and the loan of an Army mule. Within six months, forty thousand freed African Americans settled on this land. In 1866, Congress created a law reserving three million acres in five Confederate states for newly freed African Americans, who would be asked to purchase their property once they were able. President Andrew Johnson, President Lincoln's successor, vetoed both of these actions. In 1865, Congress established the Bureau of Refugees, Freedmen, and Abandoned Lands (popularly called the Freedmen's Bureau) to oversee the transition of newly emancipated Blacks from slavery to freedom. The bureau controlled some 850,000 acres of abandoned and confiscated land in the South, and its com-missioner, General O. O. Howard, was committed to creating a class of Black landowners. But in the summer of 1865, President Johnson began allowing former Confederates to reclaim their property. The Bureau was closed in 1869, three years longer than it was intended to exist but still prematurely, with its goals largely unfulfilled. Ultimately, this pattern of denied reparations con-tinued through Reconstruction when Black Codes and Jim Crow laws suc-cessfully thwarted all legislative attempts at reparations.[3]

More recently, though, the issue of reparations has been refueled by other resolved cases, here and elsewhere. In 1988, Congress apologized to Japanese Americans interned in camps during World War II and authorized payments of twenty thousand dollars each to roughly sixty thousand survivors. Canada followed with its own apology and a two hundred thirty million dollar repa-ration package to Japanese Canadians. To date, the German government, in addition to apologizing, has paid sixty billion dollars to settle claims from Jewish victims of Nazi persecution. Various groups of Inuit, Native Americans, Aleuts, as well as the Black survivors of the 1923 massacre in Rosewood, Florida, have also received restitution, totaling more than one billion dollars. In 1998, the Australian government apologized for its treatment of Aborigines after an official inquiry called past treatment genocide; financial compensation is pending. And every day, financial settlements are made for personal injuries and civil damages to individuals wrongfully harmed by corporations, institutions, or others. Certainly, these cases may be less complex as they deal with direct or surviving victims who have suffered quantifiable losses. But the question remains: What is fair compensation for the commodification and exploitation of an ancestor's humanity and labor during slavery as well as for the tangible and intangible effects of slavery, namely, institutionalized racism, on African American life in American society today?

Perhaps the discussion of reparations *is* premature if there is still not a clear understanding of what unjust damages were suffered by African Americans during slavery and continued under slavery's cousins, Jim Crow laws and segregation until the late 1960s. In her first novel, *The Price of a Child* (1995), Lorene Cary pointedly addresses the issue of what slavery cost its victims in both economic and emotional terms. Like Williams and Morrison, Lorene Cary uses an existing text of slavery, the story of Jane Johnson and her children as recorded in abolitionist William Still's *The Underground Railroad* (1872), as her source material in constructing her *lieu de mémoire*.[4] Known in her enslaved life as Ginnie Pryor, Mercer Gray, Cary's self-named and self-emancipated protagonist of *The Price of a Child*, is the mother of three children, one by her lover and two by her owner. To emancipate herself and two of her children, Mercer pays the ultimate price for her freedom—she sacrifices her third child, held ransom in bondage by her owner. In this first critical examination of Cary's liberatory narrative, I read closely Cary's depiction of the economies of bondage and freedom in Mercer's new life in Philadelphia. In this vein, Cary interrupts pedestrian thinking concerning the dialectic of bondage and freedom. Cary's liberatory narrative raises these questions: What *is* the cost of freedom? What does one continue to pay for one's humanity in a commodity-driven, free enterprise, capitalist society? I am not suggesting that Cary is arguing for reparations; rather, I offer that Cary's examination of the economies of bondage and freedom may illuminate these issues for a contemporary audience. Through a close reading of Cary's narrative, I reveal the ways in which this most recent liberatory narrative performs its liberatory work. To this end, I have emphasized words throughout this chapter to illustrate how Cary's diction helps the reader more clearly see the economies of both bondage and freedom and to expose the difficulties of establishing an absolute distinction between slavery and freedom.

Cary situates her liberatory narrative within the context of abolition. Abolitionist William Still and the Vigilance Committee in Philadelphia, where he was responsible for underground railroad activities in the 1850s, play a significant role in Cary's narrative. Having himself escaped to freedom, Still commits himself to aiding others desiring to be free. The omniscient third person narrator explains the way in which Still's documentation, which Cary uses as her narrative's source material, bears witness to his mission:

> Still had assisted or directly handled more than a hundred cases. They all intrigued him. He kept careful records of each transaction, as well as his subsequent correspondence with the fugitive. Committee members implored each other to destroy evidence as a matter of course, but . . . Still never would. . . . Still knew he must keep records. Who else . . . could help fugitive families reunite? And who else would tell the stories of their struggles to their posterity? As . . . Still was fond of repeating: "We want to plead our own cause. Too long have others spoken for us." (32)

Fortuitously, it is in Philadelphia, en route to New York, that Jackson Pryor and his entourage miss their boat and are delayed. Traveling with Pryor, the newly appointed ambassador to Nicaragua, is Ginnie, his concubine, who seizes the opportunity of extended time in Philadelphia to free herself and her two children. After she sends word through the Black hotel workers that she seeks her freedom, the Vigilance Committee members, including William Still and his partner Passmore Williamson, arrive in a scene of great drama, as the entourage is about to sail from Philadelphia. Williamson, a White man, is the official spokesperson as he has more authority than Still, even in this free state, in dealing with Whites. Although he addresses Ginnie, Pryor is his intended audience. Williamson informs Ginnie, "You are entitled to your freedom according to the laws of Pennsylvania, having been brought into the state by your owner. If you prefer freedom to slavery, as we suppose everyone does, you have the chance to accept it now" (44). Ginnie's response, and it is important that she speak publicly, is the second step to freedom. She pronounces: "I am not free. . . . But I want my freedom. I always wanted to be free. . . . But he [Pryor] holds me" (48). It is also important for Ginnie to state her desire so that no one can say that she was coerced or stolen from her owner, thus giving him a legal right to reclaim her under the Fugitive Slave Law of 1850, as seen in Morrison's *Beloved*.

This is not Ginnie's first attempt to free herself. Like Williams's Dessa Rose, Ginnie was previously inspired by her lover to seek freedom for herself and for their then-unborn daughter. Willie Cooper, her lover, had planned to run and had only included Ginnie after he discovered she was pregnant with his child. This oversight on his part "taught her something about thinking she knew somebody, and about how far to trust the tingling in her thighs and the itch at the bottom of her belly" (7). While there is pain in her "rememory," there is also pleasure. Years later, she still remembers, before that painful re- alization, "making Cooper laugh at night in the cold cabin; she remembered his hands wrapping around her waist and scooping her toward him on their pallet; she remembered the warmth of his chest against her back, the backs of her legs against the front of his; the comfort and the bullying of his body" (22). In this "rememory," the reader is privy to the consensual and satisfying physical nature of Ginnie's relationship with Cooper. Ginnie's escape with Cooper is unsuccessful as she is captured before she can meet him, and he leaves without her and their unborn child. An enlightened owner, Pryor "let it be known that he would not suffer a pregnant woman to be whipped" (8). He did, however, "mount a campaign to domesticate her," putting her under sur- veillance and reminding her frequently that Cooper *left* her and their child (8).

Cary foregrounds one of her primary sites of interrogation—the relation- ship between freedom and its cost—in Ginnie's relationship with Cooper. Al- though Pryor wants Ginnie to think begrudgingly of Cooper's action, Ginnie does not. She learns from Cooper's example that freedom exacts a great price and that one pays the price, however dear, if one means to be free. In fact, Ginnie loves Cooper *because* "he refused to settle" (8). Even though he breaks her heart, she

> loved the part of him that resolved, when the overseer threw a melon rind and spoiled his hat, to leave at any *cost*. She was the *cost*. Their daughter was the *cost*. Life together, for however long they might be together, was the *cost*. They *paid*.
>
> You don't just run. First, you make up your mind. (8; emphasis added)

Volition and agency remain the foundation of freedom. The liberatory narra- tive insists upon defining liberation in *both* physical and psychological terms because deciding to be free is the first step, and Cary's narrative is no differ- ent. The narrator reveals Ginnie's concerns:

> She might get the chance to run and miss it. She might realize her loss that moment, or never even know it had come and gone. She

might never, ever get the chance. She might try and fail. She might
die trying. She might lose the children if she tried, or lose them if she
didn't. Who knew? . . .

She began to accept the uncertainty of it, and the *costs*. (13;
emphasis added)

The process of making up one's mind to free one's self is complex, given all
the variables for failure and for success.

Ironically, the abuse and exploitation of Black female sexuality give rise
to Ginnie's self-emancipation. With those in power deciding "what [the enslaved would] eat, what they'd wear, where they'd sleep, and who they'd lay,"
(4) opportunities for escape were limited. When Pryor travels to Nicaragua,
he takes Ginnie with him even though others have warned him that she might
attempt to escape. Pryor, the narrator confides,

felt that he was entitled to a few comforts. He'd be in Nicaragua who
knew how long, and although he was a man of moderation, he wanted
his gal around. A little brownskin now and then calmed nervous
tension. It balanced the manly fluids and kept him vigorous. Jack
didn't want any nasty old whores and foreigners. He liked his gal. She
knew him. She was clean. She cooked to his liking and kept his
clothes. (17)

In this passage, Cary reveals how slavery rendered both enslaved Black female
sexuality and enslaved Black female labor unpleasant and unreciprocated. Before arriving in Philadelphia, Ginnie had wanted to escape and had heard of
people escaping: "she knew that folk had smuggled themselves onto trains and
ships out of Baltimore, that they walked the woods to Pennsylvania, rode hidden in carts and crated up in boxes to Philadelphia. Each story fed her hope"
(12). Thus, this trip provides Ginnie with a golden opportunity for escape.
Anticipating her desire for freedom, however, Pryor forces Ginnie to leave
their youngest child in Virginia under the guise that she could not do the work
Pryor required with all three of her children in tow. In actuality, her son is
held as ransom to dissuade her from attempting escape. As Jacobs also revealed,
psychological threats can work as well as physical threats when one's children
are involved. Desiring the veneer of respectability, Pryor lets two rooms. Pryor
orders her and "these *two* children" (13; emphasis added) not to leave the hotel
room. This is his way of threatening Ginnie, by indirectly reminding her that
Benjamin was still in Virginia as insurance. Nonetheless, "[s]he saw the chance
of a chance to run—and its *price*" (14; emphasis added). Her child is the price
of her freedom.

As is the case with the other enslaved mothers examined, the desire to free one's children torments the enslaved mother. Long before the trip to Philadelphia, Ginnie pleads with Pryor to emancipate her and their sons. The narrator reveals that "Ginnie kept after Jack to free the boys, and although he hadn't told her, he'd already made out a portion of land for them in his will. . . . [E]ach Christmas and Easter she'd come sidling up, worrying him about why couldn't she be free, and wouldn't he free the boys? . . . You could set your calendar by her. . . . Twice a year every year, like the equinox" (18). One imagines that Ginnie chose these religious holidays in hopes that the true meanings of the seasons would influence Pryor's decision.

In other liberatory narratives, mothers provided models of liberation; in Cary's, Ginnie's father, Virgil, provides the liberatory model for her, echoing the example of Linda Brent's father. After a cruel beating by the overseer, Virgil runs away. Enacting his own resistance, Virgil eludes the patrollers for a month. Dismissing the ineffective patrollers, Pryor's frustrated father sends a Black man to negotiate Virgil's return. With the overseer fired, Virgil returns. He was with his family less than a year when circumstance prevailed: Pryor's father died, and Virgil was sold. As the traders took him, Virgil made his wife, Lily, Ginnie's mother, "promise never to forget him and never to let them make her crawl" (9). In addition to his powerful example of selfhood, Virgil literally made it possible for Ginnie to escape. Ginnie was born with her toes stacked on top of each other, impeding her movement. Virgil corrected this impediment by crafting a splint to separate her toes. Her mother's admonition—"'Think of your daddy,' Lily said, 'every time you run'"(9)—takes on additional meaning when Ginnie frees herself. Ginnie has few memories of her mother, but she does remember Lily protecting her from sexual assault, even as she is dying from consumption. Lily strikes Ginnie's one-armed assailant with a piece of wood, saying: "Do you remember this, old man. You remember to keep your one arm and your three legs away from my girl, or I'ma kill you" (61–62). These memories of her parents, surfacing as she replays her life in her attempt to make meaning of her new life, reveal the source of Ginnie's perception of herself as worthy, valuable, and unique. These perceptions help to strengthen her resolve to live as free a life as possible.

Once she is free in Philadelphia, Ginnie's life changes in dramatic and unanticipated ways. She is befriended by a free Black family, the Quicks, some of whom work with the Vigilance Committee but whose primary function "was to make money" (78). Money means everything, including freedom, to the Quicks. In this microcosmic family, one sees divergent aspects of free Black life in an urban community. Her first free social engagement is with the Quicks at their annual picnic in the cemetery, commemorating the death of their ancestors. Symbolically, the cemetery setting is appropriate as Ginnie is dead to her former life. Thus, one of her first free acts is to change her name from Virginia Pryor to Mercer Gray: "It's the safest thing to do. And if safety had nothing to do with it, she'd still want her own name. One she picked herself and not somebody gave her" (92). The Quicks are a middle-class family: they represent the emerging, middle-class, free Black society. They are not, however, without their flaws. The patriarch and matriarch, Manny and Della, are entrepreneurs in the most flagrantly capitalist sense. Manny is scornful of all attempts to uplift and advance the race, and his chronic ill-health may be read as a metaphor for his dis-ease with race. Fitting into the school of Booker T. Washington, Manny believes, "I'm proving that colored people are not unfit for freedom. The race don't need the vote. The race needs to eat. The race needs land" (82). While she might mean well, Della is generally in agreement with Manny and, if she is not, her wishes are generally subsumed by Manny's. Thus, even as a free woman, her desires are mediated by Black patriarchy. In addition to a thriving catering business, they own rental properties. The rental properties, by and large, are slums; thus, the Quicks are guilty of exploiting their tenants, many Black and all poor. In addition to their respective employments, Manny's brother, Sharkey, and Manny's son, Tyree, are dedicated members of the Vigilance Committee, although this is a source of tension in the family as Manny and Della do not want politics to affect their business interests. After his older brother's death and with his father's failing health, Tyree assumes a great deal of familial responsibility: he marries his brother's widow, in an attempt to make up for his brother's death, and he works for his father in the rental business, even though he is greatly opposed to his father's values. Tyree and his sister, Harriet, are educated; they both wish to use their education in generative ways for the race. Harriet, a teacher, founds a school in her efforts to uplift the race through education. Tyree's work with the Vigilance Committee is his way of performing race work.

While the above might seem to be an excessive characterization of the Quick family, it is absolutely necessary because they *are* the environment in which Mercer must learn to be free. The Quick family, immediate and extended, is Mercer's first free community. They provide her with shelter and employment, and they help care for her children. They are different from all that she has known, so much so that she does not know how to feel about them initially. She feels spiteful: "They'd looked so comfortable; that's what stuck in her craw. . . . They looked like freedom too, and instead of admiring them, she resented them for it" (108). But she also feels "safe amid their freedom and wealth" (83). Her ambivalence is understandable as Mercer is learning to negotiate new emotional terrain as a free woman.

Accepting the assistance of the Vigilance Committee to free herself and her two children costs Ginnie her third child. The narrator reveals the physical and psychological trauma of this decision: "She was going to lose her baby boy. Ginnie knew it again. This time the knowledge came suddenly. She couldn't breathe. She was giving up her boy, her best baby" (48). This realization, the narrator continues, elicits a virtual out-of-body experience for Ginnie: she "almost floated up out of her body like in a dream, into the blue sky that didn't laugh or cry, to kiss her baby's fat cheek and hold her lips to the corner of his mouth and smell his breath, sweet like milk. But she held herself in; she held fast to the boat and these two children. . . . She could not run or fly or float, but she could stand. It was all she could do" (48). Like Morrison's Sethe, Mercer is haunted by his absence. "She tried not to dwell on Benjamin," the narrator confesses, "but how could she keep from moaning when she felt his absence next to her like an open wound? And there was no help for it" (63). Mercer reasons, remembering the examples of her father and her lover, Willie Cooper:

> They'd tried to hold her by holding Benjamin, but she'd pulled free
> anyway. Wasn't that what Virgil had shown her? And Willie? . . . A
> hawk would tear off its whole leg to get free. Even a scruffy old
> raccoon would have the dignity to chew off a toe if need be.
>   So. So did she. (64)

Marianne Hirsch's examination of enslaved mothers and their maternal responses in slavery may illuminate Mercer's response. Hirsch explains, "the economy of slavery circumscribes not only the process of individuation and subject-formation, but also heightens and intensifies the experience of motherhood—of connection and separation" (6). Mercer's point speaks to a fundamental issue: self-preservation. In this light, Mercer's response is understandable even though she may never see her son again; as an enslaved Black mother, her feelings are made more intense by the circumstance of her separation from him.

Rightly so, Ginnie fears what Pryor might do should her attempt at freedom fail. She risks his selling the other two children "cheap to people who would value their lives accordingly" as well as beating her "like a dog" for her perceived treachery (62). To retrieve his property, Pryor does seek legal recourse against the Vigilance Committee; Williamson is jailed for failing to produce Mercer's body. Thus her body becomes the juridical site as Pryor attempts

to reclaim it. In this setting, Saidiya Hartman would rightly identify "the captive body as the extension of the master's power" and the courtroom as the
"spatial organization of dominance" (69). But instead of transgressing the
boundaries, Mercer chooses to blur them by her presence and by her participation. Although fearful of the outcome, Mercer risks re-enslavement by tes-
tifying on Williamson's behalf. Performing freely, she produces her own body
for public consumption: "After the gasping and oohing and aahing," the narrator comments, "the spectators fell silent" (197). Thus, she takes control of
this site. More impressive than her body is her voice. Before the court, she
confirms: "Nobody forced me away. Nobody pulled me, and nobody lead me.
I went of my own free will. I always wished to be free, and meant to be free
when I came North" (199). Pryor's case is ultimately dismissed, but not without this confrontation between the perceived powerful and the powerless.

Both Mercer's escape and her work as an abolitionist involve elements
of spectatorship. During her escape, Tyree "wanted to give her a life with cur-
tains around it . . . so that [the] gathered people could not lick their lips with
the excitement of her predicament or the exquisite sweep of her bosom" (46).
Mercer's body is viewed voyeuristically in the highly politicized moment. As
in slavery, her body continues to be a blank slate on which others write their
texts of her. The narrator furthers this point, describing how "Tyree let himself feel his desire to wrap his arm around her shoulders and show her a safety
she'd never known" (46). In this instance, desire becomes mutual.

Although slavery had filled her with hate, Mercer does learn to love again.
The narrator reveals Tyree's attraction to her from the moment he sees her.
Mercer is also attracted to him; "his freedom let her admire him without re-
serve" (108). They later act upon their mutual attraction, despite the fact that
he is married and that his family has become a surrogate family for Mercer
and her children. After a lifetime of servitude and selflessness, Mercer experiences briefly the luxury of pleasure and leisure with Tyree:

> It felt good to have him, and to laugh and to forget everything but
> this moment and this pleasure. She'd never had such pleasure: it was
> rich, fat lovemaking, like gravy. This pleasure did not make her want
> to please. It did not make her worry about his delight. It did not make
> her afraid to enjoy, because the joy would be added to her account and
> taken out, double, sometime later. This pleasure made her greedy.
> (302)

When he feels the raised scars on her buttocks and thighs, Tyree is struck by
this evidence of abuse. Self-consciously, Mercer identifies this "writing" on

her body as the difference between them. This difference, however, does not impose on their lovemaking or on their plans for a future together. Mercer wants an authentic and legitimate relationship as "getting free has cost [her] dear. [She] didn't do it just to be somebody's piece of brownskin" (150). She does not want to trade one type of bondage for another. Feeling enslaved by his responsibilities, Tyree wants to end his loveless marriage to his dead brother's wife and his association with his father's businesses. Indeed, both these free individuals must constantly strive to maintain their sense of freedom and keep it alive in new and very different contexts.

In slavery, Mercer's labor had been forced from her; in freedom, she chooses how she will labor. Bearing witness to the atrocities of slavery, although painful, provides Mercer with a way to help others, as well as herself. "The more she talked," the narrator reveals, "the more she remembered" (260).[5] Thus, speaking on the abolitionist circuit serves as a kind of catharsis for Mercer. What she remembers and what she does not remember are both revealing. For example, Mercer recollects,

> My mother is dead, and the picture I have of her—the one that comes to my mind when I call her name—is I can see her sitting on that latrine, laughing. That's what I have left of my mother.
>   And I can't even see my daddy. I can't bring his face to my mind. You know when you know a word but you can't quite think to say it? That's how his face is to me. (216)

Although these are painful memories, they allow Mercer to mourn her personal losses in slavery as well as to alert those who do not know of slavery's malevolent effect on Black families.

Joining others who "came onstage to display scars . . . or to testify about the evils of slavery," Mercer attempts to explain the inexplicable to her audience (121). Slavery works, Mercer explains, because

> "[e]ither they have to look us in the face and say the truth: You a human being just like me, and I'm still gonna keep you down; or else they gotta lie and say: You a human being, but not like me and mine. You don't feel things like I do. You don't grieve like I do for your family. You don't need anything of your own to have and to keep, to feel like a man or woman. You don't need a proper marriage, 'cause you don't have no shame." (249)

Thus, slavery, according to Mercer, is built on a foundation of lies that the enslavers have to believe and to accept in order to participate in this dehumanizing institution.

Presenting one's personal history is a way not only of inserting one's self into the public narrative, amending it as it were; it is also a way to reify one's existence. Giving her first talk for the Anti-Slavery Society in Massachusetts, Mercer begins her narrative with her personal history in the same way that the nineteenth-century emancipatory narrator did. Mercer relates:

> "I was born a slave. My parents were slaves. I had an older sister, but she died in childbirth with no doctor to attend her, and my brother died of disease when he was a boy. My father was sold when I was four or five years old, and my mother died when I was ten. I have never seen my father since. I have wondered many times why I was left, but now that I stand here before you, I suppose I have been spared to tell the tale." (247)

Speaking on the abolitionist circuit, Mercer was "a lightning rod in America's race storm. . . . [as she tried] to speak freedom to power" (291). Like Baby Suggs and her big heart, Mercer uses her voice, "a voice from the South,"[6] to expose slavery: "Voice was what she had; it was all she was: her skin and sinew and bones and flesh and sex and power turned into voice and breathed through her" (264).

Mercer also uses this opportunity to teach about how disempowering historical narratives can be if told from a singular perspective and if not closely interrogated. She cautions about this danger:

> "They tell me a story that is taught to schoolchildren, that President George Washington left provisions in his will for all his personal slaves to be freed but that none of them would go. . . . Can I ask you for a moment, if you've known indenture, or known someone who had to be bound out himself or his children, can I please ask you to imagine yourself *not* accepting freedom handed to you? Can you imagine that those poor wretches, Mr. Washington's people, each and every one, had become so degraded that they would not even stretch out a hand to take the gift of freedom when it was offered? . . .
>
> That's a awful story we tell our children, ladies and gentlemen. A awful story. Stories like that are the kind of lies that grow up from the big lie we got going in slavery. The big lie just sits around making babies. And the lies don't stay down in the South. They move all over the country." (255; emphasis in original)

In all of the liberatory narratives, the novelists reveal a concern with the uses of history. In this example, Cary shows the power of narrative: ideologies are inculcated through narrative.

Cary reserves her most scathing criticism for the North and its feelings of ungrounded superiority concerning southern slavery. For Mercer, "What had started as a job had become a mission. . . . How could it not be a mission, now that she had seen their men use tobacco, their women wear cotton, and their children eat rice" (257–258). The North is not as guiltless as history would have us believe. In a lengthy passage worthy of replicating here because of its power, Mercer indicts the North and its "benign neglect":

> "We are all in this thing here together. I have been told, since I've been North, that slavery keeps prices down. I have been told that we in the North live better because three millions of Black people toil without wages in the South. I am not an educated woman, ladies and gentlemen, but I know that no one in this room would subject his sister or brother or his friend or neighbor to bondage, but we here let it go on, and the North lives better. How much better is better? Would anyone here in this room, if they saw slavery for a day, or lived it for an hour, have the heart to say: 'Let it go on, just so the price of cotton stays at four pounds to the penny. Let it go on, just so sugar stays at half a penny a pound'?
> How much better? Would anyone here say: 'Yes, sell that baby away from that mother just so I get my snuff for two bits and not two and a half?'" (264–265)

By implicating the North in its collusion with the South, Mercer asks for an examination of this nexus: economic interests in conjunction with racist ideologies in the North. Like schoolchildren accepting the story of George Washington tossing a coin across the Potomac River, the North has accepted the southern myths surrounding American slavery without carefully examining them.[7]

Mercer's work with the Anti-Slavery Society is fraught with complications due to the obliviousness and obtuseness of its members and other Northerners who do not recognize the relationship between products that they use—for example, cotton and tobacco—and slavery. Cary probes the difficulty for even well-meaning, devoted abolitionists to go beyond the abolition of slavery to the larger battle, equality between the races. For example, some Anti-Slavery Society members were shocked to think that Frederick Douglass would have preferred freedom to being "a symbol of Southern immorality" (215). Mercer struggles with finding a way to use language to enlighten her audience yet not distance those listening. She wonders, "How was she to speak to them with an honesty she knew to be impossible? They could not abide to hear the ill will that had grown up in their American soil. They didn't want to know that it was woven into their sheets of cotton picked by black fingers, as surely as it seeped into their dreams" (254). This disconnect is just as indictable as the actual offense because it allows for the institutionalizing of racist ideologies.

Mercer is aware of how resistant her audience is, even though they come to hear her. In a sense, she has to convince her audience not only of her veracity, but of the reality of sufferings in the South in which the North is complicit. She believes that the Northern Whites did not truly "want freedom for all slaves: black people free to roam the country and beat them at business and pan for gold and preach the gospel and build homes and educate children. They just didn't want them treated so bad. They wanted to sleep easier at night" (264). Even the White women who work in the Anti-Slavery Society show that they do not truly understand as they attempt to universalize the experience of women in their comparisons between Black and White women.

Mercer's body is once again displayed for public consumption through her abolitionist work. Mercer relates how the audience, after seeing her scars, used her body as a writerly and readerly text:

> [T]hey strained with attention, how they asked her one question after another: Who had done this to her? For what transgression? How long was she beaten? With what object? How old was she when it happened? What had she done about it? What did other slaves do to help her? Did it bleed? How had she healed? How much of her body did the scars cover? Were all her people treated likewise? Was that why she'd run away, to avoid more beatings? . . .
>   Had a man done this to her? Had he done it to take her virtue? Had he forced her? They filled their eyes with her. (167)

These questions are not simply interrogative; they are asked in order to confirm the answers that they think they already know. Thus, Mercer's body becomes the site of their preoccupations and needs. In this same vein, one member of the Vigilance Committee wanted "fugitives brought to meet her before they were sent on their way. She cherished their stories. She wept over their sufferings and laughed at the ruses they used to escape. Then, gleefully, she reached into her purse for a gold dollar coin to put into each palm" (128). Cary uses this example to show how similar this type of fetishizing and commodifying is to slavery. The narrator proffers that fear induces these types of behavior: "They were afraid to hear that the world was not as they'd thought it, divided up neatly with stone rows between—them up here safe and sound and loved by their special God; the Southern whites evil and greedy" (264).

Cary reframes the discussion of the enslaved and their experiences by having Mercer address the age-old questions concerning the experience of slavery: "Everyone she knew in the North looked at the slaves and said: Isn't it terrible what bondage does to people? And yes, it was. But Mercer asked another question: Wasn't it bountiful and glorious grace that some of these people even live at all? That they live and dare fight back, or dare to resist, or dare to hold the line where they would be forced no more" (262). This rhetorical turn shifts the discussion from one of object to that of subject. One must consider not only what was done to the enslaved African American, but also what enslaved African Americans did with what was done to them. Likewise, responding to the questions of why an enslaved person might betray another or participate in a fraud against the abolitionist movement, Mercer replies, "[T]he first thing that comes to my mind is not why some of us, some few, have been made into wretches by this widespread and powerful evil, but why, through the grace of a good and powerful God, more of us haven't, why all of us haven't?" (263).

At the narrative's end, love does not conquer all. Tyree and Mercer are not able to leave together because his family loses almost all of their money accidentally. He must stay in Philadelphia to support his family. Without moving to another location, they cannot afford, psychologically or morally, to be together. All that is left of the Quick family's savings is five hundred dollars. On the boat that she would have taken with Pryor, Mercer heads north, away from Tyree with a letter from him. Inside there is a note; underneath the note are five one-hundred-dollar bills, "the price of a child Bennie's age" (318). Giving the family's remaining money to Mercer may be read in this way: because money is ultimately what keeps them apart, giving her the money to purchase her son is a form of penance. This is Tyree's way of making sure that his *own* freedom has meaning. Cary broadens the scope of the liberatory narrative to question many of the larger issues relating to the construction of a free Black community and society. Ironically, freedom proves just as costly as bondage for Mercer. Money can corrupt or it can heal. The invisible costs of freedom are why eternal vigilance is needed. As the saying goes, freedom is never free. Cary constructs her liberatory narrative in ways that ask the reader, What price are you willing to pay for freedom? And the payment may not be a one-time payment.

That this narrative takes such a stance leads one to consider Cary's intent. Perhaps Cary is speaking to the more contemporary issue of economic disparity for African Americans that had its origins in slavery. She clearly shows, however, through the Quick family that economic wealth is not a panacea. Economic wealth for the individual does not necessarily translate into economic empowerment for the race. Barbara Christian reminds, "[P]ersonal empowerment cannot completely transcend the power of unjust societal law and custom" ("Beloved, She's Ours" 40). Perhaps Cary's focus is on these economies, not to advance the cause of reparations or restitution, as one might conclude, but to show how fundamental these issues are to any discussion of slavery. In showing how costly freedom is, Cary also reminds her readers that the cost of freedom is never too much. This fundamental American ideal is one that all Americans share, however contradictory our history.

"Textual Healing" and the Liberatory Narrative

*We hold these truths to be self-evident: that all men are
created equal, that they are endowed by their Creator
with certain unalienable rights, that among these are life,
liberty, and the pursuit of happiness.*

> —The Declaration of Independence

*Not everything that is faced can be changed, but nothing
can be changed until it is faced.*

> —JAMES BALDWIN

*There is not a place you or I can go, to think about, or
not think about, to summon the presence of, or recollect
the absences of slaves; nothing that reminds us of the
ones who made the journey and of those who did not
make it. There is no suitable memorial, or plaque or
wreath or wall or park or skyscraper lobby. There is no
200-foot tower. There's no small bench by the road.
There is not even a tree scored, an initial that I can visit
or you can visit in Charleston or Savannah or New York
or Providence or better still, on the banks of the
Mississippi.*

> —TONI MORRISON

"What's past is prologue."

> —The Tempest

On December 31, 1999, I attended a program interestingly entitled "The Paradox of Thomas Jefferson" at the Smithsonian Institution's America's Millennium on the Mall celebration. I found it ironic, given the range of historical
moments from which to choose, that President Jefferson's life was selected to

commemorate the millennium. This program consisted of a staged interview: Jefferson scholar Clay Jenkinson, impersonating Jefferson, was questioned by civil rights activist Julian Bond and Native American activist Richard West. As the program's title suggests, the interviewers were interested in examining the inconsistencies in Jefferson's public and personal lives. We know, for example, that, as one of the primary architects of American democracy, Jefferson also enslaved African Americans. How did Jefferson, one of the most vocal advocates of freedom in eighteenth-century America, feel about denying the "unalienable" rights of others? The interview, of course, turned to an aspect of Jefferson's life that engages these concerns and that continues to capture America's interest and imagination: Jefferson's relationship with Sally Hemings, an enslaved Black woman with whom he is believed to have had seven children. During the interview, Bond asked Jenkinson these two questions, among others: Is it possible for an enslaved woman to love? and Did Jefferson have a child with an enslaved woman? Jenkinson, as Jefferson, answered:

> "Let's say that it proves to be true. It is a subset of a much larger issue. The fact that I owned two hundred human beings, that I bought them and sold them, that I could make them do my bidding from building my house to cleaning my human waste, that I could whip them at will and kill them under certain circumstances without legal recourse tells you everything you need to know about sexual relations between master and slave. In other words, you must subordinate this to the larger evil of slavery of which it is a symbol but not a determining symbol. So let's focus on the outrage of slavery, if you want to include my sexual life in this equation that doesn't trouble me greatly, but it seems to me that the focus is wrong. That by focusing on sex you forget the larger corruption."[1]

This performance was intriguing because its enactment revealed to me why conversations surrounding the issue of slavery are doomed to failure. While some might interpret his response as a type of obfuscation, I read it as a strategy. It seems to me that in our attempt to comprehend the racist and racial ideologies that created and perpetuated the institution of slavery, ideologies that Jefferson's life represents in ironic ways, we often do so inductively, as in the above questions. By moving from the specific to the general, we hope to illuminate this complex and momentous issue one frame at a time. One imagines that, through this approach, one might subtly reveal how traumatic slavery was and perhaps initiate the long-stalled discussion of this issue without discomfort, insult, or offense. Given that we *still* have not come to terms with the significance of slavery in American life, this approach has proven to be both inefficient and ineffective. Jenkinson's response gestures toward an alternative approach. He asks, in Jefferson's stead, for a consideration of the larger, and one could argue, more substantive issues relating to slavery. In other words, he asks us to approach the issue of slavery deductively—to begin with the general and then move to the specifics. In this way, we might arrive at a more useful conversation about slavery through a discussion of the "larger corruption."

In her essay "Textual Healing: Claiming Black Women's Bodies, the Erotic and Resistance in Contemporary Novels of Slavery," Farah Jasmine Griffin coins the term "textual healing" to describe the cultural work of Black women's writing "as sites of healing, pleasure, and resistance" (521).[2] Recognizing the power of contemporary Black women's writing to effect change and healing in the lives of readers, Griffin posits, "In addition to its literary merit and theoretical implications, part of the power of some writing by black women is its transformative potential" (521). The literary project of these writers, Griffin explains, is to

> replace the dominant discourse's obsession with the visual black body
> with a perspective that privileges touch and other senses. They are
> engaged in a project of re-imagining the black female body—a project
> done in the service of those readers who have inherited the older
> legacy of the black body as despised, diseased, and ugly. (521)

With its emphasis on healing the pain of previous discourses, particularly discourses related to Black female bodies, I find Griffin's term useful to describe the cultural work of the liberatory narratives examined herein in terms of their curative value as they seek to facilitate a holistic conversation about slavery. The nineteenth-century emancipatory narrative was written to advance the cause of abolition; the twentieth-century liberatory narrative advances another cause—to liberate its readers from the shackles of the past by asking them to look at the whole of slavery, especially as it involved Black women.

Creating this discursive space as a site of interrogation, the liberatory narrative recasts and augments our understanding of our collective past; additionally, it can foster the conversation on race and race relations much wanted and needed by American society. By allowing the reader to experience with the protagonists and the characters the process of analysis, synthesis, and reorientation necessary in their quest for freedom, these writers simulate a type of liberation for their readership by employing intertextuality as a strategy. Indeed, one might argue that the intertextual nature of their writing is a direct reflection of a racial history shaped by the institution of slavery. In this way, intertextuality helps to enable discussions on race relations.

Presenting a dynamic struggle for liberation, all of the liberatory narratives have at their center Black female protagonists who subvert stereotypical configurations of Black female identity as well as who undermine the racial, gender, and economic biases of the White enslaving society. By countering the disempowering, hegemonic discourses that have been perpetuated about the enslaved Black woman and her reality, these writers create a generative genre in which they centralize the enslaved woman as the subject of her own reality. bell hooks explains the importance of this reframing: "As subjects, people have the right to define their own reality, establish their own identities, name their history. As objects, one's reality is defined by others, one's identity created by others, one's history named only in ways that define one's relationship to those who are subject" (*Talking Back* 42–43). In their revisions of the Black woman's story in slavery, these writers teach their readers how to proceed from bondage to freedom, from dispossession to repossession, and from objectification to subjectivity, either by telling the story never before told or by correcting the story as previously told.

Slavery may be considered America's greatest traumatic experience. In their revisions of the female emancipatory narrative, Black women writers expose the veneer of American reality surrounding slavery, and recent theories of trauma may offer insight to their enterprise. Certainly, the nineteenth-century emancipatory narrators bear witness to the traumas they lived. But contemporary liberatory narrative functions to bear witness to the *memories* of slavery. One might say that memory is the repository of trauma. Trauma, according to Cathy Caruth, "is not locatable in the simple violent or original event in an individual's past, but rather in the way that its very unassimilated nature—the way it is precisely *not known* in the first instance—returns to haunt the survivor later on" (4; emphasis in original). One could argue that slavery's "unassimilated" nature—the fact that our nation has never come to terms with its past—continues to haunt not only the literary imaginations of contemporary Black women writers but the national memory as well. For the actual or imaginary survivor of a traumatic experience, there is a need to bear witness in order to know the experience, a need to tell the story and to be heard. However, if the story is not heard or if there is no witness to listen and to understand, Dori Laub argues, the telling of the story "might itself be lived as a return of the trauma—*a re-experiencing of the event itself*" ("Bearing Witness" 67; emphasis in original). For Laub, the role of the listener, the witness, is crucial to the success of testimony. Indeed, he suggests that "[t]he absence of an empathic listener, or more radically, the absence of an addressable other, an other who can hear the anguish of one's memories and thus affirm and recognize their realness, annihilates the story" ("Bearing Witness" 68). I suggest that the reader of the liberatory narrative serves as a witness.

The role of the witness is essential if healing is to occur. The absence of a listener, of a reader, allows the survivor/narrator to continue to be controlled by the traumatic experience. If the survivor/narrator is unable to tell her story, she cannot understand what has happened. Instead, the survivor/narrator remains in silence which can lead to "the actual return of the trauma and through its inadvertent repetition, or transmission, from one generation to another" ("Bearing Witness" 67). For Laub, telling one's story becomes the only way to live: "[survivors] also [need] to tell their story in order to survive. There is, in each survivor, an imperative need to *tell* and thus come to *know* one's story, unimpeded by ghosts from the past against which one has to protect oneself. One has to know one's buried truth in order to live one's life" ("An Event without a Witness" 78; emphasis in original). The role of testimony centers not only on recovery from past traumatic experiences but on the recovery of the future from traumatic repetitions. Testimony is vital for the survivor to continue to survive after trauma.

Because testimony cannot happen without an audience, the role of the witness is essential to the life of the survivor. Laub warns that the witness is in a precarious position. The witness must minimize the possibility of the testimony becoming re-traumatizing. She or he must respect the silences of the survivor while at the same time helping the survivor through those silences. The witness must be able to hear the story of the survivor without resisting emotionally. Laub explains, "To a certain extent, the [witness] takes on the responsibility for bearing witness that previously the narrator felt he bore alone, and therefore could not carry out" ("An Event without a Witness" 85). Laub's theory explains why it is so difficult for Americans in contemporary society to bear witness to slavery. Most are unable to hear the story without re-traumatizing the narrator, are unable to help the narrator out of the historical silence surrounding slavery, and are unable to listen without resisting emotionally.

Slavery serves as a site of testimony for Black women writers in yet another way. Some writers construct their novels to show the lingering effects of slavery on the lives of contemporary Black women, who have not themselves experienced slavery. In *Corregidora* (1975), for example, Gayl Jones examines the continuous and inescapable influence of nineteenth-century Brazilian slavery on Ursa Corregidora, a twentieth-century African-American woman. Blues-singing Ursa is the descendant, the great-granddaughter, of an enslaver in Brazil who fathered both her grandmother and her mother. Jones triangulates her novel to reveal that Africans of the diaspora share a particular geo-political legacy in relation to chattel slavery. Ursa's familial history is her personal legacy, and it has been maintained and transmitted orally. Ursa's great-grandmother, Great Gram, teaches Ursa the importance of memory. For historically oppressed, disenfranchised people, memory is oftentimes the only source of evidence available. Great Gram testifies:

> When I'm telling you something don't you ever ask if I'm lying. Because they didn't want to leave no evidence of what they done—so it couldn't be held against them. And I'm leaving evidence. And you got to leave evidence too. And your children got to leave evidence. And when it come time to hold up the evidence, we got to have evidence to hold up. (Corregidora 14)

Great Gram charges Ursa with two tasks: to honor her familial responsibilities by remembering the horror of the past inflicted on her family so that an accounting can be given and to continue the family's lineage so that the past will never be forgotten. "The important thing," Great Gram instructs, "is making generations. They can burn the papers but they can't burn conscious, Ursa. And that what makes the evidence. And that's what makes the verdict" (22). Unfortunately, Great Gram's discourse of resistance is subverted by another form of property relations. Ursa's husband physically assaults her, causing her infertility. Thus, unable to make generations, Ursa is unable to fulfill her charge. She cannot continue her legacy by bearing generations; consequently, the weight of remembering becomes too difficult and too painful for her as she has no one to receive this testimony. Despite the reason or the circumstance, Ursa is burdened not only by a past that was not her own personal past but also by the death of memory and identity as she has no offspring.

Perhaps such torturous memories, some might say, need to die, but as Jones shows, the death of memory—be it familial or national—is not without its consequences. In the end, Ursa's story is unresolved; thus, she and the reader are left in a liminal state, much like the nation is in its lack of acknowledgment and understanding of slavery as an American phenomenon. Perhaps an apology is in order. As psychiatrist Aaron Lazare explains, "what makes an apology work is the exchange of *shame and power* between *the offender and the offended*" (42; emphasis added). With this acknowledgment and this exchange, perhaps we could learn from the past and move forward without the burden of the past. The liberatory narrative reminds us that, however traumatic, the past is memory, the past is identity, and the past is meditation.[3]

The memories of slavery are still "out there," as Sethe warns, waiting to
be encountered because memories never die. Sethe explains to Denver:

> Some things go. Pass on. Some things just stay. I used to think it was
> my rememory. . . . but it's not. Places, places are still there. If a house
> burns down, it's gone, but the place—the picture of it—stays, and not
> just in my rememory, out there, in the world. What I remember is a
> picture floating around out there outside my head. I mean, even if I
> don't think it, even if I die, the picture of what I did, or knew, or saw
> is still out there. Right in the place where it happened. . . . Someday
> you be walking down the road and you hear something or see
> something going on. So clear. And you think it's you thinking it up. A
> thought picture. But no. It's when you bump into a rememory. (36)

If memories never die, then the memories of slavery and its trauma exist forever. While this may seem futilely traumatic, it does not have to be. Because
memories always exist, there is hope. Memory allows one to acknowledge the
traumas of slavery that would be otherwise impossible to acknowledge without memory. Witnesses like Butler, Morrison, Williams, Cooper, and Cary provide testimonies of the trauma of slavery in their works. Their testimonies serve
as a weapon against forgetfulness. Ideally, the readers of the liberatory narrative will not run away, fail to listen, try to occupy the subject position of the
witness, or seek to authenticate the story. Ideally, their readers will do what
empathic witnesses do: feel, listen, and remember.

The liberatory narrative functions in two ways to emancipate its readers:
by facilitating a discussion of slavery as a *lieu de mémoire* and by defamiliarizing
slavery through illumination and interrogation. By positing slavery as a site
of memory and as a metaphor for contemporary race relations, the liberatory
narrative allows for an examination of how race operated and operates in
American history, society, and culture. In so doing, the liberatory narrative
provides the opportunity for healing the wounds, the shame, and the pain of
that past. It can serve, to use Morrison's words, as a "bench by the road" where
we can begin to talk, to listen, and to heal.

Notes

Introduction **Visions and Revisions of Slavery**

1. In addition to the five contemporary novels examined here, other novels by African American writers that engage slavery include: Arna Bontemps's *Black Thunder* (1936), Margaret Walker's *Jubilee* (1966), Ernest Gaines's *The Autobiography of Miss Jane Pittman* (1971), Gayl Jones's *Corregidora* (1975), Ishmael Reed's *Flight to Canada* (1976), Alex Haley's *Roots* (1976), Barbara Chase-Riboud's *Sally Hemings* (1979), David Bradley's *The Chaneysville Incident* (1981), and Charles Johnson's *Oxherding Tale* (1982) and *Middle Passage* (1990).

2. See Bernard W. Bell, *The Afro-American Novel and Its Tradition* (Amherst: U of Massachusetts P, 1987) 289.

   While completing this book, four books were published akin to my subject: Elizabeth Ann Beaulieu's *Black Women Writers and the American Neo-Slave Narrative: Femininity Unfettered* (Westport: Greenwood P, 1999), Venetria K. Patton's *Women in Chains: The Legacy of Slavery in Black Women's Fiction* (Albany: SUNY, 2000), Ashraf H. A. Rushdy's *Neo-slave Narratives: Studies in the Social Logic of a Literary Form* (New York: Oxford UP, 1999), and Stefanie Sievers's *Liberating Narratives: The Authorization of Black Female Voices in African American Women Writers' Novels of Slavery* (Hamburg: LIT Verlag, 1999). At first glance, it would seem that these books cover the same ground as my study; examining them, all fine studies, reveals striking and substantive differences. Beaulieu (who examines many of the works that I examine) and Patton (who includes nineteenth-century novels by Black women writers as well) are centered on issues of mothering and motherhood, and they both stay within the generic ground of Bell's *neoslave narrative*. Rushdy's work reveals how each of the novels he selects [William Styron's *The Confessions of Nat Turner* (1967), Ishmael Reed's *Flight to Canada* (1976), Williams's *Dessa Rose* (1986), and Charles Johnson's *Oxherding Tale* (1982) and *Middle Passage* (1990)] represents a range of responses to the cultural and political debates at play during their compositions. Rushdy defines his term, *neo-slave narratives*, as "contemporary novels that assume the form, adopt the conventions, and take on the first-person voice of the antebellum slave narrative" (3). Sievers's *Liberating*

Narratives has this in common with my study: she identifies these "novels of slavery," *Jubilee, Dessa Rose,* and *Beloved,* as "constructive dialogues between the writers' 20th-century present and the past—dialogues based on the presumption that what is perceived as 'the past' is largely an imaginative construction" (188). She does not, however, situate these dialogues in the literary tradition of Black women.

3. The term *emancipatory* in describing those writings traditionally known as slave narratives is a term that Toni Cade Bambara, Eleanor Traylor, and Sherley Anne Williams have all used to shift the gaze from the objectified identity of the author to the author's impetus for writing and her primary focus of the narrative—emancipation from slavery. See Bambara's *Deep Sightings and Rescue Missions* and Williams's "The Lion's History: The Ghetto Writes B[l]ack." Traylor has discussed the emancipatory narrative at numerous conferences and more thoroughly in her unpublished manuscript, *The Presence of Ancestry in African American Literature*.

4. Ironically, slavery may be the ideal ground for examining both race and gender in Black women's lives, as perhaps there is no better site where issues of both are so intricately and inextricably woven. Several Black women writers of the diaspora have also engaged slavery, for example, Maryse Condé, *I, Tituba, Black Witch of Salem* (New York: Ballantine, 1992) and Michelle Cliff, *Free Enterprise* (New York: Plume, 1993).

5. See Henry Louis Gates, Jr.'s *The Signifying Monkey: A Theory of African-American Literary Criticism* for his groundbreaking discussion of signifyin(g) as a mode of textual scaffolding and revision in African American literature.

6. See Charles T. Davis, "The Slave Narrative: First Major Art Form in an Emerging Black Tradition," in *Black Is the Color of the Cosmos* (Washington: Howard UP, 1982) 83–119; William L. Andrews, *To Tell a Free Story: The First Century of Afro-American Autobiography, 1760–1865* (Urbana: U of Illinois P, 1986) 3–31; James Olney, "'I Was Born': Slave Narratives, Their Status as Autobiography and as Literature," *The Slave's Narrative* (New York: Oxford UP, 1985) 148–175; and Deborah E. McDowell, "In the First Place: Making Frederick Douglass and the Afro-American Narrative Tradition" *Critical Essays on Frederick Douglass* (Boston: Twayne Publishers, 1991) 192–214.

7. For comprehensive bibliographies of emancipatory narratives, see Charles T. Davis and Henry Louis Gates, Jr., *The Slave's Narrative* (New York: Oxford UP, 1985) 319–327 and Marion Wilson Sterling, *The Slave Narrative: Its Place in American History* (Washington: Howard UP, 1988) 337–356.

8. For the most illuminating discussions of the differences between the emancipatory narratives by Black men and the emancipatory narratives by Black women, see Frances Foster, "'In Respect to Females . . .': Differences in the Portrayals of Women by Male and Female Narrators," *Black American Literature Forum* 15 (1981): 66–70 and Joanne M. Braxton, "Harriet Jacobs' *Incidents in the Life of a Slave Girl*: The Re-definition of the Slave Narrative Genre," *The Massachusetts Review* 27 (1986): 379–387.

9. See Barbara Welter's "The Cult of True Womanhood, 1820–1860," *American Quarterly* 18 (1966): 151–174.

10. See Margaret Walker, *How I Wrote Jubilee and Other Essays on Life and Literature* (New York: The Feminist P, 1990) 53–61. Walker describes how she began writing what would become *Jubilee* in the 1930s and continued to write until its completion in 1966. Thus, Walker wrote her novel during years of great social and political change in twentieth-century African-American history. Trudier Harris observes that Walker's *Jubilee* failed to inspire subsequent writers primarily because of its historical

context against which African Americans were still battling in the late 1960s and early 1970s. See Harris, "Black Writers in a Changed Landscape, since 1950," *The History of Southern Literature*, ed. Louis D. Rubin, Jr., et al. (Baton Rouge: Louisiana State UP, 1985) 566–577. Hortense J. Spillers also identifies *Jubilee* as lacking "ambiguity or irony or uncertainty or perhaps even 'individualism' as potentially thematic material because it is a detailed sketch of a *collective* survival" (191; emphasis in original). See Spillers, "A Hateful Passion, A Lost Love," *Feminist Issues in Literary Scholarship*, ed. Shari Benstock (Bloomington: Indiana UP, 1987) 181–207.

11. For an excellent discussion of intertextuality, see Graham Allen's *Intertextuality* (New York: Routledge, 2000).

12. Of traditions and Black women's writing, Gates explains in his foreword to the Schomburg Library of Nineteenth-Century Black Women Writer's series:

> Literary works configure into a tradition not because of some mystical collective unconscious determined by the biology of race or gender, but because writers read other writers and *ground* their representation of experience in models of language provided largely by other writers to whom they feel akin. It is through this literary revision, amply evident in the *texts* themselves—in formal echoes, recast metaphors, even in parody—that a "tradition" emerges and defines itself. (xviii; emphasis in original)

13. For an excellent discussion of the complexity of Black female subjectivity, see Ann DuCille's "The Occult of True Black Womanhood: Critical Demeanor and Black Feminist Studies," *Signs* 19.3 (1994): 591–629.

14. Of enslaved Black women writers, Hazel Carby posits,

> the authors placed in the foreground their active roles as historical agents as opposed to passive subjects; represented as acting their own visions, they are seen to take decisions over their own lives. They document their sufferings and brutal treatment but in a context that is also *the story of resistance* to that brutality. (*Reconstructing Womanhood* 36; emphasis added)

15. Hortense J. Spillers explains, "An agent endowed with the possibilities of action, or who can make her world, just as she is made by it is the crucial dialectical motion that is missing in deterministic fiction" ("Cross-Currents" 254).

16. See Pierre Nora's "Between Memory and History: *Les Lieux de Mémoire*," *History and Memory in African-American Culture*, ed. Geneviève Fabre and Robert O'Meally (New York: Oxford UP, 1994) 284–300.

Chapter 1 Harriet A. Jacobs's *Incidents in the Life of a Slave Girl*

1. Because it was originally published pseudonymously, Jacobs's narrative was long thought to be written by its editor, Lydia Maria Child, as an abolitionist novel due to its graphic revelations of the sexual abuses inflicted on enslaved Black women. Jean Fagan Yellin painstakingly authenticated the text in 1981.

2. In addition to Deborah Gray White's *Ar'n't I a Woman*, see Jacqueline Jones, *Labor of Love, Labor of Sorrow: Black Women, Work and the Family, from Slavery to the Present* (New York: Basic Books, 1985) and Patricia Morton, *Disfigured Images: The Historical Assault on Afro-American Women* (New York: Praeger, 1991).

3. This compromised situation created radical responses. There are documented cases of enslaved mothers who killed their children as a political act of resistance and of enslaved mothers whose children provided the impetus for resistance as their mothers sought to free them. Two such instances are the cases of Margaret Garner, whose life is the basis of Morrison's *Beloved*, and of Dinah, whose life is the

basis of Williams's *Dessa Rose*. See Herbert Aptheker, *American Negro Slave Revolts* (1943, New York: International, 1974) 287–288, J. Winston Coleman, *Slavery Times in Kentucky* (Chapel Hill: U of North Carolina P, 1940) 178, Stephen Middleton, "The Fugitive Slave Crisis in Cincinnati, 1850–1860: Resistance, Enforcement, and Black Refugees," *The Journal of Negro History* 62 (Winter/Spring 1987): 20–32, and Steven Weisenburger, *Modern Medea: A Family Story of Slavery and Child-Murder from the Old South* (New York: Hill and Wang, 1998). Two studies of related interest are Michael P. Johnson, "Smothered Slave Infants: Were Slave Mothers at Fault?," *The Journal of Southern History* 67 (November 1981): 493–520, and Todd L. Savitt, "Smothering and Overlaying of Virginia Slave Children: A Suggested Explanation," *Bulletin of the History of Medicine* 49 (1975): 400–404.

4. See John Sekora, "Is the Slave Narrative a Species of Autobiography?," in *Studies in Autobiography*, ed. James Olney (New York: Oxford UP, 1988) 99–111.

5. Several critics, such as Mary Helen Washington, Jean Fagan Yellin, and Valerie Smith, observe in their analyses of the text how Jacobs reappropriates the stylistic techniques of the nineteenth-century sentimental novel as well as the emancipatory narrative. See, for example, Washington, "Meditations on History: The Slave Woman's Voice" *Invented Lives: Narratives of Black Women 1860–1960*, ed. Mary Helen Washington (New York: Doubleday, 1987) 3–15; Yellin, "Texts and Contexts of Harriet Jacobs's *Incidents in the Life of a Slave Girl: Written by Herself*," *The Slave's Narrative*, ed. Charles T. Davis and Henry Louis Gates, Jr. (New York: Oxford UP, 1985) 262–282; and Smith, "'Loopholes of Retreat': Architecture and Ideology in Harriet Jacobs's *Incidents in the Life of a Slave Girl*," *Reading Black, Reading Feminist*, ed. Henry Louis Gates, Jr. (New York: A Meridian Book, 1990) 212–226.

6. In *The Slave Community* (1979), John Blassingame concluded that the narrative was inauthentic due to its orderliness and its melodrama (373).

7. After she became free, Jacobs worked as a domestic, labored for the abolition of slavery, and never married. In 1897, she died in Washington, DC.

8. This liaison could be used to give validity to the construction of the Jezebel stereotype. If so, it provides evidence that wanton sexual pleasure was not the goal of the Jezebel, but rather personal and political empowerment.

9. Sharon Davie observes in this same vein: "The female hero's quest in Jacobs's narrative is for the freedom to exercise her will. . . . Her aim is to free her children and herself from slavery, but the dramatic action focuses on Linda Brent's struggle to control access to her own body" (87). See Davie, "'Reader, my story ends with freedom': Harriet Jacobs's *Incidents in the Life of a Slave Girl*," *Famous Last Words: Changes in Gender and Narrative Closure*, ed. Alison Booth (Charlottesville: UP of Virginia, 1993) 86–109.

Chapter 2   Not Enough of the Past: Octavia E. Butler's *Kindred*

1. In *Tar Baby*, Morrison uses this phrase to describe why Jadine is a cultural orphan. For a discussion of this, see Evelyn Hawthorne, "On Gaining the Double-Vision: *Tar Baby* as Diasporean Novel," *Black American Literature Forum* 22.1 (Spring 1988): 97–107, and Marilyn S. Mobley, "Narrative Dilemma: Jadine as Cultural Orphan in *Tar Baby*," *Toni Morrison: Critical Perspectives Past and Present*, ed. Henry Louis Gates, Jr. and K. Anthony Appiah (New York: Amistad P, 1993) 284–292. One's "ancient properties" are those cultural verities that give one, to use another Morrisonian term, *rootedness* as a culturally authentic being.

2. *Sankofa*, directed and produced by Gerima, has an interesting genesis. Gerima, a Howard University professor of film, and his wife, also a filmmaker, financed and

produced *Sankofa*. This endeavor took nine years to complete. With a single copy, they arranged showings at receptive theaters until they were able to make enough money to mass produce the film. *Sankofa* had a small yet successful run as an independent and is now available for purchase. Many high schools, colleges, and universities use it in teaching about slavery. Because they do not stock movies with such graphic violence, according to one of its employees in the DC/Metropolitan area, Blockbuster Video refuses to stock it. Gerima now has a production company, Mypheduh, Inc., as well as a bookstore, Sankofa Video and Books, in Washington, DC, where he distributes his film.

3. In an interview with novelist Randall Kenan, Butler reveals that she extensively researched slavery while writing *Kindred*. The setting of the novel is an actual geographic location in Maryland—Easton—which Butler visited. Easton is not far from Frederick Douglass's birthplace of Tuckahoe. See Christine Levecq's "Power and Repetition: Philosophies of (Literary) History in Octavia E. Butler's *Kindred*," *Contemporary Literature* 41.3 (2000): 543, for a discussion of the intertextual nature of Douglass's *Narrative of the Life of Frederick Douglass, An American Slave, Written by Himself* (1845) and *Kindred*. Butler spent numerous hours in Washington-area libraries and historical societies; she also toured preserved plantations such as President George Washington's Mount Vernon. Additionally, she read numerous emancipatory narratives. Of her horrific research she comments, "One of the things I realized was that I was not going to be able to come anywhere near presenting slavery as it was. I was going to have to do a somewhat cleaned-up version of slavery, or no one would be willing to read it" (Kenan 497). Butler grounds her text, then, in historical facts. She augments factual evidence in order to give a full rendering of the enslaved Black woman's life and to give a voice to this traditionally voiceless woman.

4. Butler categorically denies that *Kindred* is science fiction because "there's no science" in it; rather, she describes it as a fantasy. See Kenan 495.

5. Ironically, Butler intended for the protagonist of *Kindred* to be a Black man. She altered her plan because she "couldn't realistically keep him alive." She says:

> So many things that he did would have been likely to get him killed. He wouldn't even have time to learn the rules . . . before he was killed for not knowing them because he would be perceived as dangerous. The female main character, who might be equally dangerous, would not be perceived so. She might be beaten, she might be abused, but she probably wouldn't be killed and that's why I wrote it. . . . That sexism, in a sense, worked in her favor. (Rowell 51)

6. Butler intimates that Kevin was involved in abolitionist activity and was injured because of his actions. Kevin's character is complex. In her contrast of Kevin and Rufus, Butler suggests that the changes Kevin experiences as a result of his time travel are not all positive as he begins to remind Dana more and more of Rufus.

7. See Spillers's "Mama's Baby, Papa's Maybe: An American Grammar Book" for her provocative discussion of Black women's bodies in terms of body and flesh.

8. I realize that this sentence may be read as essentializing motherhood. Sometimes I think it is as dangerous to remove all characteristics from subject positions as it is to affix specific and inflexible characteristics.

9. The children's names are Aaron, Miriam, Joseph, and Hagar. In the Bible, Aaron and Miriam, siblings of Moses, were enslaved in ancient Egypt. They were released by Pharaoh after God sent Moses to secure the freedom of the Israelites. Joseph, son of Jacob and Rachel, was sold into Egyptian slavery by his jealous brothers, and later he was freed by Pharaoh. Finally, Hagar was the Egyptian servant of Abraham and Sarah. Because Sarah was unable to bear children, Hagar gave birth

to a son, Ishmael, by Abraham. After Sarah miraculously conceived and delivered Isaac, Hagar was freed.

10. This is not unlike the choice that Toni Morrison's Sethe makes in *Beloved* when she attempts, as she describes it, to put her children where they will be safe. One may recall that Sethe's plan was to kill all her children as well as herself.

11. I use the term "free" loosely here because Alice's mother is certainly not free in any true, democratic sense.

12. This phrase, "the price of liberty is eternal vigilance," is from Douglass's speech, "The Glorious Morning of Liberty," delivered in Rochester, NY, on December 28, 1862, three days before the Emancipation Proclamation became law. Here he advocated steadfastness in the fight for freedom, in spite of the gains of the moment. This phrase will be significant later in my discussion of Cary's *The Price of a Child*. See Frederick Douglass, "The Glorious Morning of Liberty," *www.africana.com/ Articles/tt_342.htm*.

13. The National Advisory Commission on Civil Disorders, chaired by Illinois Governor Otto Kerner, was appointed by President Lyndon Johnson in 1967 after numerous racial upheavals in urban areas. Popularly known as the Kerner Commission, its report warned that the United States was moving toward two separate societies—one black and poor, the other affluent and white. Andrew Hacker's *Two Nations: Black and White, Separate, Hostile, Unequal* (New York: Ballantine Books, 1992) shows how accurate the Kerner Commission's findings were.

14. See Kenneth O'Reilly's *Nixon's Piano: Presidents and Racial Politics from Washington to Clinton* (New York: The Free Press, 1995) for an illuminating discussion of not only Nixon's politics and policies, but all of the presidents of the United States, through the Clinton administration.

15. Presidents Ronald Reagan and George H. W. Bush also used variants of the divisive "Southern strategy"—a strategy that basically sought to pit White against Black in terms of race and economics—to succeed in 1980, 1984, and 1988.

16. Butler has said that she wrote *Kindred* as a type of instruction for Black readers who suffered from a lack of their own historical knowledge and who exhibited impatience and intolerance about the past and its relationship to the present. *Kindred* was "a kind of reaction to some of the things going on during the '60s when people were feeling ashamed of, or more strongly angry with their parents for not having improved things faster, and I wanted to take a person from today and send that person back to slavery" (Kenan 496).

Chapter 3   History, Agency, and Subjectivity in Sherley Anne Williams's *Dessa Rose*

1. See Herbert Aptheker, *American Negro Slave Revolts* (1943, New York: International, 1974) 287–289, and Angela Davis, "Reflections on the Black Woman's Role in the Community of Slaves," *The Black Scholar* 3.4 (1971): 2–15. Of note, Davis was incarcerated, like Dessa Rose, when she wrote this essay.

2. Williams was a gifted poet, short story writer, and novelist. She created the character of Dessa Rose (who at one time is named Odessa by Williams) in each of these genres, building to the novel. See Williams's "I Sing the Song for Our Mother," *The Peacock Poems* (Hanover, NH: Wesleyan UP, 1975) and her "Meditations on History" *Midnight Birds*, ed. Mary Helen Washington (New York: Anchor, 1980).

3. Mae G. Henderson writes, "If the relationship between Styron and Turner can be described as creative misreading (misprision), I would describe that between Williams

and Styron as one of corrective rereading." See Mae G. Henderson, "(W)riting the Work and Working the Rites," *Black American Literature Forum* 23.4 (1989): 657.

4. See William L. Andrews, *To Tell a Free Story: The First Century of Afro-American Autobiography, 1760–1865* (Urbana: U of Illinois P, 1986).

5. In his examination of Styron's *Confessions* and Williams's *Dessa Rose*, John Inscoe takes issue with the criticism of Styron by pointing out that Williams "never had to make such a defense of her 'presumption' in internalizing the viewpoint of Dessa Rose" (432). He concludes that Williams's "race and sex defused any doubts about her qualifications for impersonating a slave woman" (432). He asks:

> After all, what in the experience of a late twentieth-century California native with a graduate degree from Brown University and an academic appointment at the University of California at San Diego qualifies her to write any more knowingly about an Alabama slave in the 1840s than the experiences of a white Virginian qualify him to write about a black Virginian? (432–433)

While I do not want to go down the slippery slope of essentialism, like Toni Morrison I am befuddled that "suddenly . . . 'race' does not exist . . . [after three centuries of insisting that] 'race' was *the* determining factor in human development. . . . It always seemed to me that the people who invented the hierarchy of 'race' when it was convenient for them ought not to be the ones to explain it away, now that it does not suit their purposes for it to exist" ("Unspeakable Things Unspoken" 370; emphasis in original). What Inscoe suggests is that an individual's experience is not related or connected to race and its long history in the U.S. or that regional similarities trump racial differences, or should. That Black folks' daily existence, since the end of the Civil War, in *all* parts of this country, and in *all* walks of life has been influenced, mediated, or affected by a racism born of color prejudice that either gave birth to chattel slavery or was used to justify its existence provides, I believe, some degree of authority. See John C. Inscoe, "Slave Rebellion in the First Person: The Literary 'Confessions' of Nat Turner and Dessa Rose," *The Virginia Magazine of History and Biography* 97.4 (1989): 419–436 and Toni Morrison, "Unspeakable Things Unspoken: The Afro-American Presence in American Literature," *Within the Circle: An Anthology of African American Literary Criticism from the Harlem Renaissance to the Present* (Durham: Duke UP, 1994) 368–398.

6. For his portrayal of Nat Turner in controversial ways, for example, as a religious fanatic who masturbatorily lusted for White women, Styron received a plethora of criticism from African-American writers. See *William Styron's Nat Turner: Ten Black Writers Respond*, ed. John Henrik Clarke (Boston: Beacon P, 1968). For Styron's retrospective response to this criticism, see William Styron, "Jimmy in the House," *James Baldwin: The Legacy*, ed. Quincy Troupe (New York: Simon & Schuster, 1989) 43–46. Styron also included a response in the twenty-fifth anniversary edition. Styron's *Confessions* won the Pulitzer Prize in 1968. See also Albert E. Stone, *The Return of Nat Turner: History, Literature, and Cultural Politics in Sixties America* (Athens: U of Georgia, 1992).

7. The first section is a revision of Williams's short story, "Meditations on History," whose title signifies upon the author's note of *The Confessions of Nat Turner* in which Styron offers his novel as "a meditation on history."

One might wonder, if the three sections represent the White man's story, the White woman's story, and the Black woman's story, where is the Black man's story? His story is interwoven with all three stories, signaling his significance in all three. While he is not the center of any section, he is not marginalized, effaced, or erased.

8. Dessa Rose's amanuensis, Adam Nehemiah, is an intertextual character. In her

edition of *Incidents in the Life of a Slave Girl,* Yellin identifies a minister to whom Linda Brent alludes in her discussion of slavery and religion as Rev. Nehemiah Adams, a White supporter of slavery who wrote an apologist tract, *A South-Side View of Slavery; or, Three Months in the South in 1854.* See *Incidents* 272. Mary Kemp Davis and Mae G. Henderson also note this intertexual reference in their studies of *Dessa Rose.* See Davis, "Everybody Knows Her Name: The Recovery of the Past in Sherley Anne Williams's *Dessa Rose,*" *Callaloo* 13 (1989): 544–558 and Henderson, "Speaking in Tongues: Dialogics, Dialectics, and the Black Woman Writer's Literary Tradition," *Changing Our Own Words: Essays on Criticism, Theory, and Writing by Black Women,* ed. Cheryl A. Wall (New Brunswick: Rutgers UP, 1989) 16–37.

9. Williams's use of names in *Dessa Rose* is significant. Williams signifies on the story of Nat Turner in naming her revolutionary enslaved Black men Nate and Harker, whose name signifies on Nat Turner's lieutenant, Hark. For a more general examination of names in *Dessa Rose,* see Debra Walker King, *Deep Talk: Reading African American Literary Names* (Charlottesville: UP of Virginia, 1998) 131–165.

10. Ruth's name and characterization by Williams remind the reader of the biblical Ruth, who proclaimed to her loved one as does Williams's Ruth, "thy people shall be my people." See The Book of Ruth, 1.16.

11. One of the families that Nat Turner and his followers attacked was named Vaughan.

12. In her discussion of the healing properties in *Dessa Rose,* Farah Jasmine Griffin writes, "Kaine affirms and loves those very parts of Dessa that white standards of normalcy and beauty degrade" (528).

13. Through her abbreviation of the title of Nehemiah's book, Williams may be signifying on the title of Alex Haley's *Roots* (1976), a book that inspired an important aspect of African American history long dormant—genealogical research.

14. While Styron depicts Nat Turner as a Black man who lusted for White women, Williams's Nathan (also known as Nate) enjoys a mutually desirous sexual relationship with Ruth.

15. For an illuminating discussion of this phenomenon, see Martha Hodes's *White Women, Black Men: Illicit Sex in the 19th-Century South* (New Haven: Yale UP, 1997).

16. Williams's reference to one paying a debt for one's humanity engages a recurring trope in the *oeuvre* of James Baldwin.

17. In the Bible, Elijah and Nathan are prophets and heroes as are Williams's Elijah and Nathan. Linda, the mulatto woman on the coffle from Montgomery whom the White men sexually abuse in *Dessa Rose,* brings to mind Harriet Jacobs's Linda Brent. Additionally, Styron writes in *Confessions* that "Nat alone had the key to all this ruction" (17). In her revision, Williams literally gives the keys to the coffle to Nate, the assistant to the trader.

18. Similarly, Styron's narrator characterizes Nat as a "black devil" (18).

19. In the Bible, Dorcas was resurrected from the dead by Peter. See Acts 9:36–43. Dessa resurrects Dorcas's memory in order to place Dorcas's life in a more accurate perspective.

Chapter 4 The Metaphysics of Black Female Identity in Toni Morrison's *Beloved*

1. The *griot,* in some West African cultures, is the storyteller who records, reflects, and interprets his community's history and culture. He is a wise man who functions as the cultural conservator.

2. Continuing, Christian recounts that Morrison has stated "that for African Ameri-

cans, at least until the recent past, the experience of spirits communicating with the living was a natural, rather than some kind of weird, unnatural event" ("Beloved, She's Ours" 43).

Morrison has described Beloved as "a spirit on one hand, literally she is what Sethe thinks she is, her child returned to her from the dead. And she must function like that in the text. She is also another kind of dead which is not spiritual but flesh, which is, a survivor from the true, factual slave ship" (Darling 247).

3. Studies of Morrison's *Beloved* are legion. The range of responses to this novel, nationally and internationally, is phenomenal. One collection that is representative of the burgeoning critical work on *Beloved* is eds. William L. Andrews and Nellie Y. McKay, *Toni Morrison's Beloved: A Casebook*, (New York: Oxford UP, 1999). See also ed. Carl Plasa, *Toni Morrison: Beloved*, (New York: Columbia UP, 1998).

4. To effect this, Morrison "[keeps] the reader preoccupied with the nature of the incredible spirit world while being supplied a controlled diet of the incredible political world" (396). See Toni Morrison, "Unspeakable Things Unspoken: The Afro-American Presence in American Literature," *Within the Circle: An Anthology of African American Literary Criticism from the Harlem Renaissance to the Present*, ed. Angelyn Mitchell (Durham: Duke UP, 1994) 368–98.

5. While researching materials for inclusion in *The Black Book*, the book of Black memorabilia she edited in the 1970s, Morrison discovered a newspaper clipping, originally printed in *The American Baptist* and reprinted in *The Black People's Almanac*, relating the story of Margaret Garner, the slave woman on whom *Beloved* is based. It is ironic that Morrison's Sethe remains physically free when, in fact, Margaret Garner was returned to slavery. See P. S. Bassett, "A Visit to the Slave Mother Who Killed Her Child," *The Black Book* (New York: Random, 1974) 10.

6. For a historical study of Margaret Garner, see Stephen Middleton, "The Fugitive Slave Crisis in Cincinnati, 1850–1860: Resistance, Enforcement, and Black Refugees," *The Journal of Negro History* 62 (1987): 20–32 as well as Steven Weisenburger, *Modern Medea: A Family Story of Slavery and Child-Murder from the Old South* (New York: Hill and Wang, 1998).

7. Morrison stated that she intended to give the house a separate identity, to personify it "by its own activity, not the pasted on desire for personality" (395). See Toni Morrison, "Unspeakable Things Unspoken: The Afro-American Presence in American Literature," in *Within the Circle: An Anthology of African American Literary Criticism from the Harlem Renaissance to the Present* (Durham: Duke UP, 1994) 368–98.

In a conversation with my mother I learned that, once upon a time, bluestone was prescribed by healers, both schooled and unschooled, for its curative properties. For example, if one suffered from a rash on one's foot, the doctor might prescribe that one soak the affected area in water containing bluestone, which was available for purchase at the pharmacy. One wonders, then, about the healing properties of 124 Bluestone Road. Although it is troubled, 124 Bluestone is the site of Sethe's healing and the impetus for Denver's healing. I thank Evelyn W. Mitchell for this insight.

8. In this way, Morrison takes the enslaved Black man's narrative in new directions. We see in *Beloved* episodes of dehumanizing brutality and sexual assault, but we also see a son's love for his mother, the respect for Black womanhood as they wait for Sethe to choose, and the vulnerability of Black manhood when unable to protect loved ones.

9. Employing such elements as claustrophobic enclosures and personification of inanimate objects, Morrison employs elements of the Gothic to engage her reader's narrative imagination.

10. Schoolteacher is summoned because the widowed Mrs. Garner, a White woman, needs a White man to run her plantation.

11. For a discussion of the psychological effects of Sethe's complicity in her dehumanization by making the ink (or the milk), see Anne E. Goldman, "'I Made the Ink': (Literary) Production and Reproduction in *Dessa Rose* and *Beloved*," *Feminist Studies* 16 (1990): 313–330.

12. Of Sethe, Jennifer Fitzgerald writes:

> Because slavery denies parental claims, Sethe insists upon her role as mother. She thus refutes her position as object in the discourse of slavery by asserting her position as subject in the discourse of good mother. But the version of motherhood she articulates offers an exaggerated, idealized view of exclusive maternal responsibility (677).

See Jennifer Fitzgerald, "Selfhood and Community: Psychoanalysis and Discourse in *Beloved*," *Modern Fiction Studies* 39 (1993): 669–687.

13. Because of Morrison's description of his indigo skin, as well as her description of his cultural and spiritual rootedness, I read Sixo as an African man.

Chapter 5   J. California Cooper's *Family*

1. A prolific writer, J. California Cooper has received surprisingly little scholar: attention. In addition to her three novels, she has written several collections of short stories and many award-winning plays. In reviews of her work, Cooper has been favorably compared with Zora Neale Hurston in her use of figurative language.

2. See Elizabeth Beaulieu, *Black Women Writers and the American Neo-Slave Narrative: Femininity Unfettered* (Westport: Greenwood P, 1999) especially 83–108.

3. See, for example, Cathy Caruth, *Unclaimed Experience: Trauma, Narrative, and History* (Baltimore: Johns Hopkins UP, 1996) as well as *Testimony: Crises of Witnessing in Literature, Psychoanalysis, and History*, eds. Shoshana Felman and Dori Laub (New York: Routledge, 1992).

4. This passage brings to mind Paul D's observation about the rooster, Mister: "Mister, he looked so . . . free. Better than me. Stronger, tougher. Son a bitch couldn't even get out the shell by hisself but he was still king. . . . Mister was allowed to be and stay what he was. But I wasn't allowed to be and stay what I was" (*Beloved* 72). I thank Farah Jasmine Griffin for suggesting this parallel.

5. Sue's ancestor had been sent, we are told, to America as a White bondswoman and had served seven years in hard labor. But her "need turned to opportunity and a good solid marriage with a hard-working man" (70). Thus, Cooper weaves the indentured White servant's narrative, as Morrison does with the character of Amy Denver, into her liberatory narrative, showing that all who came to North America did not come under the same conditions and circumstances.

6. One thinks here of the first example of an interracial couple in African American literature, Mag Smith and Jim, Frado's parents, in Harriet E. Wilson's *Our Nig; or, Sketches from the Life of a Free Black* (1859; New York: Vintage, 1983).

7. For an excellent discussion of the "mammy" figure in *Dessa Rose*, see Ashraf H. A. Rushdy, "Reading Mammy: The Subject of Relation in Sherley Anne Williams' *Dessa Rose*," *African American Review* 27.3 (1992): 365–389.

8. Twain's construction of the enslaved mother is satirical; Cooper's is not.

Chapter 6   The Economies of Bondage and Freedom in Lorene Cary's *The Price of a Child*

1. In a 1999 interview, Mr. Conyers candidly revealed that, while he hopes his legislation will one day be successful, he is content for now if it will cause people to

discuss the issues it raises. See Kevin Merida, "Did Freedom Alone Pay a Nation's Debt? Rep. John Conyers Jr. Has a Question. He's Willing to Wait a Long Time for the Right Answer," *The Washington Post* 23 Nov. 1999: C1.

2. See ed. Roy L. Brooks, *When Sorry Isn't Enough: The Controversy Over Apologies and Reparations for Human Injustices* (New York: New York UP, 1999).

3. For additional information concerning Reconstruction, see Eric Foner and Olivia Mahoney, *America's Reconstruction: People and Politics after the Civil War* (New York: HarperCollins, 1995), Claude F. Oubre, *Forty Acres and a Mule: The Freedmen's Bureau and Black Land Ownership* (Baton Rouge: Louisiana State UP, 1978), and Ira Berlin, et al., *Free at Last: A Documentary History of Slavery, Freedom, and the Civil War* (New York: New Press, 1993). See also Randall Robinson, *The Debt: What America Owes to Blacks* (New York: Dutton, 2000).

4. William Still's *The Underground Railroad* (1872) remains the best source of information concerning the Underground Railroad and the African Americans who emancipated themselves.

5. This line brings to mind how Williams's Dessa better understood her life as she remembered and recounted her life's story. The equation seems to be memory and orality equal knowing one's self.

6. I am signifying here on Anna Julia Cooper's *A Voice from the South* (1892), one of the first works of Black feminist thought.

7. Our country continues to mythologize our past as it relates to slavery. For example, the relationship between Sally Hemings and Thomas Jefferson remains a site of contestation because of our inability to reconcile Jefferson's public work with his private self. Thus, some choose to accept the narrative that better fits the myth of American democracy. That eight of the first twelve Presidents of the United States owned enslaved African Americans is not a fact widely known or advanced. We know, however, that all were freedom fighters. Some clarity is emerging in spite of our illusory veneer of American history. Until recently, the existence of enslaved African Americans went without comment during tours of George Washington's Mount Vernon, and Congress mandated that Civil War battleground tours now include, because they did not before, commentary on the relationship of slavery to the War and to the battleground sites.

Epilogue "Textual Healing" and the Liberatory Narrative

1. I thank the Smithsonian Institution and Dr. Richard Kurin and staff for permission to use this excerpt from the program. America's Millennium was a project of The White House Millennium Council, the Smithsonian Institution, the National Park Service, and the National Park Foundation, in conjunction with the District of Columbia government.

2. I borrow the epilogue's title and its underlying premise from Farah Jasmine Griffin's "Textual Healing: Claiming Black Women's Bodies, the Erotic and Resistance in Contemporary Novels of Slavery," *Callaloo* 19.2 (1996): 519–536. Of course, Griffin's title signifies on Marvin Gaye's 1984 hit "Sexual Healing."

3. Perhaps we are beginning to face our history of slavery. In 2000, Congress approved H.R. 5157: *The Freedmen's Bureau Records Preservation Act of 2000*. This bill requires the government to preserve and to catalog existing documents from the United States Freedmen's Bureau, the official clearinghouse for the formerly enslaved African Americans in the nineteenth century. These documents, now languishing and deteriorating in local field offices as well in the National Archives, are a historical treasure trove as they contain valuable information and documentation about all aspects of slavery, its participants, and its victims. Overall, these

documents chart the everyday movement of African Americans from slavery to freedom. For example, information concerning enslaved African Americans, their enslavers, Civil War veterans, plantation owners, and anyone who may have had dealings with the formerly enslaved is recorded in these official documents. Preserving this history may signal a step in the right direction: that we are ready to learn from our history of slavery, instead of ignoring it and leaving it to decay.

The World Conference Against Racism, Racial Discrimination, Xenophobia, and Related Intolerance met August 31–September 7, 2001, in Durban, South Africa. Two of the many issues discussed were an apology for slavery and a call for reparations. On September 8, the delegation issued the following declaration on slavery: "We acknowledge that slavery and the slave trade, including the trans-Atlantic slave trade, were appalling tragedies in the history of humanity not only because of their abhorrent barbarism but also in terms of their magnitude, organized nature and especially their negation of the essence of the victims and further acknowledge that slavery and the slave trade are a crime against humanity and should always have been so, especially the trans-Atlantic slave trade, and are among the major sources and manifestations of racism, racial discrimination, xenophobia and related intolerance, and that Africans and people of African descent, Asians and people of Asian descent and indigenous peoples were victims of these acts and continue to be victims of their consequences." On the issue of reparations, the conference recognized the relationship between the past injustices of slavery and current economics. However, it did not issue a statement of support for specific reparations. Perhaps this type of global attention will help the United States in its attempt to come to terms with our history of slavery. Dilday, Erika. "Conference Concludes with Some Agreement, Some Disappointments," *www.confnews.com/sep/thedurbanconferenceconcludessep_10.htm* (2001).

Works Cited

Allen, Graham. *Intertextuality*. New York: Routledge, 2000.

Alter, Jonathan. "The Long Shadow of Slavery." *Newsweek*. 08 December 1997: 58–63.

Andrews, William L. *To Tell a Free Story: The First Century of Afro-American Autobiography, 1760–1865*. Urbana: U of Illinois P, 1986.

Aptheker, Herbert. *American Negro Slave Revolts*. 1943. New York: International, 1974.

Bakhtin, Mikhail. *The Dialogic Imagination*. Trans. Caryl Emerson and Michael Holquist. Ed. Michael Holquist. Austin: U of Texas P, 1981.

Ball, Edward. *Slaves in the Family*. New York: Ballantine Books, 1999.

Bambara, Toni Cade. *Deep Sightings and Rescue Missions: Fiction, Essays, and Conversations*. New York: Vintage, 1999.

———. *The Salt Eaters*. 1980. New York: Vintage, 1992.

Barthes, Roland. "Theory of the Text." *Untying the Text*. Ed. Robert Young. New York: Routledge, 1981. 31–47.

Beaulieu, Elizabeth Ann. *Black Women Writers and the American Neo-Slave Narrative: Femininity Unfettered*. Westport: Greenwood P, 1999.

Bell, Bernard W. *The Afro-American Novel and Its Tradition*. Amherst: U of Massachusetts P, 1987.

Blassingame, John. *The Slave Community: Plantation Life in the Antebellum South*. 1972. New York: Oxford, 1979.

Braxton, Joanne. "Harriet Jacobs' *Incidents in the Life of a Slave Girl*: The Re-definition of the Slave Narrative Genre." *The Massachusetts Review* 27 (1986): 379–387.

Bulworth. Dir. and prod. Warren Beatty. Perf. Warren Beatty and Halle Berry. Twentieth-Century Fox, 1998.

Butler, Octavia. *Kindred*. 1979. Boston: Beacon P, 1988.

Butterfield, Stephen. *Black Autobiography in America*. Amherst: U of Massachusetts P, 1974.

Calinescu, Matei. *Five Faces of Modernity: Modernism, Avant-Garde, Decadence, Kitsch, Postmodernism*. Durham: Duke UP, 1987.

Callahan, John F. *In the African-American Grain: The Pursuit of Voice in Twentieth-Century Black Fiction*. Urbana: U of Illinois P, 1988.

Carby, Hazel V. "Ideologies of Black Folk: The Historical Novel of Slavery." *Slavery and the Literary Imagination*. Eds. Deborah E. McDowell and Arnold Rampersad. Baltimore: Johns Hopkins UP, 1989. 125–143.

———. *Reconstructing Womanhood: The Emergence of the Afro-American Woman Novelist*. New York: Oxford UP, 1987.

Caruth, Cathy. *Unclaimed Experience: Trauma, Narrative, and History*. Baltimore: Johns Hopkins UP, 1996.

Cary, Lorene. *The Price of a Child*. New York: Vintage, 1995.

Christian, Barbara. "Beloved, She's Ours." *Narrative* 5.1 (January 1997): 36–49.

———. "'Somebody Forgot to Tell Somebody Something': African-American Women's Historical Novels." *Wild Women in the Whirlwind: Afra-American Culture and the Contemporary Literary Renaissance*. Eds. Joanne M. Braxton and Andree Nicola McLaughlin. New Brunswick: Rutgers UP, 1990. 326–341.

Clarke, John Henrik, ed. *William Styron's Nat Turner: Ten Black Writers Respond*. Boston: Beacon P, 1968.

Clinton, Catherine. "'With a Whip in His Hand': Rape, Memory, and African American Women." *History and Memory in African American Culture*. Eds. Geneviève Fabre and Robert O'Meally. New York: Oxford UP, 1994. 205–218.

Cooper, Anna Julia. *A Voice from the South*. 1892. Intro. Mary Helen Washington. New York: Oxford UP, 1988.

Cooper, J. California. *Family*. New York: Doubleday, 1991.

Crossley, Robert. Introduction. *Kindred*. By Octavia Butler. Boston: Beacon P, 1988. ix–xxvii.

Darling, Marsha. "In the Realm of Responsibility: A Conversation with Toni Morrison." *Women's Review of Books* 5 (March 1978): 5–6. Rpt. in *Conversations with Toni Morrison*. Ed. Danille Taylor-Guthrie. Jackson: UP of Mississippi, 1994. 246–254.

Davis, Angela. "Reflections on the Black Woman's Role in the Community of Slaves." *The Black Scholar* 3.4 (1971): 2–15.

———. *Woman, Race and Class*. New York: Vintage, 1983.

Davis, Mary Kemp. "Everybody Knows Her Name: The Recovery of the Past in Sherley Anne Williams's *Dessa Rose*." *Callaloo* 13 (1989): 544–558.

Dobson, Joanne. "The American Renaissance Reenvisioned." *The (Other) American Traditions: Nineteenth-Century Women Writers*. Ed. Joyce Warren. New Brunswick: Rutgers UP, 1993. 164–182.

Doriani, Beth M. "Black Womanhood in Nineteenth-Century America: Subversion and Self-Construction in Two Women's Autobiographies." *American Quarterly* 43 (1991): 199–222.

Doyle, Laura. *Bordering on the Body: The Racial Matrix of Modern Fiction and Culture*. New York: Oxford UP, 1994.

Du Bois, W.E.B. *The Souls of Black Folk*. 1903. Eds. Henry Louis Gates, Jr. and Terri Hume Oliver. New York: Norton, 1999.

Finney, Brian. "Temporal Defamiliarization in Toni Morrison's *Beloved*." *Obsidian II* 5 (1990): 20–36.

Fitzgerald, Jennifer. "Selfhood and Community: Psychoanalysis and Discourse in *Beloved*," *Modern Fiction Studies* 39 (1993): 669–687.

Foster, Frances Smith. "Resisting *Incidents*." *Harriet Jacobs and Incidents in the Life of a Slave Girl*. Eds. Deborah M. Garfield and Rafia Zafar. New York: Cambridge UP, 1996. 57–75.

———. *Witnessing Slavery: The Development of Ante-bellum Slave Narratives*. Westport: Greenwood P, 1979.

Friend, Beverly. "Time Travel as a Feminist Didactic in Works by Phyllis Eisenstein,

Marlys Millhiser, and Octavia Butler." *Extrapolation: A Journal of Science Fiction and Fantasy* 23 (1982): 50–55.

Gates, Henry Louis, Jr. *Figures in Black: Words, Signs and the Racial Self.* New York: Oxford UP, 1987.

———. Introduction. *Reading Black, Reading Feminist: A Critical Anthology.* Ed. Henry Louis Gates, Jr. New York: A Meridian Book, 1990. 1–17.

———. *The Signifying Monkey: A Theory of African-American Literary Criticism.* New York: Oxford UP, 1988.

Goldman, Anne E. "'I Made the Ink': (Literary) Production and Reproduction in *Dessa Rose* and *Beloved.*" *Feminist Studies* 16 (Summer 1990): 313–330.

Govan, Sandra Y. "Homage to Tradition: Octavia Butler Renovates the Historical Novel." *MELUS* 13 (1986): 79–96.

Griffin, Farah Jasmine. "Textual Healing: Claiming Black Women's Bodies, the Erotic and Resistance in Contemporary Novels of Slavery." *Callaloo* 19.2 (1996): 519–536.

Haisty, Donna. "Cries of Outrage: Three Novelists' Use of History." *Mississippi Quarterly* 49.4 (Fall 1996): 727–741.

Harris, Trudier. "Escaping Slavery but Not Its Images." *Toni Morrison: Critical Perspectives Past and Present.* Eds. Henry Louis Gates, Jr. and K. A. Appiah. New York: Amistad, 1993. 330–341.

Hartman, Saidiya V. *Scenes of Subjection: Terror, Slavery, and Self-Making in Nineteenth-Century America.* New York: Oxford UP, 1997.

Heller, Dana. "Reconstructing Kin: Family, History, and Narrative in Toni Morrison's *Beloved.*" *College Literature* 21.2 (June 1994): 105–117.

Henderson, Mae G. "Speaking in Tongues: Dialogics, Dialectics, and the Black Woman Writer's Literary Tradition." *Changing Our Own Words: Essays on Criticism, Theory, and Writing by Black Women.* Ed. Cheryl A. Wall. New Brunswick: Rutgers UP, 1989. 16–37.

———. "Toni Morrison's *Beloved*: Re-Membering the Body as Historical Text." *Comparative American Identities: Race, Sex, and Nationality in the Modern Text.* Ed. Hortense J. Spillers. New York: Routledge, 1991. 63–86.

Hirsch, Marianne. *The Mother/Daughter Plot: Narrative, Psychoanalysis, Feminism.* Bloomington: Indiana UP, 1989.

Holloway, Karla F. C. "*Beloved*: A Spiritual." *Callaloo* 13.3 (Summer 1990): 516–525.

hooks, bell. *Black Looks: Race and Representation.* Boston: South End P, 1992.

———. *Talking Back: Thinking Feminist, Thinking Black.* Boston: South End P, 1989.

House, Elizabeth B. "Toni Morrison's Ghost: The Beloved Who Is Not Beloved." *Studies in American Fiction* 18 (1990): 17–26.

Hurston, Zora Neale. *Their Eyes Were Watching God.* 1937. Urbana: U of Illinois P, 1978.

Hutcheon, Linda. *A Poetics of Postmodernism: History, Theory, Fiction.* New York: Routledge, 1989.

Jacobs, Harriet A. [Linda Brent]. *Incidents in the Life of a Slave Girl: Written by Herself.* 1861. Ed. Jean Fagan Yellin. Cambridge: Harvard UP, 1987.

Jones, Gayl. *Corregidora.* 1975. Boston: Beacon P, 1986.

Jones, Jacqueline. *Labor of Love, Labor of Sorrow: Black Women, Work and the Family, from Slavery to the Present.* New York: Basic Books, 1985.

Kaplan, Carla. "Narrative Contracts and Emancipatory Readers: *Incidents in the Life of a Slave Girl.*" *The Yale Journal of Criticism: Interpretation in the Humanities* 6.1 (Spring 1993): 93–120.

Kenan, Randall. "An Interview with Octavia E. Butler." *Callaloo* 14 (1991): 495–504.

King, Nicole. "Meditations and Mediations: Issues of History and Fiction in *Dessa Rose*." *Soundings* 76.2–3 (Summer/Fall 1993): 351–368.

Kristeva, Julia. *Desire in Language: A Semiotic Approach to Literature and Art*. Trans. Thomas Gora, Alice Jardine, and Leon S. Roudiez. New York: Columbia UP, 1984.

Krumholz, Linda. "The Ghosts of Slavery: Historical Recovery in Toni Morrison's *Beloved*." *African American Review* 26 (1992): 395–408.

Kubitschek, Missy Dehn. *Claiming the Heritage: African-American Women Novelists and History*. Jackson: UP of Mississippi, 1991.

Laub, Dori. "Bearing Witness, or the Vicissitudes of Listening." *Testimony: Crises of Witnessing in Literature, Psychoanalysis, and History*. Eds. Shoshana Felman and Dori Laub. New York: Routledge, 1992. 57–74.

———. "An Event without a Witness: Truth, Testimony and Survival." *Testimony: Crises of Witnessing in Literature, Psychoanalysis, and History*. Eds. Shoshana Felman and Dori Laub. New York: Routledge, 1992. 75–92.

Lazare, Aaron. "Go Ahead, Say You're Sorry." *Psychology Today*. 28.1 (January/February, 1995): 40–43, 76–78.

Lerner, Gerda. *Why History Matters: Life and Thought*. New York: Oxford UP, 1997.

Levecq, Christine. "Power and Repetition: Philosophies of (Literary) History in Octavia E. Butler's *Kindred*." *Contemporary Literature* 41.3 (2000): 525–553.

Levine, Michael L. *African Americans and Civil Rights: From 1619 to the Present*. Phoenix: The Oryx Press, 1996.

The Long Walk Home. Dir. Richard Pearce. Perf. Whoopi Goldberg and Sissy Spacek. Miramax, 1990.

Lorde, Audre. "Age, Race, Class, and Sex: Women Redefining Difference." *Sister Outsider*. Freedom, CA: The Crossing Past, 1984. 114–123.

Lukács, Georg. *The Historical Novel*. 1962. Trans. Hannah and Stanley Mitchell. Lincoln: U of Nebraska P, 1983.

Maida, Patricia. "*Kindred* and *Dessa Rose*: Two Novels that Reinvent Slavery." *CEA Magazine* 4 (1991): 43–52.

Marshall, Brenda K. *Teaching the Postmodern: Fiction and Theory*. New York: Routledge, 1992.

Marshall, Paule. *Praisesong for the Widow*. New York: Plume, 1984.

McCafferty, Larry. *Across the Wounded Galaxies: Interviews with Modern Science Fiction Writers*. Urbana: University of Illinois P, 1990. 54–70.

McDowell, Deborah E. "'The Changing Same': Generational Connections and Black Women Novelists." *Reading Black, Reading Feminist*. Ed. Henry Louis Gates, Jr. New York: A Meridian Book, 1990. 91–115.

———. "Negotiating between Tenses: Witnessing Slavery after Freedom—*Dessa Rose*." *Slavery and the Literary Imagination*. Eds. Deborah E. McDowell and Arnold Rampersad. Baltimore: Johns Hopkins UP, 1989. 144–163.

Meese, Elizabeth. *(Ex)Tensions: Re-Figuring Feminist Criticism*. Urbana: U of Illinois P, 1990. 129–54.

Mitchell, Margaret. *Gone with the Wind*. 1937. New York: Warner Books, 1993.

Morrison, Toni. *Beloved*. New York: Knopf, 1987.

———. *The Bluest Eye*. New York: Washington Square Press, 1970.

———. *Jazz*. New York: Knopf, 1992.

———. *The Nobel Lecture in Literature*. New York: Knopf, 1993.

———. *Playing in the Dark: Whiteness and the Literary Imagination*. Cambridge: Harvard UP, 1992.

———. "The Site of Memory." *Inventing the Truth: The Art and Craft of Memories*. Ed. William Zinsser. Boston: Houghton Mifflin Co., 1987. 103–124.

————. *Song of Solomon*. New York: Knopf, 1977.

————. *Sula*. New York: Knopf, 1973.

————. *Tar Baby*. New York: Knopf, 1981.

————. "Unspeakable Things Unspoken: The Afro-American Presence in American Literature." *Michigan Quarterly Review* 28.1 (Winter 1989): 1–34. Rpt. in *Within the Circle: An Anthology of African American Literary Criticism from the Harlem Renaissance to the Present*. Ed. Angelyn Mitchell. Durham: Duke UP, 1994. 368–398.

Morrison, Toni, and Robert Richardson. "A Bench by the Road: *Beloved*." *The World* 3.1 (January/February 1989): 4, 5, 37–41.

Naylor, Gloria. *Linden Hills*. New York: Penguin, 1986.

————. *The Women of Brewster Place*. New York: Penguin, 1983.

Nora, Pierre. "Between Memory and History: Les Lieux de Mémoire." Trans. Marc Roudebush. *History and Memory in African-American Culture*. Eds. Geneviève Fabre and Robert O'Meally. New York: Oxford UP, 1994. 284–300.

O'Donnell, Patrick, and Robert C. Davis, eds. *Intertextuality and Contemporary American Fiction*. Baltimore: Johns Hopkins UP, 1989.

O'Reilly, Kenneth. *Nixon's Piano: Presidents and Racial Politics from Washington to Clinton*. New York: The Free Press, 1995.

"The Paradox of Thomas Jefferson." Perf. Julian Bond, Clay Jenkinson, and Richard West. Smithsonian Institution's Baird Auditorium, Washington DC. 31 December 1999.

Paulin, Diana R. "De-Essentializing Interracial Representations: Black and White Border Crossings in Spike Lee's *Jungle Fever* and Octavia Butler's *Kindred*." *Cultural Critique* 36 (1997): 168–193.

Perez-Torres, Rafael. "Knitting and Knotting the Narrative Thread—*Beloved* as Postmodern Novel." *Modern Fiction Studies* 39 (1993): 689–707.

Riberio, Orquidea. "History and Memory in Toni Morrison's *Beloved*." *Mapping African America: History, Narrative Formation, and the Production of Knowledge*. Eds. Maria Diedrich, Carl Pedersen, and Justine Tally. Hamburg: LIT Verlag, 1999. 163–173.

Robinson, Patricia M. "The Historical Repression of Women's Sexuality." *Pleasure and Danger: Exploring Female Sexuality*. Ed. Carole Vance. Boston: Routledge, 1984. 251–266.

Rowell, Charles. "An Interview with Octavia E. Butler." *Callaloo* 20 (1997): 47–66.

Rushdy, Ashraf H. A. "Families of Orphans: Relation and Disrelation in Octavia Butler's *Kindred*." *College English* 55.2 (February 1993): 135–157.

Sanchez-Eppler, Karen. *Touching Liberty: Abolition, Feminism, and the Politics of the Body*. Berkeley: U of California P, 1993.

Sankofa. Dir. and prod. Haile Gerima. Mypheduh, Inc., 1993.

Sekora, John. "Comprehending Slavery: Language and Personal History in the *Narrative*." *Frederick Douglass's Narrative of the Life of Frederick Douglass*. Ed. and intro. Harold Bloom. New York: Chelsea House, 1988. 153–164.

————. "Is the Slave Narrative a Species of Autobiography?" *Studies in Autobiography*. Ed. James Olney. New York: Oxford UP, 1988. 99–111.

Sirgo, Henry B. "Blacks and Presidential Politics." *Blacks and the American Political System*. Eds. Huey L. Perry and Wayne Parent. Gainesville: UP of Florida, 1995. 75–104.

Smith, Valerie. "'Circling the Subject': History and Narrative in *Beloved*." *Toni Morrison: Critical Perspectives Past and Present*. Eds. Henry Louis Gates, Jr. and K. A. Appiah. New York: Amistad, 1993. 342–355.

————. "'Loopholes of Retreat:' Architecture and Ideology in Harriet Jacobs's *Incidents in the Life of a Slave Girl.*" *Reading Black, Reading Feminist.* Ed. Henry Louis Gates, Jr. New York: A Meridian Book, 1990. 212–226.

Spillers, Hortense J. "Changing the Letter: The Yokes, The Jokes of Discourse, or, Mrs. Stowe, Mr. Reed." *Slavery and the Literary Imagination.* Eds. Deborah E. McDowell and Arnold Rampersad. Baltimore: Johns Hopkins UP, 1987. 25–61.

———. "Cross-Currents, Discontinuities: Black Women's Fiction." *Conjuring: Black Women, Fiction, and Literary Tradition.* Eds. Marjorie Pryse and Hortense J. Spillers. Bloomington: Indiana UP, 1985.

———. "Mama's Baby, Papa's Maybe: An American Grammar Book." *diacritics* 17 (1987): 65–81. Rpt. in *Within the Circle: An Anthology of African American Literary Criticism from the Harlem Renaissance to the Present.* Ed. Angelyn Mitchell. Durham: Duke UP, 1994. 454–81.

Still, William. *The Underground Railroad.* 1872. New York: Arno P, 1968.

Stowe, Harriet Beecher. *Uncle Tom's Cabin.* 1852. New York: Bantam, 1981.

Styron, William. *The Confessions of Nat Turner.* New York: Random House, 1967.

Tate, Claudia. *Domestic Allegories of Political Desire: The Black Heroine's Text at the Turn of the Century.* New York: Oxford UP, 1992.

Tate, Claudia, ed. *Black Women Writers at Work.* New York: Continuum, 1983.

Trapasso, Ann E. "Returning to the Site of Violence: The Restructuring of Slavery's Legacy in Sherley Anne Williams's *Dessa Rose.*" *Violence, Silence, and Anger: Women's Writing as Transgression.* Ed. Dierdre Lashgari. Charlottesville: UP of Virginia, 1995. 219–230.

Traylor, Eleanor W. "The Presence of Ancestry in African American Literature." Unpublished manuscript, 2000.

Twain, Mark. *Pudd'nhead Wilson.* 1892. New York: Bantam, 1984.

United States. The House of Representatives. 105th Congress. H. Con. Res. 96. Washington DC: GPO, 1997.

United States. The House of Representatives. 106th Congress. H. Con. Res. 40. Washington DC: GPO, 1999.

Vance, Carole. "Pleasure and Danger: Toward a Politics of Sexuality." *Pleasure and Danger: Exploring Female Sexuality.* Ed. Carole Vance. Boston: Routledge, 1984. 1–27.

Verney, Kevern. *Black Civil Rights in America.* New York: Routledge, 2000.

Vrettos, Athena. "Curative Domains: Women, Healing, and History in Black Women's Narratives." *Women's Studies* 16 (1989): 455–473.

Walker, Alice. *The Color Purple.* New York: Harcourt, 1982.

———. *Meridian.* New York: Simon and Schuster, 1977.

———. *The Third Life of Grange Copeland.* New York: Harcourt, 1970.

Walker, Margaret. *Jubilee.* New York: Bantam, 1966.

Walker, Melissa. *Down from the Mountaintop: Black Women's Novels in the Wake of the Civil Rights Movement, 1966–1989.* New Haven: Yale UP, 1991.

Wallace, Michele. *Invisibility Blues: From Pop to Theory.* New York: Verso, 1990.

Washington, Mary Helen. "'The Darkened Eye Restored': Notes Toward a Literary History of Black Women." *Invented Lives: Narratives of Black Women 1860–1960.* Ed. Mary Helen Washington. New York: Doubleday, 1987. xv–xxxi.

———. "Meditations on History: The Slave Woman's Voice." *Invented Lives: Narratives of Black Women 1860–1960.* Ed. Mary Helen Washington. New York: Doubleday, 1987. 3–15.

Welter, Barbara. "The Cult of True Womanhood, 1820–1860." *American Quarterly* 18 (1966): 151–174.

White, Deborah Gray. *Ar'n't I a Woman: Female Slaves in the Plantation South.* New York: Norton, 1985.

Wiencek, Henry. *The Hairstons: An American Family in Black and White.* New York: St. Martin's Press, 2000.

Williams, Sherley Anne. *Dessa Rose.* New York: Morrow, 1986.

———. "The Lion's History: The Ghetto Writes B[l]ack." *Soundings* 76.2–3 (Summer/Fall 1993): 245–260.

Yellin, Jean Fagan. "Texts and Contexts of Harriet Jacobs's *Incidents in the Life of a Slave Girl: Written by Herself.*" *The Slave's Narrative.* Eds. Charles T. Davis and Henry Louis Gates, Jr. New York: Oxford UP, 1985. 262–282.

Index

About the Author

Angelyn Mitchell is an associate professor of English at Georgetown University, Washington, D.C., where she teaches African American and American literatures. She is the editor of *Within the Circle: An Anthology of African American Literary Criticism from the Harlem Renaissance to the Present* (1994).

CPSIA information can be obtained
at www.ICGtesting.com
Printed in the USA
LVHW040708270220
648320LV00001B/6